IN THE MINDS OF EXTREMISTS

Complimentary copy.
To: Shahbar Dhalla.
From: Dr Mahmood Y. Abdulla

IN THE MINDS OF EXTREMISTS

Exposition of Multifaced Psychotic Extremism

DR. MAHMOOD YOOSUF ABDULLA

A cataloguing-in-Publications Data entry for this title is available from the British Library.

ISBN: 1535001305
ISBN 13: 9781535001304
Library of Congress Control Number: 2016911362
CreateSpace Independent Publishing Platform
North Charleston, South Carolina

CONTENTS

ABOUT THE AUTHOR

Dr Mahmood Yoosuf Abdulla earned his master of arts from Portsmouth University and a PhD from Loughborough University in the United Kingdom. Awarded the Diploma with Distinction Award in freelance writing from the London School of Journalism, the author has dedicated the past thirty-five years of his career as a fellow of the Association of Chartered Certified Accountants in London.

Academic qualifications and professional experience apart, Dr Abdulla has participated in community charitable activities since the age of sixteen. He held several voluntary executive posts in the community organizations. During the course of forty-five years, after completing his studies, he lectured in eighty community centres across four continents.

AUTHOR'S NOTE

The integral part of extremism is jihadist militancy, which has been bred and buttressed in the East in some Muslim countries. This reality has now reached the Western shores. The concerns about national security and the challenges of extremism and terrorism are now very much in public domain. These issues had been nurtured in their present form over the past few centuries. They have emerged in recent years as a perceptible reality in developed countries. Nobody seems to be safe from this new phenomenon thanks to globalization and the love affair between oil riches and arms supplies.

This work examines the rising trend of extremism and its repercussions. It consists of researched material which will be of interest to academics, scholars, and readers in general. The subject matter is informative in the context of violence perpetrated in the name of religion. The callous violence has terrorized and victimized people and posed dilemmas for human-rights agencies, governments, and the international community. This aspect has been analysed under its politicoreligious causes and consequences.

This work investigates extremism in its historic and current contexts. It traces back in history and in yesteryears the development of acute obsession and phobia in the minds of religious extremists. This book critically explores the brutal means conceived in the minds of psychotic extremists in violation of international norms to justify the aim of coercing their hegemony upon others who might have different belief systems and political outlooks.

This is an empirical-cum-academic study. The objective is to present a variety of perspectives on how the Muslim public opinion is manoeuvred and manipulated by the media, elites, and radical court clerics, resulting in far-reaching impacts on the lives of the victimized communities.

In a nutshell, the author deliberates on a hitherto unexplored paradigm of institutional extremism, which has given rise to bigotry and ethnic cleansing of religious minorities through indiscriminate killings and suicide bombings. The rising trend of violent extremism legitimizes shedding the blood of its adversaries, including innocent civilians. There is a new imperialism of ideology in the offing which has reached the West after spreading far and wide in the East.

The discourse in this work also incorporates an exposé on human-rights abuses, discrimination, and outright violence targeting a particular ethnic community whose tragic plight has been ignored for too long. Turning a blind eye towards a humanitarian tragedy might motivate the violent organized groups to target other communities, too, because the common denominator they use is the same. Their political philosophy is based on 'either my way or no way' simply because they conceive themselves to be all-knowing and all-wise, those who have a divine authority to decide the fate of other nations and communities. Their obsession has led to genocide in some countries. This book traces and critically analyses the roots of this intolerant ideology.

AUTHOR'S NOTE

In this study, transliterations of Arabic words and expressions are avoided in order to keep the text as reader-friendly as possible. Non-English characters and symbols and non-English names follow phonetic sounds. The author quotes passages from the Quran to illustrate his points. The reference to the passages appears like 11:11, where the first number indicates chapter number, and the second number indicates verse number. Throughout the book, the city of Mecca has been spelled Makkah, not Mecca; the city of Madina has been spelled Madinah, not Madina; the Kaba has been spelled Ka'bah, not Kaba; the word Quran has been used, not Koran; and the name of the Prophet appears as Muhammad, not Mohamed. The first name of the founder of the Wahhabi movement has been avoided. Instead, he is referred to as Ibn Abd al-Wahhab or the son of Abd al-Wahhab.

PREFACE

Warfare and bloodshed have existed in the human race since time immemorial. Gone are the days when the warring parties used to meet each other face to face on battlefields and the combatants used to recognise their foes in armed conflicts. As warfare evolved and became more sophisticated, the triumphant exercised control over the lives and properties of the vanquished. Proxy wars became a common feature. In the last few centuries, ferocious devises and deadly weapons have been developed and employed to win wars and control others for political, economic, and ideological reasons. The overwhelming victims of the armed conflicts are civilians who are caught up on both sides. This study focuses on the tragic plight of innocent people who are not parties to the conflict and who do not even understand the nature of the conflict imposed upon them.

In the present world, it is civilians who suffer the disastrous effects of battles and wars which are fought without their mandate. Nations around the world have resorted, in the words of Amnesty International, to 'injustice, brutality and a complete disregard for human rights' despite the fact that the offending nations are members of the United Nations and are signatories to human-rights accords.

On the other side of the spectrum, the outlaws and militants are resorting to deliberate, indiscriminate, and brutal targeting of civilians with complete disregard for international law and the UN Charter of Human Rights. They use religious rhetoric and slogans to justify suicide bombing, although they are aware that acts of committing suicide and killing civilians indiscriminately violate religious and secular laws. By its very nature, suicide bombing is meant to cause maximum mayhem to human lives. This does not mean that other devices are humane. Modern warfare by its very nature is void of fairness and bravery. Wars are fought through proxies, or by the click of a button, or by remote control. In all cases, innocent lives are victimised and scars of pain are left permanently on the victims' physiques and psyches.

The threat of weapons of mass destruction is still looming over the heads of certain nations which have experienced their disastrous effects. Equally lethal is a warfare which has been triggered by fanatical groups in the name of religion. Its effects are long lasting. The seeds of hatred implanted in the minds of indoctrinated men and women can be observed in their willingness to blow up even babies and children. They remain indifferent to whether their victims are combatants in the field or are weaning infants in the laps of their mothers. Their barbaric measures deliberately target schoolchildren, especially girls at school, as happened under the reign of the Taliban and after their removal from power.

The sponsors of the fanatical zealots contribute generous support from public treasuries and from the funds collected in mosques, despite being aware that these are used for violent activities and intimidation. If the victims of indiscriminate attacks are from ethnic communities or from differing religious sects (whom the sponsors and financiers of the outlaws see as their political rivals), then not a word of condemnation is heard at the governmental level or in the popular media against the perpetrators of heinous crimes. On the contrary, suicide bombings and indiscriminate killings are excused in some of the most popular Arabic satellite channels. Not only have these channels provided a platform for the Taliban and Al-Qaeda extremists for winning public sympathy, but sometimes they have acted as their spokesmen. It is observed that their reporters are the first to appear on the scene wherefrom the fighters of the Taliban and Al-Qaeda operate. These facts can be verified from several documentaries shown on these channels.

In Islamic polity, there is a strictly laid-down code of conduct in the sacred sources of the Quran and the Sunnah[1] in relation to armed conflicts, wars, and disputes. But these are being violated or ignored by the extremist groups. Islam has always faced the dilemma that its core teachings, guidance, and values have been misapplied by the ones who claim to be holier than thou. Nobody in his right state of mind can approve mass killings and genocide, where the killers are motivated by sectarian hatred and religious bigotry.

When the names of Islam and Muslims are associated with inhumane measures in furtherance of political objectives, through violence, power struggle, hegemony, and domination over others, this leads other communities of the world to form wrong ideas about Muslims and their faith. The irony of the situation is that the militant groups, despite their gross disregard for human lives and human rights, enjoy strong backing from their fellow ideologues, known on the international scene as 'conservatives' and 'moderates'. It is now an open secret that most of the financial support for the radical activities comes from the inner circles of the so-called conservatives and moderates. One may wonder why the absolute majority among Muslims remain oblivious to the deeds of the violent extremists, which tend to offend the basic teachings and tenets of Islam. Why isn't there meaningful and audible public outcry

---

1 Defined as traditions, Hadiths, or sayings and practices of the Prophet Muhammad, which form the second most authentic source of guidance, according to the Muslim faith, the first being the Quran, which, according to the Islamic faith, is the revealed word of God.

or mass protest against the extremists for misusing the names of Islam and Muslims to justify extreme actions? Why do the militant groups resort to indiscriminate killings? The answer may not lie in the trail of money paid through the middlemen or the offshore companies to the dependants of the so-called martyrs and their recruiters. The real cost is disguised in the indoctrination process which the vulnerable and uninformed youths undergo to turn into extremists, who are then prepared to destroy innocent human lives while believing that their salvation lies in completing their deadly missions.

The training of these young men and women for ill-conceived causes constricts their thoughts. They are not able to see beyond the slogans and selected verses from the Quran, which are often misinterpreted to suit the preconceived ideological and political interest of their mentors, supporters, and financiers. Yet in the minds of the non-Muslim communities, there is a terrible muddle between Islam as a religion and Muslims, who have never been a homogeneous community because of their different backgrounds. But knowingly or unknowingly, there is a tendency to blame Islam and the Quran for the actions of the radicals due to the obvious flaws in thinking, understanding, and interpreting the sources.

'Human dignity', 'human values', 'tolerance', and 'respect for others' are words and expressions that do not exist in the vocabulary of the militant extremists. They bestow upon themselves the right to decide who in the human race is entitled to live and who needs to be disposed of. The ideology that they espouse turns perfectly normal and intelligent youths into murderers and suicide bombers. They believe that they are performing a religious duty, opening for them the gates of Paradise in the company of the *houris* (heavenly brides).

Since the oil-price hike of the '70s in the last century, phenomenal oil wealth—and charity and religious alms deriving from such wealth—have been lavishly showered upon the radical religious groups for promoting a particular ideology as the vast majority of the Muslim countries have been living on the edge of poverty. These excess revenues could have been equitably spent for helping the poor and downtrodden in the wider community, or in order to reconcile nations in dispute, or for the promotion of peace in the region rather than in the pursuit of political and ideological domination.

Some of the richest countries in the world are homes to people who live below the poverty line in substandard living conditions, while the elites of these countries enjoy the most extravagant and lavish lifestyles. Their clerics make loud noises in the name of the shariah (Islamic or divine law) but overlook the contradictions that characterise the gluttony and greed of the elites, which results in the wastage of national resources. In this way, the societies replete with injustices, human-rights abuses, and corruption pave the way for extremism.

An individual may be a leftist or a rightist extremist. He may be a radicalised political or religious extremist. As long as his extremism does not infringe upon everybody else's rights to live their lives peacefully, nobody would care. But as soon as extremism erupts into violence and usurps the rights of others to peaceful living and practising their own creed, it is bound to lead to a range of abuses. These abuses—whether in social, economic, or religious spheres—may result in a vicious spiral of violence and counter violence. This is precisely what is happening in a number of Muslim countries affected by violent extremism. This culture of intolerance and violence has now spilled over to the countries of the West.

✼

The term 'extremism' is used frequently in this work. Hence, the term shall be defined at the outset. Extremism is understood to be the measure adopted outside the normal behaviour in political, social, or religious matters to achieve a set purpose. It incorporates unusual means chosen by certain individuals, groups, or nations in pursuance of their objectives.

Muslims have been feeling for a long time that whenever this term is mentioned, the mental picture or perception shifts to them, although all other communities have their own share of extremists. There is no denial that in the present Muslim world, extremist trends are perceptible in media, in state policies, among splinter groups, and even among court jurists. At times, they adopt bullying and coercive tactics to mould political and religious concepts in their favour. These facts will be demonstrated later on through case studies.

Another term that has attracted much furore is 'terrorism'. It refers to the use of violence, or threat of violence, against civilians in order to attain political, religious, or ideological objectives. This applies not only to individuals but also to organised militants and nations, whose reckless policies endanger human lives and their means of livelihood. The killing of innocent civilians, Muslims or non-Muslims, by any political power in the world cannot be condoned. Under no circumstances and under no pretext can deliberate killing of children be tolerated in the theatre of war or otherwise. But history bears testimony that certain ideologues and fanatical groups have laid down a precedent in history of massacring children in furtherance of their political and ideological goals.

Terrorism is one of the corollaries of extremism. Again, Muslims have expressed their grievances that terrorism is unfairly associated with Islam. Neither all Muslims are terrorists, nor are all terrorists Muslim. Indeed, the overwhelming majority in the world communities are neither extremists nor terrorists.

There are a number of religious, political, social, and economic factors which amalgamate to cause unusual or abnormal behaviour in individuals and groups. Extremism is responsible for nurturing violence, promoting hatred, causing persecution of political or religious opponents, and demonising ethnic communities on the basis of differences in faith and beliefs. The essential features of extremism are bigotry against political rivals, intolerance towards the viewpoints of others, and disregard for fairness and justice in interhuman relations. When the campaign of hatred intensifies, rational faculties of the extremists tend to become dysfunctional and, consequently, they cannot distinguish between what is right and what is wrong or what is an acceptable behaviour and what is an unacceptable behaviour in society. This leads to the use of force and violence, which eventually leads to terrorism.

Broadly speaking, in the context of Islam and Muslims, the first cause of extremism is injustice perpetrated by the nations and their despotic rulers. The second cause is the court clerics who mislead people to gain favours from their paymasters. The third cause is the religious fanatics. At times, the three elements in the triangle change role among themselves although they may not necessarily be in direct contact with each other.

There are certain terms which are frivolously used in the media and press. They portray what they call 'moderates' as a homogeneous entity, whereas there is a notable projection towards heterogeneity in the behaviour and outlook of the so-called moderates. In the moderate camp, there are many who hold uncompromising attitudes on a number of juristic political issues. Within the so-called conservative puritan camp, there are extremists who support militancy morally, religiously, and financially. The 'conservatives', who are averse to changes and are intolerant of all other faiths, believe that they are the sole representatives of God on earth and have an almighty right of being judgmental against every other soul except themselves.

Even the baby-killers among the extremists believe that they are on their way to entering paradise. They memorise the Quran in parrotlike fashion, but the message of the Quran does not go beyond their melodious voices. Every infant or child killed, wherever in the world, in their terrorist attacks is enough to earn them an eternal damnation. It would seem that the militants have found a shortcut to wash off the burden of guilt for their crimes by misusing the name of '*jihad*' for their terrorist activities.

Within the Muslim ranks, from the earliest times, from the times of the Prophet Muhammad, Muslims have been divided into two distinct categories: *muminun* (believers) and *munafiqun* (hypocrites). There are separate chapters in the Quran in the name of both groups, describing the essential characteristics of each. In as much as they existed in the time of the Prophet, the hypocrites have multiplied many times since then and will continue to exist and spread their mischief, which has become a perceptible reality in the modern world.

According to the Quran, the status of the believers is higher than the status of Muslims in general. The believing Muslims respect and practise the tenets of religion with faith and sincerity. The most unreliable and untrustworthy of the lot are hypocrites. That is why the Quran declares, 'The hypocrites will be in the lowest depths of the Fire: no helper will you find for them' (4:145). They are in the habit of committing treacheries and betrayals. Their deeds contradict their words. They wear two different masks on their faces. They read and memorise the verse of the Quran which says, '...and if any one saved a life, it would be as if he saved the life of all people...' (5:32). Killing an innocent soul is like killing the entire humankind, and saving an innocent soul is like saving the entire humankind, according to the Quran. Therefore, the mass killers and sponsors of international terrorism can only fall in the category of hypocrites because their verbal testimony contradicts their actions.

Violence against minorities, whom the extremists consider infidels, is encouraged and perpetrated not only through underground groups but through state organs, as in Afghanistan under the reign of the Taliban. In a number of countries which house violent extremists, funding plays a crucial role in nurturing them. Some nations do not believe in liberty or human rights or rights of citizenry. Therefore, they try to derail any political reforms taking place elsewhere in the region, lest their own citizens wake up from the slumber and start demanding their civil and human rights.

On monitoring the popular media in the Arab world, one cannot help but observe a distinct bias in political commentary, news, and views. The state-run media are affiliated with political or religious interests. One of their noticeable features is to mix up facts with propaganda to demonise political opponents.

〜〃〆〜

This work seeks to explore the outlook and attitude of certain religious ideologues that have given rise to extremism in Muslim society. These ideologues have distorted the sanctity attributed by Islam to human life and neglected the Islamic exhortations for tolerance and moderation. Historically, a number of theological and political factors have given rise to dichotomy in the Muslim community. This study examines the double standards practised in the name of Islam under the garb of Islamic piety. It investigates religious and political issues which have created a rift, widely polarising the Muslims into factions. This work represents a protest and outcry against the agony and indiscriminate killing of civilians.

A major part of this study is empirical, gradually evolving into critical academic discussion and discourse. The role of the media, the role of the preachers and clerics in the mosques, and the role of the ideologues are analysed to demonstrate the correlation among the three.

One of the essential aspects of this discourse is to critically review some of the published academic studies relevant to the subject. This research will be of interest to students of politics, academics, scholars, and lay-persons. This work focuses on the predicament of the Shia Muslims, the minority among the wider Muslim community, who have suffered persistently from targeted killings and genocide by militants in several countries. This can provide a vital lead to other communities of the world to learn from the precedent set by the indoctrinated *takfiris* (those declaring others to be nonbelievers or infidels) and, hence, permitting their bloodshed.

In a number of countries, the backbone of political despotism is the growing despotism of radical ideology. This scenario is reminis-cent of enforcing hegemony over all other schools of thought in Islam, under the banner of a particular school, which has a history of sup-pressing popular movements and opposing public demands for free-dom and civil rights. Hence, to stand any chance of success, political manoeuvring is dressed up in the garb of religion. State jurists are ordered to pass juristic rulings stating that to rise against the rulers, however oppressive and unrepresentative they may be, is prohibited in the religion of Islam.

Paradoxically, the same ideologically motivated states and their court clerics take a turn in the opposite direction and change position when their own political interests are sensed to be at stake. Hence, what is impermissible for their own public becomes quite permissible for the public of their adversaries. They do not have any qualms about support-ing uprising, instigating rebellion, and financing the rebels in other na-tions which they consider to be their political foes.

In this work, for precision and ease of verification, the dates of the events are identified wherever possible, though not in chronological or-der. 'AH' refers to the Islamic *hijri* calendar (i.e. *anno Hegirae*) and 'CE' refers to the Christian era. The term 'Wahhabis' refers to the followers of Muhammad ibn Abd al-Wahhab (d. 1206 AH–1792 CE). They, however, prefer to call themselves 'Salafis'.

The term 'Salafis' in this work is used for the followers of the theology of Taqi al-Din Ahmad ibn Taymiyyah (d. 728 AH–1328 CE). Modern Salafis follow his teachings and consider themselves the true representatives of the Sunnis.

'Salaf' literally means predecessor. The Salafis prefer to be known as the followers of *al-salaf al-salih* (the virtuous predecessors, dating back to the companions of the Prophet). The followers of the Wahhabi/Salafi school of Saudi Arabia are obliged to swear an oath of allegiance to the Saudi monarchs. The Salafis elsewhere are required to give allegiance to their own rulers.

A common error occurs in the books authored by Western writers on this movement. They use the name Abd al-Wahhab for the founder of the movement, whereas this was the first name of his father. Hence, wherever the founder of the Wahhabi movement is mentioned in this work, he is referred to as Ibn Abd al-Wahhab ('son of Abd al-Wahhab'), and his followers are referred as Wahhabis.

The term Sunnis refers to the *ahl al-sunnah wa al-jama'ah* (the followers of the tradition and the community), who are in the majority among Muslims. Conventionally, the Sunnis subscribe to one of the four legal schools of Abu Hanifah (699–767 CE), Malik (711–795 CE), Shafi'i (767–820 CE), and Ibn Hanbal (780–855 CE). All the four legal schools follow the Asha'irah (Ash'arite) creed.

All references in this work to Salafis and Wahhabis exclusively refer to the radical and extremist elements among them, not to their moderates.

Unless otherwise stated, the term Shias refers to the followers of the school of the Twelvers or Ithna'asharis, who believe in the successive imamate or leadership of the twelve Imams as the testamentary successors of the Prophet Muhammad. They follow the jurisprudential school of Imam Ja'far al-Sadiq (702–765 CE). The leadership of the twelve Imams extends to religious and temporal guidance, according to the Shia faith.

A well-known and influential Salafi cleric has featured prominently in this work simply because he has played a crucial role in contemporary Muslim politics. Everything that has been said is based on well-documented facts.

The exposé presented in this work necessitated for the author to monitor the Arabic media and Friday sermons from mosques over a number of years. What this work does not do is defend the record of any government.

Chapter 1

EXTREMISM AND FALSE
SENSE OF HEROISM

Extremism is multifaceted. In theory, the life of a Muslim is regulated by religious piety. In practice, there are many contradictions. On observing these contradictions in the negative behaviour of Muslim extremists, the outside world takes the impression that this is what Islamic piety is all about. Nothing can be further from the truth. Islamic piety is not dependant on any individual, group, or national policies of Muslim countries. It is directly associated with Islamic teachings of the Quran and the authentic traditions of the Prophet Muhammad. At times, the conduct of Muslims is in wide disparity with the basic and root teachings of Islam.

If Islam is to be blamed for the unusual and irrational behaviour of the Muslim extremists, then Christianity has to take the blame for the scandals that have rocked the Catholic Church by the paedophile Catholic priests. If it is justified to call the actions of Muslim militants 'Islamic terrorism', then it is justified to call the violence of the Irish militant groups in Northern Ireland 'Christian terrorism'. In as much as Christianity cannot be blamed for the terror of Timothy McVeigh, the

Oklahoma City bomber, Islam cannot be blamed for the terror of, for instance, the Boston Marathon bombers. Hence, those who have coined the term 'Islamic terrorism' are motivated by some ulterior motives to accuse the Muslims en bloc for the deeds of the outlaws among them.

MUSLIM EXTREMISM AND ITS REPERCUSSIONS

Muslims like to present themselves under the banner of one *ummah* (community of believers). They like to pose as a united community, whereas the concept of unity is vitiated by the behaviour of vocal extremists. All the niceties and courtesies hailing 'unity' fade away when the reality on the ground reveals its ugly face. The bigots carry daggers in their hearts against their own fellow believers. The ideologues among them preach intolerance, knowing very well that the community is divided into different schools of law, sects, and factions. In their own school of thought or sect, many rival splinter groups emerge, each vying for an exclusive right to speak for everybody else. They like to pretend that the community, in its present state, provides the best of models for other communities of the world. The radicals like to see others succumb blindly to their interpretations and pretensions. They use blackmail, branding anybody who does not consent to their viewpoint as a *kafir* (infidel). They excommunicate many Muslims on account of differences in beliefs, thought, and approach.

Most Muslims find it very offensive to hear the non-Muslim critics arguing that Islam approves taking of hostages and beheading them, committing mass murders and suicide bombings, and brutalising civilians. Islam does not approve these acts. Yet the fact remains that the ideological complacency of some Muslim extremist groups encourages despicable misconceptions.[2] These have become a matter of deep con-

---

2 See Henry McDonald, 'Hostage-taking "legitimate"', http://www.theguardian.com/world/2004/nov/07/terrorism.iraq, 7 November 2004.

cern for the overwhelming majority of Muslims, who feel that their religion and traditions are being hijacked by a minority of militants.

Extremism has not emerged in the bazaars and alleyways of impoverished Muslim cities. It has emerged from the lavish and flamboyant palaces of those who, for ideological reasons, have chosen the path of asserting their hegemony through uncompromising radical thought. In religious matters, they act as the 'all-knowing, all-wise' deputies of God on earth, and anybody who does not see eye to eye with them has to be nothing but misguided and heretic, according to their perverted thought.

In the political world, they and their supporters readily breach international law, human-rights accords, and civilised code of conduct to retain power all to themselves, which they believe has been granted by God to their family and dynasty. In this age and time, when the rights and duties of citizenry are recognised through international covenants, the citizens of some countries are deprived of their basic rights. They are forced to succumb to the will of the despots; otherwise, they are thrown in jails without trial, tortured, and killed.

Irrespective of whether these nations are run as a family business or hereditary enterprise, the citizens are expected to obey the despots, with a guarantee from their court clerics that they will be rewarded abundantly in the afterlife for their patience or, more appropriately, for remaining subdued and obedient to the repressive policies of the autocrats. In this century of civil rights and sweeping changes which are affecting every aspect of human life, Western nations do not tolerate for themselves dictatorial and absolute rule concentrated in the hands of a few. In their own systems of governance, they look down upon dictatorships as detrimental to their national interests. But the same nations do not have any qualms if their clients in the Middle

East, intoxicated with absolute power, are actively engaged in suppressing civil liberties. One cannot imagine that any prime minister in the West would retain his or her post for more than forty years. But one of their client nations in the Arab world, like Bahrain, has the longest-serving prime minister on the face of the earth. He may even be preparing to leave the premiership in inheritance to his eldest son, or if he does not have one, then to his eldest son-in-law, or perhaps take his post with him to his grave.

Violence is being perpetrated, on the one hand, by despotic regimes against their own citizens and, on the other hand, by the extremist militants who kill indiscriminately. In doing so, they blaspheme Islam and Islamic values. They trample upon human compassion and mercy preached by Islam. They pave the way for barbarity manifested in blowing up innocent men, women, and children in crowded markets and in places of worship of their opponents. They all are graduates of the school of radicalism, which has been proficient at making Muslims enemies to one another. Apart from strong financial backing, they also muster support from fabricators who distort the established facts of history. They interpret the Quran and the traditions of the Prophet selectively as it suits their interests and preconceived notions. They portray the criminals of history as heroes and turn the mass murderers into role models.

The clerical establishment supporting the militants preach sectarian rifts. The extremists would never have succeeded in their evil endeavours if they had not undergone systematic indoctrination. The ideology that was fed into their hearts and minds left its destructive repercussions upon their own lives. This is the reason that Bin Laden was successful in recruiting fanatical extremists to his cause because they had not been groomed on any rational and constructive purpose in life. Their overemphasis on jihad according to the interpretation peculiar to them, which has nothing to do with jihad as prescribed by Islam (this subject is covered in greater detail in my study *Bankruptcy of the Extremist Ideology: How Divorced Are Muslims from Islam?*, to be published later), qualified them as the most likely candidates to dominate the world of militancy for dirty power politics. They were, therefore, used for fighting proxy wars, which still continue with renewed ferocity, as in Afghanistan, Iraq, Syria, Yemen, and Somalia.

Professor Mahmood Mamdani writes, 'Bin Laden was recruited, with US approval at the highest level, by Prince Turki al-Faisal, then head of Saudi intelligence...Bin Laden emerged as the organizer and patron of the most prominent privatized arm of the American jihad'.[3] During the Afghani jihad, Bin Laden was an indispensable asset bequeathed by the Saudi establishment to the United States.

In the aftermath of the Soviet invasion and occupation of Afghanistan in the '80s, the United States trained and funded Bin Laden and his followers for jihad against the Soviets. The babies born out of the womb of this jihad were Al-Qaeda and Taliban. The Arab Afghans had to be accommodated after the end of the Soviet occupation. Their countries of origin did not want them. By this time, under whatever pretext, Bin Laden turned his guns against the United States. Hence, the power that had trained, nurtured, and financed him and his organisation in the first place became his avowed enemy. The time bomb was set to explode. It detonated itself and caused mayhem on 9/11 in the United States, on 7/7 in London, in the Madrid train bombing, and thereafter in hundreds of suicide attacks on civilian targets in Iraq, Pakistan, Syria, Yemen, Somalia, and Afghanistan—all with the blessings of the militants, who habitually justify their terror in the name of religion.

In the aftermath of the 9/11 and 7/7 carnage, the extremists claimed on their websites and through video messages that the

---

3 Mamdani, pp. 132–133.

civilians killed in the attacks were legitimate targets for having voted their governments into power. They did not have any imagination to think that the victims might not have voted at all in general elections in their countries. Nevertheless, on the basis of a highly uncertain and presumptuous matter, they justified killing and maiming innocent civilians.

At least three decades before the militants targeted the West, they had prepared an army of terrorists who were well trained in terrorizing innocent people. The backlash on the Muslim community after the 9/11[4] and 7/7[5] terrorist attacks gave rise to Islamophobia. Although ordinary Muslim masses in the West had stood against violence and extremism, they became targets of the homebred extremists of Europe and the United States. Untold damage was done to the community relations when mosques in the United States were attacked and there were random attacks on women in hijab (Islamic dress). This state of affairs was repeated after the savage attack on a soldier in Woolwich, London, in May 2013.

The attackers were least concerned that their actions were bound to create negative ramifications and violence from the racist groups who were waiting for such opportunities to vent their prejudices against Muslims. Despite the fact that the Muslim community joined hands in condemning the Woolwich terrorist attack, there followed assaults on Muslim women in hijab and malicious attacks on mosques and on individuals going about their work. This shows that irrational and violent elements are found in all communities, and their conduct is an affront to civilised behaviour.

---

4 The 9/11 attacks were a series of coordinated terrorist attacks by al-Qaeda on the United States on the morning of 11 September, 2001.

5 The 7 July 2005 London bombings, referred to as 7/7, were a series of coordinated terrorist suicide bomb attacks in Central London which targeted civilians using the public transport system.

EXTREMISM IN NON-MUSLIM SOCIETIES

Extremism is rampant in non-Muslim societies too. There are wide-ranging causes interconnected with each other which lead towards extremism and violence. A few illustrations would prove the point. Nobody would have expected the Buddhists, who portray themselves to the world as ascetics and as a nonviolent religious community, to resort to brutal violence against the Rohingya Muslims in Myanmar in Burma. They expressed their economic and political frustration against the policies of their government by victimising the poor and destitute ethnic community of Muslims. The unruly mob of Buddhists went on a rampage, burning houses, looting properties, killing hundreds, and injuring thousands of Rohingya Muslims in what became some of the most shocking scenes of barbarism in the twenty-first century. The graphic scenes of casualties and the eyewitness reports of merciless mob attacks on helpless Muslims will remain a dark side of the Buddhist extremism that the world had not hitherto seen.

The pre-partition India and the post partition Indo-Pak subcontinent have witnessed many violent clashes and murdering sprees between Hindus and Muslims, between the upper-class and the lower-class Hindus, between Hindus and Sikhs, and between different sects of Muslims. The agent provocateurs, often affluent members in their communities, implant the seeds of commotion and violence by feeding the minds of the ignorant masses with hate speech. Once the violence erupts, it is followed by the spiral of negative effects and counter effects. It results in intolerance in society, and intolerance paves way for extremism. It is a vicious cycle which continues until the agent provocateurs are brought to their senses by the force of law. This phenomenon is also becoming very much visible in Western societies, where there is a rise in racist and fascist groups and political parties.

There existed a campaign against Islam and Muslims in the West long before 9/11 was even conceived. But since 9/11, this campaign has been reactivated in the public domain. It has been able to win on its side some public figures and opinion makers. During the presidency of President George W. Bush, these personalities succeeded in gaining proximity to the US administration and raised public paranoia over what they called the 'Islamic threat'.

Hence, in the developed world, a new form of extremism was taking shape from the top of the pyramid. When Rev. Jerry Falwell branded the Prophet Muhammad with the most derogatory expressions[6] which defy civilised behaviour, or when Franklin Graham slandered Islam, or when Pat Robertson said that Islam is the root of 'terrorism', these outrageous slanders seriously damaged coherent community relations in the United States.

As if the damage done by the bigots was not enough, twelve years down the line, the personality of the Prophet Muhammad, loved and revered by all Muslims, was targeted in an anti-Islamic indecent movie in the United States with the intention of offending Islam and promoting Islamophobia. The provocateurs behind the production of this offensive movie wanted to provoke Muslims and incite violence. Yet the blasphemy was categorised in the United States and Europe as 'freedom of thought'! But if a living politician in Europe or the United States is defamed in a similar outrageous manner, the perpetrator will not be able to get away without facing legal consequences.

When Muslim leaders challenged Franklin Graham over his allegations against the Islamic faith, he reiterated his bizarre claims: 'The God of Islam is not the same God. He's not the Son of God of the Christian or Judeo-Christian faith. It's a different God, and I believe

---

6 Michael Gillespie, 'Jerry Falwell attempts to incite religious and racial violence in America', *Media Monitors Network* (8 October 2002), http://www.mediamonitors.net/gillespie9.html, accessed 10 May 2014; 'NCC Board Repudiates Falwell's "60 Minutes" Comments on Islam,' *National Council of Churches* (7 October 2002), http://www.ncccu-sa.org/news/02news86.html, accessed 11 May 2014.

it is a very evil and wicked religion'.[7] It was hypocritical of this clergy-man to drag the Judaic faith into the doctrine of 'Son of God' when people of his own faith had been accusing the Jews for centuries of crucifying Jesus, on the basis of which the Jews were savagely perse-cuted in Europe by no other than Christians. Unfortunately, these religiofascists became the rising stars in President George W. Bush's administration.

In the category of religiofascism, the writings of Dr Daniel Pipes warrant a separate study altogether. The antagonistic policies adopted by the neoconservatives in the Bush administration were represented in the writings of Dr Pipes. When he emerged as the most-favoured candi-date to head the US Institute of Peace, the move was not only rejected by the university professors in the United States but by the late Senator Edward Kennedy, who considered his writings to be offensive.[8] Professor John Esposito observes, 'Anti-Americanism is also fed by leaders of the Christian Right such as Pat Robertson, Jerry Falwell, and Franklin Graham,'[9] who were in a favourable position to offer prayers at President Bush's inauguration.

When the former secretary of state Madeleine Albright asserted that the US policy objectives were worth the sacrifice of half a million Iraqi children under the UN sanctions, this was a case of extremism cam-ouflaged in the garb of moderation. The number of children killed in

---

7 'U.S. Evangelist Graham Says Islam Is an "Evil & Wicked" Religion', *Islam Daily* (19 November 2004), http://www.islamdaily.org/en/islam/2015.us-evangelist-graham-says-islam-is-an-evil--wicked.htm, accessed 11 May 2014.

8 Statement of Senator Edward M. Kennedy on the nomination of Daniel Pipes to the board of the US Institute of Peace, http://votesmart.org/public-statement/17524/statement-of-senator-edward-m-kennedy-on-the-nomination-of-daniel-pipes-to-the-board-of-the-us-institute-of-peace#.U6w_SSgquiA, 23 July 2003.

9 Esposito (2002), p. ix.

Iraq as a result of the US-sponsored policy of sanctions was greater than those killed in Hiroshima.[10]

In addition to political and religious causes, there are social and cultural factors that pave the way for diverse forms of extremism in non-Muslim societies. These have negative impacts even on the domestic lives of members of the community and their future generations. In this context, several case studies will be presented illustrating the exploitation and victimisation of children and women in non-Muslim societies. As a prelude, it can be said that there is a comprehensive website (HELPGUIDE.org) which covers in great detail the types of abuses prevailing in domestic life. This results in violating the rights of individuals and damaging them physically, emotionally, and psychologically. The victims may either become totally submissive or end up doing some unusual things outside of the orbit of normal and acceptable behaviour in society. Violence breeds violence. At times, because of the sufferings that the victims undergo at the hands of their spouses, parents, guardians, teachers, or peer groups, they may end up taking revenge against society at large by abusing other individuals.

The growing extremism in the Jewish communities has been brought to light in the international press. This is expressed in 'violence' and 'vulgarity' of the ultra-Orthodox men against women.[11] It may have developed as a result of a history of sexual abuse of Jewish children back to the Nazi period by their own guardians and protectors. It has repercussions in the ongoing abuse under official cover-up, whereby the silent victims continue to suffer and are deprived of justice.

Haaretz.com reported widespread sexual abuse in Brooklyn's ultra-Orthodox Jewish community, including child sex abuse, often by adults

---

10 Rahul Mahajan, 'We Think the Price Is Worth It', *Fairness and Accuracy in Reporting* (November/December 2001), http://www.fair.org/index.php?page=1084.

11 Noga Tarnopolsky, 'Israel protests rising Jewish extremism', *GlobalPost*, 28 December 2011.

in the family. The report says, 'Some 37 percent of more than 516,000 Jews in Brooklyn are Orthodox...' A case is cited of a rabbi who used to sexually abuse boys in Orthodox school. He admitted doing nothing wrong but pleaded guilty! Another case is cited where an ultra-Orthodox rabbi had sexually abused his own daughter throughout her childhood. A third case is cited where New York Police investigated a Jewish man who had raped a number of boys and then absconded to Israel. One of his victims commented, '[The rabbis] paralyzed an entire generation. When one of them destroys another person, they do nothing'.[12] This sounds as if these rabbis were no less competent than those Catholic priests who made a history of child sex abuse for decades or perhaps centuries and had enjoyed an official cover-up from Catholic Church for the sake of saving the reputation of the Church and not the reputation of the victims.

These types of tragic incidents have been uncovered in Western media through several TV documentaries. Some legal measures were taken by the American courts in ordering the insolvency of churches which could not meet the financial claims arising from child-abuse cases. Until then, the only solution the Catholic Church establishment proposed was to preach to the victims to forget and forgive. These are not decade-old cases. Even today, new cases of abuses are uncovered. Hannah Osborne writes in *International Business Times* (30 January 2013) about a Channel 4 Dispatches investigation titled 'Child Abuse Hidden in London's Strict Orthodox Jewish Community'.[13] Strange types of extremism are emerging, sometimes from well-known and sometimes from less well-known communities. For instance, one would not have expected in any normal situation for a mother to consent to the burning of her child alive just

---

12 'N.Y. to battle sexual abuse among ultra-Orthodox Jews', *Haaretz.com* (1 April 2009), http://www.haaretz.com/hasen/spages/1075535.html, accessed 11 May 2014.
13 Hannah Osborne, 'Child abuse hidden in London's strict Orthodox Jewish community', *International Business Times* (30 January 2013), http://www.ibtimes.co.uk/articles/429593/20130130/child-sex-abuse-dispaches-hidden-britain-jewish.htm, accessed 27 April 2013.

because her cult leader believed that the child was the antichrist,[14] but it did happen.

The *Jewish Week* revealed the plague of child sex abuse that has inflicted the Orthodox Jewish community in New York. This has been worsened by the institutional injustice in covering up the crime and its effects on the victims. The law-enforcement agencies rebuked the community for the cover-up.[15]

By citing these examples, it is not implied that because of the misdeeds of certain rabbis and priests, all the rabbis and priests in the world are blameworthy. It would be irresponsible to imply that these types of behaviour emanate from the teachings of Christianity and Judaism. Hence, in as much as Christianity and Judaism cannot be blamed for the deplorable behaviour of their followers, Islam cannot be blamed for the misconduct of any Muslims. Yet, under the pretext of freedom of speech, Muslims are vilified by filmmakers, cartoonists, and novelists in Western societies.

In the United States, over 3 million reports of child abuse are received annually; about 30 per cent of abused children end up abusing their own children; a report of child abuse is made every ten seconds; 14 per cent of all men and 36 per cent of all women in prison were abused as children.[16] Additionally, abuse against the elderly is also reported in many Western societies.

Even in the matter of a widely publicised furore created in some biased Western media branding Muslims as being wife-bashers, statistics

---

14 *International Business Times*, http://www.ibtimes.co.uk/articles/461651/20130426/chile-burn-baby-bonfire-antichrist.htm, accessed 27 April 2013.

15 Hella Winston, 'Judge Lashes Out at Orthodox Community in Sex-Abuse Case; Says It Protects Abusers, Not Victims', *Jewish Week*, 10 February 2009.

16 Child-abuse statistics and facts website, http://www.childhelp.org/pages/statistics, accessed 28 May, 2013.

show that there is a rising number of cases in the West where not only wives are beaten up by their husbands, but husbands are beaten up by their wives. Sometimes the assaults are so violent that husbands end up in hospitals, according to the reported cases. Many cases of husband-bashing remain unreported because of the shame they are likely to attract. But the biased media are more likely to publicise abuses taking place in Muslim societies only, whereas both Muslim and non-Muslim communities may have been matching each other in this type of extremism.

Naomi Graetz reports from Ben Gurion University of the Negev that the myth of a kind and gentle Jewish husband towards his wife is over. He writes, '"One out of six" or "one out of seven" Israeli woman is regularly beaten up at home. The estimated minimum figure is 100,000 battered women in Israel (of whom 40,000 end up hospitalized)...'[17] But no caricatures are likely to be drawn by Danish cartoonists and the very offensive *Fitna* Dutch filmmakers accusing Jews and Christians of committing domestic cruelties and violence, similar to their enthusiasm in accusing and vilifying the Muslim offenders; although there has been a lot of backlash to the Christian church's cover-up of child sex abuse.

The examples cited are meant to highlight the fact that there are plenty of incidents outside the Muslim communities which have the potential of creating a media circus and facilitating the production of offensive cartoons and novels. Yet Muslims are singled out for witch-hunting.

In any event, the case studies taken from real-life problems prove that extremism in religious, social, and political arenas is not restricted to a particular religious group or community but is shared among people of different ethnic backgrounds.

---

17 Naomi Gaetz, 'Judaism Confronts Wife-beating', *Women in Judaism* (vol. 1, no. 2, 1998), http://wjudaism.library.utoronto.ca/index.php/wjudaism/article/viewArticle/172/205, accessed 11 May, 2014.

DEFORMED SENSE OF HEROISM

Many Muslim opinion makers and men of religion have fallen into another type of extremism. They permit themselves a pattern of behaviour which they dislike in others. They do not like anybody to be bigoted against them, whereas they themselves are bigoted against their opponents. They like to see others judge them with fairness and justice, whereas they themselves are divorced from a sense of justice. If the clerics, who have given themselves the right to speak in the name of the shariah law, cannot be fair to those having different views and outlooks, then their judgment cannot be trusted. Their judgment becomes unreliable when they glorify publicly the worst criminals and terrorists in modern times just because they share the same ideology with each other and are obsessed by the phobia of a common enemy.

The global community views with abhorrence any attempt at condoning acts of violence and outright terrorism against innocent souls. But this is precisely what some Muslim opinion makers and clerics are engaged in doing. It is stressed that what the Muslims do or say is not necessarily Islamic. Islam as a religion and a set of values is miles away from the strange and abnormal ways in which Muslims sometimes think and behave. This may be motivated by sectarian and racial prejudice, malice against certain ethnic communities, and a misconceived concept of jihad.

In the context of Muslim extremism, an overview would speak volumes about the eccentric and deviant sense of heroism promulgated in glorifying criminals and terrorists. No conscientious human being could accept that mass murderers of innocent people be portrayed as role models. If the opinion makers are prepared to stoop to this level of thinking, then this portrays their gross prejudice.

The Salafi extremists, in the 'moderate' Hashemite Kingdom of Jordan, publicly celebrated the bridal parties for their 'martyr'—the

inhuman and notorious criminal and terrorist Abu Musab al-Zarqawi—
as he was envisaged to have been welcomed by the houris in the garden
of paradise. Bin Laden paid him a warm tribute. In a video message
televised on Al-Qaeda and Taliban-sympathetic 'independent' popular
Arab media, he conveyed condolences to the worldwide Muslim community for a 'great loss' they suffered by losing Al-Zarqawi. According
to the standards laid down by Bin Laden, the heinous criminals like
Al-Zarqawi were guaranteed an exalted status in paradise. At the advent
of the Muslim holy month of Ramadan in August 2011, the late President
Gaddafi's mufti (jurist who issues religious rulings or edicts) issued
a fatwa (religious ruling) that those who have been fighting Gaddafi
should not bother to fast because, according to him, their fasts are not
acceptable by God. Hence, even worshipping God was perceived to be
held hostage by succumbing to the authority of the despot and dictator.
Just before his downfall, again the mufti made his desperate appeal that
Gaddafi is the representative of God on earth. But the Libyan people
did not bother to pay attention to his insane plea.

Shaykh Salman al-Awdah, the famous cleric from Saudi Arabia, said
on *The Shariah and the Life* programme on Al Jazeera Arabic TV on 20
February, 2011, that the good thing about Libya is that the entire population is of Sunnis and all of them are from the Maliki madhhab (school
of law). The homogeneous picture painted by Al-Awdah did not comply
with the situation on the ground, where interfighting flared up between
people of the same school. The clerics got divided into pro- and anti-
Gaddafi factions. These factions fought each other in a brutal civil war,
causing tens of thousands of deaths and injuries. But no united stance
was heard from the country's clerics who were presumed to be of the
same school of law.

From February 2011 onwards, the diplomats, military personnel,
ambassadors, ministers, and army generals of Libya started deserting
Gaddafi's evil regime, together with some of his personal advisors and

top officials. The dictator was a fan of his fellow power maniac and dictator Saddam of Iraq but had learned nothing from his downfall. He had built a big idol in the memory of his hero. But with the way Gaddafi himself fell from grace and met his destiny, no surviving dictator would dare to build an idol or monument in his memory. His death was a sigh of relief for his countrymen, who had suffered throughout his autocratic reign of forty-two years.

A senior minister in the Gaddafi regime disclosed after his defection that he carried evidence that the dictator had personally ordered the bombing of the Pan Am flight over Lockerbie in 1988. Anybody who had observed his behaviour and arrogance since he grabbed power in 1969 could have deduced that he was quite capable of doing very unusual things. If Nero could rejoice at the burning of Rome, other tyrants are not less capable of doing it.

The West should have known that nobody in Libya could have taken the initiative of blowing up a civilian aircraft and killing innocent travellers without a direct order from the dictator himself. Yet, as soon as Gaddafi opened the treasury of his nation to pay over two billion dollars in compensation for his crime, he became very respectable. The heads of state of some European countries queued up for pilgrimage to his Bedouin tent. One head of state even bowed down to kiss his hands respectfully for winning lucrative contracts for his private companies. This proves how insensitive some heads of state of civilised nations are towards the sufferings of the people at the hands of the dictatorial regimes as long as they end up milking benefits from them.

For over three decades, Saddam, the dictator of Iraq, enjoyed unqualified support from many Arab and European countries. In his eight-year war against Iran, some countries supplied him with strategic military intelligence and chemical weapons, which he frivolously used against the Kurds and the Shias. The dictator was given a free reign to carry out his brutal suppression at home. He even summoned the support of international Muslim clergy, who met in Baghdad. The clerics participating in the conference allowed themselves to be exploited by the dictator, who banked on sectarian differences. The oil-rich Arab nations were looking for a buffer zone with Iran, and their clerics wanted to assert their sectarian supremacy over a non-Arab regional power of Shia Iran. But their ambition remains unfulfilled to this day.

The present situation in Iraq demonstrates that militant extremists and outlaws share the same ambition. Saddam and Bin Laden departed from this world without coming anywhere nearer to fulfilment of their objectives. In the process, thousands of innocent people have been killed indiscriminately, thanks to the strong Arab media backing and financial aid from petro dollars that both Saddam and Bin Laden enjoyed.

After the killing of Bin Laden, the radical Salafi establishment across the world paid him a warm tribute and hailed him as a '*mujahid*' (fighter in the cause of God) notwithstanding the fact that the overwhelming majority of Bin Laden's victims were Muslims and his hands were stained with the blood of innocent people. Yet, to his fellow psychotic extremists, he was a 'hero' and 'martyr'. His fans held his funeral prayers in absentia in their mosques in several countries, but they never had the courtesy of holding prayers in absentia for thousands of innocent victims of Bin Laden.

Even now, some of the most popular Arab satellite TV channels are vigilant never to call Al-Qaeda and the Taliban 'terrorists'. They are always referred to as 'Al-Qaeda' or the 'Taliban organisation'. Their acts of mass killings are referred to as 'so-called terrorism' and the fight against them as 'so-called war on terrorism'.

An imam in one of the mosques in Karachi spoke after the killing of Bin Laden about the lessons to be learnt from his *'shahadat'* ('martyrdom'). He said, as Salah al-Din (Saladin) had fought the Jews to liberate Jerusalem, so did 'Shaykh' Osama Bin Laden. This is a sample of the babble which the congregation is fed in some mosques. Taking undue advantage of the unawareness of many Muslims, such declarations are meant to glorify terrorists and to portray them as heroes.

If only the clerics had taken the lead in denouncing the violent extremist groups clearly and without double talk from the pulpits, much of the misunderstanding prevailing at the grassroots level would have been cleared, and thousands of innocent lives would have been saved. But, unfortunately, some popular clerics use the podium or the pulpits in their mosques to glorify terrorists, which is equivalent to praising the devil in the house of God.

In Pakistan, the ideologues subscribing to Bin Laden's subnormal beliefs wept openly amidst prayers in absentia in the memory of their 'martyr'. The Islamic etiquette of prayers demands that the believers must focus all their attention towards God only. Paradoxically, the same ideologues have been persistently accusing the Shia Muslims that they have created *bidah* (innovation) in Islam by commemorating and weeping over the massacre of Karbala, in which the grandson of the Prophet, Imam Husayn, was brutally killed with his children and small entourage. But when it comes to their heroes, even the sanctities of the mosques and prayers are breached in memory of their 'martyrs' or mass murderers. What is prohibited for others becomes quite permissible for them and that, too, for the sake of a notorious outlaw. In this way, day in and day out, the uninformed Sunnis are misled by the extremist clerics, who maintain double standards.

Books with innuendos against the Shia Muslims are distributed free of charge every year to the pilgrims in the pilgrimage season in Saudi

Arabia, alerting them that there are 'misguided' people around them and advising them to avoid these people. Such is the campaign that the radical ideologues undertake, with state support, taking undue advantage of the pilgrimage season to market their brand of Islam. Said K. Aburish, in his book *The House of Saud*, cites several cases of persecution for bringing into the country Shia literature (p. 74). Saud Al Ahmad was executed in a much-publicised case in 1981 for a similar offence.

In contrast, Bin Laden, whose violence claimed mostly the lives of innocent civilians, is still portrayed as a 'hero' and 'martyr' by his followers. This attitude of the extremists is an affront to the dignity of thousands of souls, Muslims and non-Muslims alike, who were killed mercilessly by the militants.

The video tapes of Bin Laden were shown as breaking news on the most popular Arab satellite TVs. In his video recordings, Bin Laden praised and glorified the criminals who blew up the World Trade Centre twin towers in New York. Yet the Indian Salafi intellectual and celebrity Dr Zakir Naik, in his Q&A programmes on Al-Salam (Peace) TV, on which he appears regularly, totally rejected any allegation that Bin Laden had any involvement in the 9/11 attacks.

Bin Laden himself had eulogised the 9/11 hijackers in his recordings and appealed to the global Muslim youths to emulate their example. In his audio broadcast on Al Jazeera Arabic TV on May 24, 2006, he bluntly confessed that he had personally assigned this duty to the hijackers. Yet the video in which the confession of the crime came directly from the horse's mouth was considered by the devotees of Bin Laden not sufficient proof of his involvement in the savage crime.

Dr Naik, a missionary public speaker who has fans in the thousands, is on record as having said that if Osama bin Laden is a terrorist, then all Muslims are terrorists. Before passing such loose statements on a public platform, he should have asked himself who had given him a mandate or authority to speak on behalf of all Muslims. If he felt strongly about an issue, the most he could have done was to speak for himself or for the Deobandi ideology (the Indo-Pak version of Wahhabism or Salafism) that he espouses. Many Muslims felt very offended that he had the audacity of associating the name of an outlaw with the reputation of the global Muslim community.

One of the features of mob mentality, of which some celebrity opinion makers seem to be taking full advantage, is manifested in the huge gatherings of the fans of Dr Naik. The mob almost always reacts with claps and cheers as soon as the celebrity answers the questions from the audience. The mob is groomed to believe that the celebrity has always to be the winner in his gathering and his opponents have to be the losers. His opinion is portrayed as perfect.

Under normal circumstances, people take offence at being associated with mass murderers. But no eyebrows were raised by the mob of Dr Naik when he linked a known international terrorist with the good name of the global Muslim community. Those who depend on mob mentality are quite aware that the mob cannot think for itself. In response to a question from the audience enquiring about his sect, Dr Naik replied that there are no sects in Islam. He claimed that Islam is one religion, as in Saudi Arabia. As simple as this! The mob cheered. Even a naïve observer could tell that in Saudi Arabia, the Wahhabi sect is dominant and state sponsored. The state clerics belong to this school throughout the Saudi Kingdom. The non-Wahhabis are persecuted and suppressed, as in the eastern region of Saudi Arabia. Many reports produced by human-rights agencies bear witness to this fact.

Having realised that his claim was grossly exaggerated, he immediately tried to justify the existence of the four legal schools in Sunni Islam by saying that all the four imams, Abu Hanifah, Malik,

Shafi'I, and Ibn Hanbal, had done a great job to convey the 'right Islam' to people. But nobody in his mob questioned him that if the 'right Islam' was already conveyed by the four imams of the Sunnis, then which Islam did Ibn Taymiyyah and Ibn Abd al-Wahhab seek to convey much later, which created a permanent rift within the Sunni schools?

Under the Saudi system, poverty is widespread, even in the capital Riyadh, although it is the largest oil-producing country in the Middle East and one of the richest in the world. The extravagance of the Saudi royals has been widely covered in the international Arabic and English media since the oil-price boom of the 1970s. The Quran specifically prohibits wastage and extravagant spending. Yet Dr Naik had the audacity of claiming that the Saudi system is a 'pure Islamic order'. Under the same logic, perhaps the 9/11 victims should have shown some gratitude that fifteen out of nineteen hijackers involved in the massacre of innocent people were the products of this so-called 'pure Islamic system'.

When a celebrity, respected by thousands of his fans, expresses biased opinions on contestable political issues, his stance is bound to cause controversy. The Indian TV channels have produced and shown documentaries publicising Dr Naik's sympathy with Bin Laden, the globally implicated terrorist.

Celebrity culture is a tangible reality, not only in the glamour of the celebrity world in the West but also in religious gatherings, where people tend to surrender their faculty of thinking by blindly succumbing to what the celebrity speaker says. Since World War II, the churches in the United States had depended on celebrity speakers to spread their message, and they had achieved enormous success. For instance, Dr. Norman Vincent Peale, a prolific writer and speaker, achieved a celebrity status as a preacher and minister. In some other religious denominations, too, this culture has prevailed, like with the mass-religious rituals and spiritual exercises led by Swamis in open-air gatherings of Hindu devotees in India and elsewhere.

In recent years, celebrity culture has shifted to the huge religious gatherings of Muslims, especially in India and Pakistan, where it attracts thousands of people. The speaker conveys his message to his crowd. This impresses the members of his audience, who, in any case, are unlikely to verify the facts they hear or to conduct independent research of their own. This method best suits the ideologues. They capitalise on the half knowledge of the mob, knowing very well that in the heat of the moment, their mob would accept at face value whatever the celebrity speaker chooses to say.

Through celebrity culture and personality cult, some segments of Muslims may well be heading towards a new phenomenon in Islamic preaching. This culture has worked very well for Dr Zakir Naik in India and Dr Mohammad Tahir al-Qadri, formerly of Pakistan but now living in Canada, although both are at the opposing ends of Sunni Islam. Dr Naik is closely associated with the Salafis, and Dr Qadri is closely allied with the Sufis. The Salafis consider the Sufis misguided and heretics. Dr Naik takes his religious *fatwas* from the Deobandi establishment, and Dr Qadri is a Sufi authority among the Barelvis, a major grouping of Hanafi Sufis in Pakistan.

The mobs are highly unlikely to realise what the celebrity speaker selectively reveals or conceals. He might get away with hiding loads of facts or disclosing the facts that he wants to promote. In this way, the agenda of a particular school or sect takes momentum. The celebrity is then projected as leaving his opponents speechless. In fact, the opponents might not have been given enough time and opportunity to express their views.

At times, the mob gives the celebrity speaker an exclusive prerogative to declare who are qualified to be raised to the status of heroes and martyrs and who are to be demeaned and demonised, especially those that are seen as the opponents. This is the grim reality of the mob culture, which results in stagnation of individuality of a person, whose voice is lost in the garbled noises of the mob. It might be interesting to explore how the psychology of the mob works. A keen observer can almost accurately say when the mob is going to react with cheers and claps and burst out in laughter. The judgment of the mob is not determined by rational thinking but by emotions.

Unsurprisingly, Dr Naik got away with associating the terror activities of Bin Laden with the Muslim community, the overwhelming majority of which abhors and condemns violence and terrorism. This encouraged him to take another bold step by praying for the mercy and pleasure of God for the most heinous criminal that Islamic history has ever known—Yazid, the son of Mu'awiyah, who had carried out the most dreadful massacre of the holy progeny of the Prophet Muhammad in 61 AH–680 CE in the city of Karbala in Iraq. With the exception of the followers of Salafi, Wahhabi, and Deobandi brands of Islam, the heinous crime of the caliph of the Umayyad dynasty (661–750 CE) has been attracting condemnation to this very day from the worldwide Muslim communities and from most of the Sunni imams, except the followers of Ibn Taymiyyah and Ibn Abd al-Wahhab.

In conclusion, the examples cited of Bin Laden and Yazid, the son of Mu'awiyah, are instances of fake heroism with which the psyche of Muslim mobs is afflicted because of the effects of propaganda and, at times, due to sheer ignorance, as a result of which the outlaws are projected as heroes of Islam.

Chapter 2

UPRISING OF THE MASSES

Two thousand eleven is said to be the year of resuscitation of the suppressed Arab masses after they had remained in a comatose state lasting many decades. The rapidity with which the events in the Arab world unfolded from January 2011 onwards took many observers aback. Some states revolted against the unrepresentative reigns of regional dictators who had usurped the rights of the people and misappropriated the resources and wealth of their nations. This uprising did not take place overnight; it was the product of grievances which had piled up for many years because of widely prevailing injustices.

Revolutions are triggered by masses against violations of civil rights and freedom. They are against repression, unemployment, and poverty. They are against corruption of top government officials and civil servants. They are against treacheries committed by the officials of the state against the people. They are against betrayals committed by dictators for the sake of preserving and protecting their power base. When the bottled-up grievances of the poor and deprived masses explode in the faces of the oppressors, this becomes a warning call to the dictators that either they have to mend their ways or face the consequences.

Saddam, the Nero of modern Arab history, fell unceremoniously from power after ruling Iraq for over three decades. This was followed by the fall of the dictator of Tunisia, Zine El Abidine Ben Ali. He fled the country with enormous loot from the public treasury. Soon after the Tunisian revolution, the youth revolution in Liberty Square in Cairo succeeded in toppling the Egyptian dictator Husni Mubarak; and then came Gaddafi's turn, the dictator of Libya. He was captured in over ground sewage pipes, similar to Saddam, who was captured underground. Both were sixty-nine at the time of their deaths. The policies of both were based on double-crossing and betraying their own people.

The Tunisian dictator, unsurprisingly, was given a safe haven and refuge in Saudi Arabia, similar to Idi Amin Dada, the late tyrant of Uganda. The Saudis pressurised the new Egyptian military regime not to put Husni Mubarak on trial for corruption, bribery, and murder. But the deposed dictator had to face trial under the elected regime of the Muslim Brotherhood, which itself fell from grace within a year of assuming power.

An official of the Muslim Brotherhood movement issued a statement on 11 May, 2012, that, in 2011, Saudi Arabia offered four billion US dollars to the Egyptian authorities in return for setting the former dictator free. Later, Saudi Arabia emerged as the main supporter of the anti-Muslim Brotherhood camp and offered billions of dollars in aid to the regime which succeeded in toppling President Morsi.

Gaddafi was determined that if he could not rule over his people for life, then he would rather fight them, which he did, and was killed in disgrace. Forty-two years of absolute dictatorship were not enough, so he groomed his eight sons and a daughter to inherit the country after him. Instead, he lost some of his sons and grandsons in his own lifetime in a battle which he could never have won against the will of his people.

It has become customary among Muslim dictators that they put up stern resistance against relinquishing power until either they kick the bucket in office or are kicked out of office. There are some common features which the totalitarian regimes share with each other. They are unrepresentative and unaccountable to their people for whatever they do and in whichever ways they fill their coffers from the public treasury. Their personal wealth, smuggled out of the country, runs into hundreds of millions of dollars. They tolerate corruption in the organs of the state in order to remain in power.

In one of his public addresses, Gaddafi said that he had created modern Libya and his grandfather had fallen martyr for the sake of Libya and that he, too, would rather die than relinquish his position. But as he was intoxicated with self-aggrandisement, he did not realise that he had robbed his people of their fundamental rights. For every single drop of blood that his grandfather may have shed for Libya, he and his sons and daughter had already sucked it from the veins of the Libyan people.

After his downfall, it transpired that Gaddafi's desert tent was a big hoax. The tent was built in the compound of his palace. This was meant to deceive the Libyans that their ruler was living in simplicity. But when the doors of his palace and that of his sons and daughter were opened after his downfall, the world saw the super-luxurious life enjoyed by the dictator and his children, with crates of wine discovered in their palaces. One after another, as the dictators of Tunisia, Egypt, and Libya fell, their personal wealth smuggled out of the country was being discovered and disclosed to the public. What remains undisclosed might be far more shocking than what has been disclosed. The Arab world is still suffering from a very high rate of illiteracy and poverty. This predicament could have been solved a generation ago if the resources of the Muslims had not been dumped into prestigious projects and the arms industry for the benefit of the ruling elites.

HIJACKING THE REVOLUTIONS

Initially, revolutions may succeed in toppling dictators. But counter-revolutionary measures are set out almost immediately. The most extreme measures to hijack the revolution are adopted by some religious extremists who endeavour to control the state for imposing their own ideologies. They are not interested in the democratic process or in democracy. In some countries that witnessed mass movements and revolutions, these elements played the role of replacing one tyranny with another.

The vacuum created is filled by the militants, who tend to make lots of noises and claims in the name of jihad—the jihad of cutting the throats of and disfiguring the dead bodies of their enemies, of slashing the chests and chewing the mutilated body parts of the dead, and the jihad of what their muftis call *munakahah*, permitting the raping of women of the enemy camp. All of these acts have been conducted by the militant ideologues in Syria and Iraq and publicised on the Internet, with harrowing scenes posted on YouTube and on the websites of the extremist groups.

Syrian society had been multireligious, multiethnic, and multicultural. Before the current political turmoil, Syrian religious communities, of which there are several, had enjoyed freedom to practise their beliefs, religious rites, and cultural traditions. But the political upheaval in the country since March 2011 and the influx of Salafi militants and armed insurgents from different nationalities changed the scene. The *takfiri*s have torn Syrian society and its people apart. They have been supported generously by some oil-rich countries in the Middle East. For the first time in many decades, the minorities were being targeted on sectarian grounds in Syria. Members of the minority sects were being killed by the militants under the pretext that they were infidels. Many were kidnapped with Taliban-style terror.

There are videos that the militants of the terrorist group Al-Nusra Front have posted on YouTube, showing savage mutilation of a dead Syrian soldier, where the killer takes pride in eating his bodily organs after ripping his chest apart. Shocking scenes have been posted by both sides showing massacres of children. It is now an open secret, widely publicised on international forums and newspapers that most, if not all, of the foreign insurgents in Syria, whose illegal entry was facilitated from eighty-three countries, were, at one time or another, supported by countries neighbouring Syria like Turkey, Saudi Arabia, Qatar, and the tyrants of Bahrain.

One of the radical clerics issued a fatwa that the insurgents fighting in Syria, who are deprived of sexual pleasure, can marry Syrian women who are on the side of the Syrian regime only for a few hours so that they could fight with renewed vigour. In this way, they would also be able to open up the doors of paradise for these women for rendering such an invaluable service. He had earlier issued a fatwa that a girl must not sit alone with her father except in the presence of her mother or brothers until she gets married,[18] lest her father decides to rape her.

Turning a blind eye to the atrocities and crimes against humanity committed by the so-called mujahidin (those who fight jihad) in Syria, the well-known Egyptian cleric based in Qatar, Shaykh Yusuf al-Qaradawi, president of the International Association of Muslim Ulama (scholars), issued a fatwa that the civilians and religious scholars who are on the side of the Syrian regime have to be fought. They are a legitimate target, he declared in his interview on Al Jazeera Arabic TV.[19] Al-Qaradawi conveniently forgot that only a few years ago, he himself was on very friendly terms with the tyrannical Gaddafi, and the emir of Qatar and his family were enjoying friendly relations with the president of Syria and his family.

---

18 http://www.youtube.com/watch?v=zAG72Dq9rW4, accessed 1 June 2013.
19 http://www.youtube.com/watch?v=-e-J2977xB4, accessed 1 June 2013.

Advocating violence against civilians is a flagrant violation of international and Islamic law, of which Al-Qaradawi is supposed to be an expert par excellence. But history is full of instances where Islam and the shariah (Islamic law) have been made subservient to the political interests and wishes of the ruling elites. Instead of permitting violence, he should have preached that violence is not a solution to any crisis, especially in modern times, in which the policies of nations are based solely on selfish political and strategic interests. Violence breeds violence, and, in the end, everybody loses.

Al-Qaradawi's fatwa attracted widespread condemnation. According to the statement of the Association of Religious Scholars in Syria, it was in breach of the traditions of the Prophet and the shariah law. But as it was issued under the environment of the Muslim Brotherhood reign in Cairo, the Muslim Brotherhood's ex-president Morsi added his voice by describing in his address the Shia community as *anjas* (impure).

Shaykh Al-Qaradawi was quick to rightly condemn the Boston Marathon terror attacks. But in the same period, Al-Qaradawi did not raise a voice of condemnation when civilians were being randomly killed in cold blood in a series of suicide bombings in Iraq and Pakistan simply because the victims were Shia Muslims. In early July 2016, at the end of the Muslim holy month of Ramadan, on the eve of Eid al-Fitr, the Muslim feast of celebration, like Christmas is for the Christians, as the children and their mothers were doing Eid shopping in the Karrada area of Baghdad, four suicide bombers from ISIL carried out a most bestial massacre, where children were turned into charcoal and hundreds of civilians were killed and maimed. The savage massacre shocked the world, but these clerics who espouse the same ideology as ISIL did not have the moral decency to condemn the massacre just because the overwhelming majority of their victims were Shia Muslims. The amount of sectarian hatred and malice that these types of clerics espouse has surpassed the hatred and malice that their progenitors in the pre-Islamic Era of Ignorance used to espouse against their foes and rivals. But the religious mantle that these clerics wear carries religious responsibility. If they cannot live up to the responsibility, they should not deceive the simple-minded masses, who tend to pay them respect.

Al-Qaradawi had in the past achieved much publicity when he had permitted suicide bombings against Israeli civilians, saying that in Israeli occupied land, there are no civilian targets; all targets are military. At that time, the United States was a sworn enemy in his sight. But in the context of crisis in Syria, he appealed to the United States to get its act together and to intervene militarily. The video of his Friday sermon is posted on YouTube, where he is pleading to the United States that it is wrong to say that the mujahidin in Syria, after defeating the regime, are going to be a threat to Israel and would attack Israel.[20]

Political leaders in Arab countries are aware that if the militants succeed in creating the Islamic Emirate in Syria, then they will be the next target. They know that the godfathers of the movement have issued instructions that, wherever there is a potential of establishing an Islamic state, as in Afghanistan, the mujahidin from all around the world must all proceed in that direction, which they have been doing in Syria from many countries in the East and West.

COUNTERING MASS MOVEMENTS WITH SECTARIAN STRIFE

Oppression is the antithesis of justice, and justice is the basic need of human society. No society or community can survive without justice. The oppressors are seen as the enemies of people because they believe in coercing their wills on others.

---

20 https://www.youtube.com/watch?v=Wp3B4p-iorw, accessed 21 June 2013.

As much as the ultranationalists are intolerant and coercive in their political philosophies, the radical ideologues, too, have shown no tolerance for people of different beliefs. They take for granted that they are right, and, therefore, others should take religious guidance exclusively from them.

Traditionally and historically, the Egyptian and Yemeni Sunnis have been following the Shafi'i, and not Salafi, school; the Sunnis in North Africa have been following the Maliki, and not Salafi, school; the Iraqi Sunnis have been following the Hanafi, and not Salafi, school; the Saudi Sunnis have been following the Hanbali, and not Salafi, school. This means that the organised Salafism, inspired by Ibn Taymiyyah and Ibn Abd al-Wahhab, is a relatively new phenomenon in the Sunni world. These figures have acquired prominence only after the influx of petro dollars in Saudi Arabia.

All the Sunni schools—Hanafi, Maliki, Shafi'i, and Hanbali—closed the doors of *ijtihad* (independent reasoning in jurisprudential matters). Nevertheless, it was deemed necessary for their disciples to follow one of the four jurisprudential schools of Sunni Islam. The Shia Jafari School (the Twelvers) do not deem the doors of *ijtihad* to be closed. Most rules of jurisprudence are common between the Sunni and the Shia schools to the extent that the renowned Sunni seminary Al-Azhar in Cairo has rejected the intransigent attitude of the Salafis and Wahhabis against Shia jurisprudence. It issued its approval that one may follow the Shia Jafari jurisprudential rules, amidst objections from the Wahhabi establishment.[21] The Wahhabis reject *taqlid* (imitation of the jurisprudential schools), but they did not hesitate to form their own school based on the rigid interpretations of Ibn Taymiyyah and Ibn Abd al-Wahhab.

---

21 http://www.human-rights-in islam.co.uk/ index.php?option=com_content&view=art icle&id=250:sheikh-al-azhar-rejects-wahabi-extremist-call-for-withdrawal-of-recognition-shia-doctrine&catid=34:religious&Itemid=53, accessed 4 June 2013.

Since the influx of petro dollars, scholarships have been offered around the Muslim world for studies at religious seminaries in Saudi Arabia. These seminaries and universities are administered and managed by the Wahhabi system. Their syllabi and educational systems are built upon the Wahhabi ideology. Literature is constantly published, translated into several languages, and distributed free charge around the world for preaching the Wahhabi creed and its interpretations of the Quran and Sunnah. Consequently, the four traditional schools of law of the Sunnis have come under heavy Salafi and Wahhabi influence. The latter, in turn, have come under heavy influence of the *nasibi*s (those who harbour intense hatred against the nearest kith and kin and progeny of the Prophet) and the Kharijis (the violent insurgents and secessionists from the community of believers), who rebelled against the caliph Ali ibn Abi Talib (656–661 CE), the first imam in Shia faith and beliefs.

The globalised Salafi/Wahhabi movement is trying to establish its hegemony and monopoly over all other schools or sects in Islam by offering handsome stipends and scholarships to Muslim organisations. The only stumbling block standing in its way is the Shia bloc, which is not prepared to give way or succumb to any pressure, even at the cost of ethnic cleansing perpetrated against the Shia community in several countries by their extremist elements. There have been many violent attempts in recent years to subdue the Shia bloc. In Iraq and Pakistan, ethnic cleansing has not worked, although thousands have been killed and many are being killed on regular basis in targeted attacks.

The religious extremists act as if they have a mandate to admit into paradise people of their own pervert ilk, even if they are drowned in crimes and vices. They condemn others into hell, even if they are full of good deeds and virtues. Their backbones are their muftis who give them the mandate to invade foreign countries like the poverty-stricken Yemen. With a sense of self-righteousness, like the Taliban and Al-Qaeda, they are involved in burning hundreds of copies of the Quran when they attack the mosques of the rival sects, as they have been doing in Bahrain by destroying more than thirty mosques belonging to the Shia and desecrating copies of the Quran stored therein.

The incident of burning copies of the Quran by the American troops in Afghanistan in February 2012 provoked storms of violent protests around the world. But when the Saudi Wahhabis and the Bahraini government forces destroyed the mosques of the Shia, the same copies of the Quran were set on fire. Neither the militants nor their sponsors showed any respect for the sanctity of the mosques and the sacredness of the Quran when they carried out their mission, under the auspices of the so-called pure Islamic system that they claim to espouse. The suicide bombers, who blow themselves up in the midst of the congregational prayers in Shia mosques, also destroy copies of the Quran in the process.

The mental complex of the extremists gives them the exclusive right to decide which people are Muslims and which are infidels. On the international scene, this ideology showed its true effect in Egypt, when their ideologues desecrated the shrines of Sunni Sufi shaykhs after the fall of the dictator Mubarak. At almost the same time in April 2011, the Taliban of Pakistan caused harrowing carnage by killing and maiming hundreds of innocent people when their suicide bombers blew up a Sunni Sufi shrine. In Egypt, the extremists failed to steer mass movement in their favour. Therefore, they stirred up trouble between Christians and Muslims as they had done in Lebanon many times in the past.

In Egypt, fanatics were released from the cocoon and provoked into attacking places of worship and desecrating tombs and shrines. More than one hundred shrines were destroyed across Egypt. In April 2011, the religious scholars of Al-Azhar, the highest religious authority of Sunni Muslims, issued a ruling that it is totally prohibited in Islam to desecrate shrines of the saints and virtuous souls. The scholars of Al-Azhar decreed that those who desecrate the holy shrines are outside the fold of Islam. The Egyptian people demanded the military regime to take strict measures against the fanatics, who were bent on igniting sectarian strife among the Egyptians.

WRONG CHOICES AND INFECTIOUS POLITICS

In recent years, a popular and respected figure like Shaykh Yusuf al-Qaradawi has joined the trumpets calling against the spread of Shia teachings in Sunni countries. Al-Qaradawi must have been aware that this is a century of technological revolution and fast communication, which has broken down the borders between nations. Gone are the days when the rulers and their clerics used to decide how the masses must and must not think.

In a century when people are bombarded on cyberspace with a host of ideas of atheistic, agnostic, and nonreligious natures, a responsible man of religion should have refrained from creating a phobia against other schools or sects. He should have been worried about the spread of nudity, indecency, immorality, and sexual promiscuity in Muslim countries. He should have been worried about the widespread child poverty and sickening scenes of child beggars in many Muslim and Arab capitals. He should have been concerned that even in the oil-rich Arab countries, children are being abused and foreign workers are being exploited and deprived of their fair wages.

In March 2012, the chief of police of Dubai warned Al-Qaradawi that he would not be permitted to enter the country because of his ill-informed attack on the police of Dubai. In May 2012, the Tunisian authorities warned that they would bring a legal action against him for provoking the Salafis in the country and for instigating sectarian trouble. In early February 2014, the ambassador of Qatar was called to the Foreign Office of the United Arab Emirates in Abu Dhabi, where a protest was launched against Al-Qaradawi's offensive attack on UAE from Qatar's soil. He is based in Qatar, from where his Friday sermons are aired on the state TV. Previously, the post-Morsi regime in Egypt banned him from entering Egyptian land. Palestinian Authority President Mahmoud Abbas withdrew an honorary Palestinian nationality granted to him by Hamas.

Qatar was involved in financing the Salafis in Egypt and supporting the Muslim Brotherhood movement. Qatar was accused by the regimes of Tunisia and Libya, not to mention Syria, of meddling in their internal affairs by financing the Salafi extremists and setting the scenario for igniting sectarian trouble. In the pre-election campaign for France's president, Qatar was singled out by the opposition parties for funding the penetration of the extremist Salafis into the French society and supporting Nicolas Sarkozy in the French presidential election campaign.

With the blessings of the court clerics, the two excellencies, the ex-emir (or ruler), and the ex-prime minister and foreign minister of Qatar spent three billion US dollars to support the rebels in Syria and eight billion US dollars to support the Muslim Brotherhood projects in Egypt. Whatever the motivation might have been, it was badly thwarted as Saudi Arabia and other Persian Gulf countries emerged as the principal providers of aid to the new regime which took over from the Muslim Brotherhood.

The two hamads had to hand over power to the young emir, although compared to the aging leadership in Saudi Arabia, the former were construed to be in their teens. But they had to relinquish power because their ambition was getting on the nerves of their close foreign allies. Their ambition of playing a superpower game in international politics had gone too far, and some foreign powers were clearly annoyed with them. One of the reasons the ex-ruler abdicated in favour of the young emir was to ensure that the heir to the throne becomes a new ruler in his lifetime.

Coming back to the role of Al-Qaradawi in regional politics, by February 2014, a political row was developing between Qatar and Saudi Arabia, following Al-Qaradawi's attack in his Friday sermon. He criticised Saudi Arabia for donating $3 billion to the post-Morsi Egyptian regime. He alleged that the regime was directly involved in killing Egyptian people.

On August 25, 2013, in an episode of an *Al-Shariah wa al-Hayat* (*The Shariah and Life*) programme on Al Jazeera Arabic TV, under the topic 'Who are the Kharijis?', Al-Qaradawi completely evaded the answer in its historical context. Instead, he discussed it solely in the context of power struggle between the Muslim Brotherhood movement and the secular parties, branding General Abd al-Fattah al-Sisi, now the new president elect but at the time the defence minister of Egypt, and his supporters as '*kharijis*' (outside the fold of the community of believers). He emphasised that anybody not working for restoration of the elected President Morsi to his post is a khariji. The political bias of Qatar's media and the clerics in favour of the Muslim Brotherhood and in favour of violent organisations such as the Taliban puzzles many analysts and observers.

The Taliban had not in any manner changed their militancy and terrorism against civilians. But this did not deter Qatar from giving them recognition and opening up a representative office for them in the capital, Doha, under the name of the Islamic Emirate of Afghanistan. Since then, the office has been closed. Initially, however, this was the most undiplomatic move against Afghanistan's sovereignty. On 18 June, 2013, as the Taliban's office was being inaugurated, they were involved in killing NATO troops on the ground in Afghanistan. But according to the bizarre standards set, neither the violence of the Taliban nor that of Al-Qaeda and its sister militant groups is called terrorism in the popular Arab media.

Soeren Kern writes, 'Qatar, the most fraudulent "moderate", is "sparing no effort" to spread Wahhabi Islam across "the whole world", discouraging integration, encouraging jihad'.[22] But Al-Qaradawi was blind to all these interferences into the affairs of the European nations and of attempts at pitting Sunnis against fellow Sunnis and Sunnis against Shias.

Qatar and Saudi Arabia had publicly declared their policy of financing and arming the militants in Syria. Since then, Qatar has taken a backseat, and Saudi Arabia is in control of the steering as a leading supporter of insurgency in Syria. There has been rivalry between Qatar and Saudi Arabia in regard to who is more Salafi than the other. Qatar's rulers claim to be the progeny of Ibn Abd al-Wahhab, as the Saudi rulers do. Both have been in the forefronts in supporting Salafi movements around the world.

The Washington Post reports the arming of rebels with advanced weapons, stockpiled on the Turkish border and financed by Persian Gulf states.[23]

Michael Stephens writes in BBC News, 'Qatar's position and influence in the region would be irreparably damaged should the rebels [in Syria] it has backed so openly be defeated...distrust clouds Western interpretations of Qatar's intentions, and its relationships with hard-line

---

22 'Qatar Financing Wahhabi Islam in France, Italy, Ireland and Spain', *Gatestone Institute International Policy Council* http://www.gatestoneinstitute.org/2833/qatar-financing-wahhabi-islam-europe, 9 February 2012.

23 Karen DeYoung and Liz Sly, 'Syrian rebels get influx of arms with Gulf neighbors' money, U.S. coordination', *The Washington Post*, 16 May 2012.

Islamists in Libya and Syria as well as the country's links with Hamas are troubling Washington and its allies'.[24]

The Independent newspaper reports that Saudi Arabian, Qatari, and Turkish intelligence was heavily involved in arming the Muslim Brotherhood of Syria across the Turkish borders.[25] According to other newspaper reports, transfer of militants is facilitated from Saudi Arabia, Qatar, Turkey, Kuwait, Libya, Tunisia, Algeria, Morocco, Jordan, Lebanon, Iraq, Yemen, Somalia, Chechnya, Pakistan, Afghanistan, and from different countries, including several Western countries, into Syria. The militants joining Al-Nusra Front, allied with Al-Qaeda, are covered in detail in an informative article in *The New York Times*.[26] In some countries, convicted murderers were released from prisons under the condition of joining the insurgents in Syria. In Saudi Arabia, Yemeni workers with work permit problems were threatened with deportation if they refused to join the militants in Syria.[27]

The Financial Times magazine reports from its informed sources that Qatar injected $3 billion for the insurgents in Syria. It also discusses the Saudi and Turkish aid for the insurgents. This analytical report reveals, 'The Stockholm International Peace Research Institute, which tracks arms transfers, says that between April 2012 and March [2013], more than 70 military cargo flights from Qatar landed in Turkey for Syrian militant groups. Some of these Al-Qaeda affiliated groups are involved in terrorising civilians, according to the UN Human Rights reports'.[28]

---

24 http://www.bbc.co.uk/news/world-middle-east-22875409, 16 June 2013.

25 'Exclusive: Arab states arm rebels as UN talks of Syrian civil war', http://www.independent.co.uk/news/world/middle-east/exclusive-arab-states-arm-rebels-as-un-talks-of-syrian-civil-war-7845026.html, 13 June 2012.

26 Eric Schmitt, 'Worries Mount As Syria Lures West's Muslims', *The New York Times*, 27 July 2013.

27 'Riyadh sends Yemeni workers to fight in Syria', http://india.shafaqna.com/shafaq/item/9963-riyadh-sends-yemeni-workers-to-fight-in-syria.html, 20 July 2013.

28 Roula Khalaf and Abigail Fielding-Smith, 'How Qatar seized control of the Syrian revolution', *FT Magazine*, 17 May 2013.

The purpose of such colossal spending was to promote and serve the narrow political and sectarian interests of the donors. If it was meant solely for humanitarian relief, then the aid money should have been spent to relieve the sufferings of millions of Syrian refugees, who lived under subhuman conditions in refugee camps. If there was any motive for saving Syria's future generation, then children in refugee camps, who were growing up with no educational facilities and no schooling, deserved most of it. Their tragic plight in refugee camps was covered in detail in Al Jazeera Arabic TV documentaries. But not a fraction of money spent on the supply of arms and ammunitions to the terrorists is spent on salvaging the future of these innocent children, who are the main victims of inhuman carnage and disaster in Syria. Consequently, a whole generation of Syria's juveniles is facing annihilation.

Since the invasion and occupation of Iraq in 2003, and especially since the Shia majority in the country dominated the government of Iraq, the Wahhabis and Salafis and their media started their open campaign against what they called the dangers of the spread of Shia thought in Sunni countries. Shaykh Al-Qaradawi and many Saudi Wahhabi clerics played a leading role in this campaign. They provoked the sentiments of half-informed and emotional youths and gave the impression that the Shias have set out to invade the Sunni countries.

King Abdullah of Jordan was the first to create a public phobia of the rise of 'Shia Crescent', as he called it. Since then, the Shia-phobic people have lined up to face what they consider to be the challenge of the spread of Shia teachings in the Sunni world. It is not unlikely that Abu Musab al-Zarqawi, the notorious criminal and terrorist, took up the fight against the Shia Crescent after coming out of prison in Jordan. He was committed to creating mayhem in Iraq.

The London Arabic daily *Al Hayat* published a document authored by Al-Zarqawi on February 12, 2004. It carried a blueprint for triggering civil war in Iraq, which could go on for years and years. It unveiled the extreme spite that his group sought to implant among the masses in an effort to ignite sectarian war simply because he considered the Shia Muslims to be infidels.

On a separate front, in Bahrain, the authorities broke the record of cruelty by kidnapping injured patients, doctors, nurses, and other medical personnel from hospitals in the early days of the uprising in 2011. The government forces attacked the ladies on the streets. They used tear gas in their faces. Boys and women were tortured in prison. They applied inhuman measures against the people who were peacefully demanding their civil rights and provoked them into violence so that they could use live weapons against them, which they did. These facts are well documented in the reports of human-rights agencies.

The masses have been defrauded into believing that their despots are great achievers and, hence, they qualify for unaccountability. The court clerics claim that the unjust and oppressors are equally entitled to enter paradise along with the virtuous and pious souls. Historically, the Umayyad dynasty invented this belief, and it perfectly suited the interest of all other tyrants who succeeded them. The Shias rejected these claims, which, according to them, betray common sense and contradict basic Islamic teachings and values. So, as a result, they are called *rafidah* (rejectionists). The ruling elites and their clerics go as far as misinterpreting the Quranic verse which says, 'O you who believe! Obey God, and obey the Messenger, and those charged with authority among you' (4:59).

The court clerics historically interpreted 'those charged with authority' as their rulers in whatever ways they grab power—through force or intimidation, through sword or gun, through terror or military takeover, through civil war or suppressive measures, or through oppression and crimes against humanity. Once they are on the seat of power, dictators are glorified and become 'commanders of the believers'. The cronies of the rulers among the court clerics and intellectuals form an orchestra praising the dictators and giving them legitimacy.

The youth uprisings of 2011 proved that the Sunni masses for once completely rejected lame justifications to endure unrepresentative and dictatorial regimes. But the unelected rulers and their clerics kept on insisting that it is mandatory in the shariah law to follow the rulers, no matter how oppressive they are.

According to the Islamic faith, obedience to the Messenger of God (the Prophet) is essential because it is tantamount to obeying God. The Messenger never acts against the will of God. He translates the will of God through his actions, deeds, and admonitions. Under the same logic, if 'those charged with authority' follow God and His Messenger, then well and good. But if they defy, deny, and deface the commandments of God, then they have neither obeyed God nor His Messenger. So they cannot occupy an exalted position, as they end up betraying the very essence of the message of the Quran.

But the granting of general immunity to the despots by the court clerics, who are partners in misinterpreting the verse of the Quran, has backfired. For once, all the youth revolutionaries in the Sunni world became rejectionists. The revolutions in Tunisia, Egypt, Libya, and Yemen rendered null and void the historic position taken by the unrepresentative regimes and their muftis.

A line of demarcation was drawn by the devotees of the Household of the Prophet (namely, the Shia) to prove that 'those vested in authority' were not the ones whose reign was founded on massacres, raids, and banditry. From the times of the Umayyad dynasty and thereafter, their supporters portray the same characteristic traits of suppression of freedom and usurpation of the rights of the people.

No power can survive by waging war against its own citizens. Any power that suppresses freedom is bound to end up in a situation where its closest allies turn away their faces in the other direction at crunch time, as the world powers did with the shah of Iran when he was rejected asylum in countries closely allied with him during his hay days.

The people of Bahrain have lived in their country for generations, long before the dynastic rulers arrived, and will remain in the country for generations to come. Wounds inflicted on the body may heal, but wounds inflicted on the heart and soul through systematic torture, imprisonment without trial, and the killing of loved ones are difficult to heal. If the civilised nations of the world remain oblivious to these realities, then they are passing wrong messages to the people of Bahrain, who are facing constant repression.

The devotees of the totalitarian Al-Khalifah dynasty of Bahrain believe that the country, under its absolute dictatorial rule, cannot be more democratic than it already is. Once upon a time, the late King Fahd of Saudi Arabia said, 'The election system has no place in the Islamic creed, which calls for a government of advice and consultation...and holds the ruler fully responsible before his people'.[29]

The late Prince Nayif ibn Abd al-Aziz, the minister of interior in Saudi Arabia for a very long time and the heir to the thrown for a short while, supported repression against any demand for democracy and freedom of speech in his country. His austerity measures were abhorred by the people of eastern Saudi Arabia. His extreme obsession against Bahrain's Shia majority resulted in the invasion of that country by the Saudi forces, in breach of international law. He was behind the decision to give asylum to the ousted despot Zine El Abidine Ben Ali of Tunisia, who is wanted by his country's judicial system for crimes committed against the state, including walking away with many million dollars from

---

29 Esposito, 'Practice and Theory', in Abou El Fadl (2004).

the public treasury. Prince Nayif was behind the suppression of women's rights in Saudi Arabia. If this is what is called 'government of advice and consultation', as the late King Fahd had portrayed, then this type of system and governance ought to be in the *Guinness Book of Records*.

Chapter 3

POLITICAL AND IDEOLOGICAL MANIPULATIONS

I n the aftermath of the 11 September, 2001 terrorist attacks on US soil, the attention of the international community focused on indoctrination administered inside the *madrasahs* (religious schools) in Pakistan, Afghanistan, and Saudi Arabia. Fifteen out of nineteen hijackers were citizens of Saudi Arabia.[30] Many charities in the United States were discovered to have a direct link with terrorism; hence, their funds were frozen by the US government.[31] In the wake of the onslaught from the international community and adverse publicity in the Western media to the sponsors of international terrorism, the radicals had to revamp their policies and change tactics.

---

30 USATODAY.com, http://usatoday30.usatoday.com/news/world/2002/02/06/saudi.htm, 6 February, 2002.

31 See detailed paper on terrorist financing: Mathew A Levitt, 'The Political Economy of Middle East Terrorism', *MERIA Middle East Review of International Affairs*, vol. 6, no. 4, http://meria.idc.ac.il/journal/2002/issue4/jv6n4a3.html, December 2002, and 'Two Saudi nationals named as terrorist financiers', USINFO.STATE.GOV, http://usinfo.state.gov/ei/Archive/2004/Dec/22-862859.html.

Normally, Saudis are very sensitive to any negative publicity because it hampers the cordial relation they enjoy with their main ally, the US administration. In the aftermath of 9/11, the radical Wahhabis suffered a very bad international image from 2001 to 2003. The invasion of Iraq in 2003 opened up opportunities for them to turn the tables and divert the attention of their ideologues from the setbacks. They started feeding them with propaganda against Shia Muslims under the pretext that it was the Shias who invited non-Muslim foreign troops to invade a Muslim country. The *takfiri* clerics claimed that 'those who seek help from infidels are themselves infidels', notwithstanding the fact that Qatar, Bahrain, and Saudi Arabia were directly involved in providing all the help and logistics from military bases on their territories to the occupation forces to launch attacks on Iraq and occupy the country. But it seems, in their dictionary, hypocrisy is an art of behaviour.

IRAQ: THE STRATEGY OF TRIGGERING SECTARIAN WAR

Since the invasion of Iraq by the coalition forces in 2003, the militants and their regional supporters focused on creating upheavals in this country for the main reason that the Shias are in the majority. Al-Qaeda and Saddamites were, and are, heavily involved in insurgency in Iraq. This has been fuelled by the arrival of the Wahhabi ISIL. The Salafi oil powers stood as their principal backers in finance and weaponry, as they do in Syria.

There are serious ideological differences between Al-Qaeda and Saddamites. Yet both have found a common ground for instigating sectarian violence. Their hate campaigns, aimed at triggering sectarian war, extend to despatching suicide bombers into Shia-populated areas for committing genocide. Under their strategy, they have targeted the sacred cities of Karbala and Najaf many times and killed and maimed hundreds of civilians, without a word of condemnation from the radical clerics and politicians. Some popular Arabic channels have dedicated themselves to providing the propaganda, which acts as a backbone for the cause of the insurgents, both in Syria and Iraq. But not even by a slip of the tongue do these channels dare to disclose or discuss the aid package of billions of dollars being pumped to the militants and terrorists.

Hundreds of suicide bombings have taken place since 2003 in Iraq. In their zeal to kill Shias, they end up killing Sunnis too. This is the innate nature of these murderous cliques. The Iraqi government has claimed time and again that it possesses documentary proof and witnesses that some neighbouring countries, mainly Turkey and Saudi Arabia, are involved in the conspiracy of creating chaos in Iraq as they have done in Syria. Lately, after the public confession of the terrorists caught in action, top government officials of both Syria and Iraq have named Saudi Arabia and its security agencies for being directly involved in financing and arming the insurgents. After the surge in terrorist activities in Caucasia, which is under the jurisdiction of the Russian Federation, the commentators on Russian Television (RT) have also blamed Saudi Arabia for financing the insurgents.

In Iraq, the local pawns of some rich foreign powers among the members of parliament and clerics advocated the separation of Sunni areas. Of course, they do not represent the Sunni population, which is committed to a unified country. But the ordinary people do not realise that the opportunists have their own hidden agenda of dividing the second-largest oil-producing country in the Middle East into fragments.

For the love of Saddam, the most popular nationalist Arabic TV channels, which themselves have yet to establish their proper Islamic credentials, provide platforms for Al-Qaeda's *takfiri*s and Saddamites. They are not interested at all in ballot papers, as is the Taliban in Afghanistan. Any process which does not end up in their favour is considered fake and fraudulent. Their bullying tactics are aimed at derailing any peaceful political process in the country.

For centuries, Sunnis and Shias have lived together peacefully in Iraq and Syria. But the ultra extremist elements among the *takfiris* are introducing a dangerous strategy which may become a prelude to creating sectarian divisions in the entire Arab world. This has already begun by demonising the Shias and other minorities and desecrating places of worship and shrines of their religious personages. This has been happening in broad daylight in both countries. In Syria, the militants of the Al-Nusra terrorist front, which had publicly declared allegiance to Al-Qaeda, are involved in the destruction of Shia religious monuments as well as ancient historic relics and churches.

By the end of 2011, US troops withdrew from Iraq. On 5 January, 2012, after the withdrawal of foreign troops, a series of deadly bomb attacks followed on the Iraqi pilgrims going to the sacred city of Karbala for religious commemorations. This caused hundreds of deaths and casualties. This proves that the cause of violence in Iraq had never been to fight foreign occupation, as the militants and their supporters kept on claiming hypocritically. The main cause was to stop the Shia majority from retaining power in the country. On this basis, terrorist activities were geared to using notorious criminals from neighbouring countries.

In Iraq, some political parties moaned and groaned over the withdrawal of the US troops and started speaking about civil war breaking out in the absence of the occupation forces. The same parties until yesteryear were making noises for the need to liberate Iraq. They accused the United States of the unforgivable offence of bringing the Shia political parties into power. They turned a blind eye that the Shias had won a fair and free general election under the observation of international monitors.

Without any respect for the law, they violated the country's legal system and insulted the judiciary by assisting the fugitive vice president, Tariq al-Hashimi, to escape justice for allegedly running death squads. The vice president was charged by the courts of the country, and not the government, for being involved in terrorist activities, according to the confessions of his bodyguards and other evidence presented to the judges. But for sectarian reasons, Saudi Arabia, Qatar, and Turkey were determined to help him evade the law of his country.

A keen observer and monitor of popular Arabic TV channels and Friday sermons from mosques cannot escape observing the resentment of the bigots against the Shias being in power in Iraq despite being the absolute majority in the country and winning a fair general election under international observers. The bigots prefer to view the matter in the context of the overall majority of the Sunni Arab population in the world. This means that the Shia Arabs, being in the minority in the wider Arab world, should never have been in power in Iraq. Contrary to the census of population, some bigoted channels claimed that the Shia Arabs are in minority in Iraq. They are quite capable of twisting the facts and lying bluntly in front of the world even in this enlightened century. When it is in their political interest, they disregard the boundaries between the nations, as if individual states are not independent and sovereign members of the United Nations. Some of their bigoted politicians even lamented, blaming the United States for presenting Iraq on a golden plate to Iran. This means that if the Shias had not assumed power under free and fair election, they and their terrorists would have used all the repressive and criminal measures, as they do in their own territories, in suppressing the majority.

The extent to which their sense of proportion is blurred can be perceived by referring to the main news bulletin on BBC-Arabic TV on 3 April, 2012. The news commentator said that the Saudi media had mounted a strong attack on Prime Minister Nuri al-Maliki of Iraq for condemning the arming of insurgents in Syria. In his earlier news conference, the prime minister of Iraq did not even name Qatar and Saudi Arabia, which, at the Friends of Syria Conference in Istanbul, were pushing the agenda for arming the insurgents and rebels, many of whom turned out to be members of the Al-Nusra terrorist organisation and ISIL. The former is affiliated to Al-Qaeda, and the latter has international coalition forces under US leadership fighting it. It is claimed in the media that due to its brutality even Al-Qaeda had to disown ISIL, although none of the acts of the parent organisation were any less brutal.

In analysing the said news item, the BBC reporter questioned a Saudi newspaper editor about the reason for mounting such a strong attack on Prime Minister Maliki when Qatar had officially received the fugitive vice president of Iraq, Tariq al-Hashimi, who was wanted in Iraq to face charges for his alleged involvement in death squads. The newspaper editor could not answer the question. He evaded the answer altogether by saying that the editors are quite free to mount such attacks, and there is no government pressure on them. This apologist answer itself indicated that there is government pressure on newspapers to carry out their tirade with amazing unanimity among the editors.

After a few days, Tariq al-Hashimi was officially received by the foreign minister of Saudi Arabia. No one could have known better than the fugitive vice president about the hostile policies of Qatar and Saudi Arabia against Iraq since the downfall of the dictator Saddam. Yet this did not deter him from seeking political support from these countries as if there was some common denominator between them. Ever since 2003, Saudi citizens have been arrested in Iraq for their active involvement in terrorism in the name of jihad. They have given themselves the right to cross the borders illegally and sabotage the country's security. In May 2013, trucks with Saudi number plates, carrying heavy arms and heading towards the Sunni areas, were intercepted by Iraqi security at the Jordanian–Iraqi border.

Qatar declared that it still recognises Tariq al-Hashimi as the vice president of Iraq. But nobody dares criticise the undiplomatic actions of the Qatari authorities because this country is still in the mourning period over the execution of the tyrannical Saddam, the architect of mass graves, who, among others, was defended by the former US attorney general, and prominent lawyers from Qatar and Jordan joined the defence team in Saddam's trial.[32] Any politician having a Saddamite perversion, therefore, could expect a safe refuge in Qatar. Paradoxically, the countries which are hereditary absolute monarchies, with no constitution, with no elections, and with no interest in democracy, are pressing for human rights, freedom, and democracy in Syria.

In Iraq, had Prime Minister Maliki turned a blind eye towards the conspiracy of some Iraqi politicians who had one leg in the parliament and another in the world of terror, then no protests would have been instigated against him. His fault was that he had the courage to lift the veil of hypocrisy and treachery from the faces of the opportunists, who have been conspiring with some neighbouring Arab and foreign countries to divide Iraq on sectarian grounds. The violence and killings witnessed in both Syria and Iraq have nothing to do with liberating them or seeking political freedom for their people. Political freedom is the concept of aliens in the parlance of certain nations that have been financing insurgency in these countries.

If we go back twenty years from now, the Saudi Wahhabis had remained mute to every atrocity and crime committed by the dictator Saddam because they did not want the Shias to takeover power in Iraq, notwithstanding the fact that under international convention, majority rule is well recognised. Even after the invasion of Kuwait by Saddam's forces in 1990 and his attacks on the Saudi borders, as soon as he was

---

32 The University of Iowa, http://www.uiowa.edu/~c030070/warstories04/aljazeera051129/src/english.aljazeera.net/NR/exeres/5C22C24D-2A5B-4391-9450-748EA05225FE.htm, 25 November 2005.

kicked out of Kuwait with disgrace, the Saudis put pressure on the United States not to allow the *intifada* (uprising) against him to succeed as this would have meant victory for the Shia Muslims. The US administration of Bush (senior) succumbed to Saudi pressure. He permitted the disgraced and defeated Saddam to carry out aerial bombardment. The result was the most heinous crime against humanity in the form of a massacre of Shias in the south and Kurds in the north of Iraq.

Following the terrorist attacks on Saudi soil, there was an unprecedented condemnation against militants in Friday sermons relayed from the Grand Mosques of Makkah and Madinah. Yet, as disclosed on the British television Channel 4, on April 19, 2006, 60 per cent of all the foreign insurgents killed in Iraq were Saudi citizens. The ratio has increased substantially since then.

In his Friday sermon on March 2, 2012, from the Grand Mosque in Makkah, the leader of the congregation dedicated his prayers for the militants in Syria. The insurgents in Syria, being Salafi armed groups, enjoyed the full moral and material support of the Salafi oil powers and qualified for special prayers in the sacred environment. In contrast, the Bahraini and Yemeni peaceful protesters, who were being violently assaulted in public squares, did not qualify for any prayers in the city of Makkah. Hence, even the holy sanctuary of Islam was being politicised by the court clerics in sympathy with the foreign policy of their regime.

In Saudi Arabia itself, peaceful protesters and demonstrators in Al-Awwamiyyah and Qatif in the eastern region were mainly Shia Muslims. The court jurists, therefore, wasted no time in branding them 'traitors', 'terrorists', and 'agents of Iran'. These jurists issued religious edicts that to come out in demonstrations in the kingdom is against the Islamic shariah. Hence, anything that clashed with their ideological and political interests was immediately labelled as 'against the shariah'. This means that even the law is used as a pawn in the game to be manipulated by the politicians and court clerics at their will.

GUILLOTINE OVER THE HEADS OF THE ADVERSARIES

The 'moderate' Salafi cleric Shaykh Yusuf al-Qaradawi has emerged as a leading *takfiri* cleric, who has become furious after a bad defeat suffered by the militants in Qusayr in Syria. He assembled his fellow Salafi clerics from around the world in Cairo, under the auspices of the Muslim Brotherhood, the political party that he supported vehemently during the elections and thereafter.

In the conference, the Salafi clerics canvassed military and financial aid for the rebels in Syria. On the international scene, his fatwa, declaring the Shias 'heretics' and permitting murder of their civilians and religious scholars, did not go unheeded. In the village of Hatla on the outskirts of Deir al-Zur, Shias were massacred, and many were kidnapped. A videotape of a Saudi cleric has been posted on YouTube in which he proudly declares that he has slaughtered Shia clerics, whom the terrorists got hold of in Hatla. But Al-Qaradawi and his fellow *takfiri* clerics were determined to portray the crisis in Syria as a Shia–Sunni conflict, notwithstanding the fact that the Syrian Shias are hardly 2 per cent of the total population in the country. Anybody having rudimentary knowledge about the geopolitical nature of the conflict and the involvement of several Arab and foreign powers would not have viewed the Syrian crisis from the narrow prism of sectarian politics. But the Salafi establishment that Al-Qaradawi and his clerics represented knew that it would be difficult to raise finance and motivate fighters under anything other than the sectarian pretexts and slogans.

From June 2013, indiscriminate suicide bombings intensified in Iraq, Syria, and Pakistan mainly on civilian targets, including assassination of religious scholars. According to the United Nations, in Iraq, 1,045 people were killed and 2,400 injured in a series of bomb attacks and suicide bombings in the month of May 2013 alone. The months that followed were no less atrocious, especially since the commencement of the Islamic holy month of Ramadan. Members of the public and security personnel observing the fast were attacked at the time of breaking the fast. One would not have expected this type of behaviour even from the deadliest enemies of Islam. Yet it happened under the watchful eyes of the world. A terrorist operation on this scale could cost thousands of dollars. To sponsor hundreds of operations since 2003 in Iraq, there must have been a budget allocated by some nations for the vile and evil purpose.

The clerics attending the Cairo conference were not true to their words. They did not volunteer to send their own sons or relatives. As long as they could induce others to risk their lives in the mouth of danger, this was the best option they could hope for. This unrepresentative assembly had not been given any mandate to speak on behalf of the Sunni communities.

There was no condemnation in the conference against the beastly behaviour that the insurgents had displayed in the field against their opponents to the extent of eating organs of the dead Syrian soldier, beheading a sixteen-year-old boy in front of his parents after accusing him of apostasy, holding hostages, and raping women. These incidents should have sent shivers down the spines of the clerics with an iota of responsibility towards the community.

The worst affected in the Syrian crisis are the innocent children, who have been deprived of schooling and are growing up to become illiterate. The prime concern of the clerics meeting in the conference should have been to talk peace and to invest all their efforts in reconciling the warring parties rather than adding fuel to fire and exploiting sectarian sentiments.

In contrast to this group of Salafi scholars, there was another group of conscientious, responsible, and respectable Sunni clerics, called the Ulama of Sham (Scholars of Levant), which held its conference in early July 2013 in Beirut. Together with the Shia scholars, they deliberated upon the increasing challenge that the *takfiris* pose to Islam and to the global Muslim community. Needless to mention, the Salafi clerics boycotted this conference.

The overwhelming majority of the global Muslim communities are against bloodshed anywhere and for whatever purpose. Yet this did not stop the agent provocateurs like a Kuwaiti Salafi cleric and others like him to announce in public handsome stipends for anyone volunteering to go to Syria for fighting. For the unemployed youths who were not likely to get employment in their countries, this initial offer was too lucrative to miss.

Within a few days of the fatwa of Al-Qaradawi, an act of extreme savagery took place against Shaykh Hasan Shihatah, a prominent Shia scholar in Egypt and a graduate of the reputable Al-Azhar seminary. He used to preach against radicalisation of Egyptian society at the hands of the extremist Salafis. He was an imam of a mosque in Cairo and did not make a secret of his adherence to the Shia theology. The eve of 15 Shaban in the Shia calendar is considered to be one of the most sacred nights, according to the tradition of the Prophet, narrated by his wife, Ayishah, in addition to other memorable events associated with that night. The helpless scholar was dragged out from his home and brutally murdered in front of his children and family members on that sacred night. This crime was followed by mutilation and lynching of his dead body. This became a public event, where a mob of hundreds of Salafi *takfiris* gathered to watch and celebrate the ghastly incident.

The incident took place in the village of Abu Mussalam in Giza Province near the capital, Cairo. While Shaykh Shihatah was holding religious vigil with his friends and family in the privacy of his house on 23 June, 2013, he was attacked by a mob carrying sticks, swords, and machetes. The reason was the same old lunatic phobia initiated by the *takfiri* clerics in Saudi Arabia and Qatar that the Shias are invading Sunni countries. No sensible person would have accepted that the Shias, who are less than 1 per cent of the total population in Egypt, posed any threat worth mentioning to that nation. But this is how the minds of the extremists work in creating demons out of shadows.

Shaykh Shihatah was dragged in the streets in front of a cheering crowd. The savagery of the scale of pre-Islamic era of ignorance (*jahiliyyah*) was revived in the name of Islam and jihad. But history speaks profoundly for itself that this is the type of heritage that the brutal Umayyad and Abbasid dynasties have left for their faithful devotees.

Under the watchful eyes of the authorities and in the presence of the police force gathered on the scene, Islam was being defamed—if not in words then in action. The assailants were not satisfied in mutilating the dead body of a very respectable scholar but kicked and jumped on his chest, which the videos posted on YouTube and shown on several TV channels clearly show. This was the result of malevolence fed into the minds of people through systematic indoctrination by the Salafi clerics in the surrounding mosques. They were confident that being in alliance with the then-president's Muslim Brotherhood party, they would escape accountability.

Joe Stork, deputy Middle East director at Human Rights Watch, said, 'The brutal sectarian lynching of four Shia comes after two years of hate speech against the minority religious group, which the Muslim Brotherhood condoned and at times participated in'. He continued, 'This horrific incident...shows that Shia can't even gather in the privacy of their homes to celebrate and heightens fear of persecution among all religious minorities in Egypt'. Witnesses told Human Rights Watch that three vans of riot police were stationed nearby from the outset but failed to intervene to disperse the mob.

According to the AhlulBayt News Agency,[33] President Morsi personally participated in events at which there was violent hate speech against the Shias. His party and movement were at times directly involved in hate speech against the Shias, opposing their right to religious freedom. In April, the Muslim Brotherhood Guidance Bureau member and the head of its pedagogy department, Dr Muhammad Wahdan, said at a Freedom and Justice Party event in the governorate of Sharqiyyah that the Egyptian people and government would not allow the spread of Shi'ism in Egypt. This was also reported on the website Ikhwanonline under the title 'There is no place for Shi'ism in Egypt'.

On 1 June, 2013, President Morsi spoke at a conference supporting the Syrian opposition at which a Shia-phobic Saudi *takfiri* cleric, Muhammad al-Arifi, described the Shias as 'non-believers who must be killed'. Under their weird standards, there was nothing wrong with inciting people to commit murder. In April, the Salafi Nur Party, which had won 25 per cent of parliamentary seats in the 2012 general election, according to the report of ABNA, began a series of rallies in Alexandria, Kafr al-Shaykh, and other cities, raising the slogan, 'Shia are the enemy, so beware of them'. Also in April, posters appeared in Alexandria with the logo of Nur Party saying, 'Together against the Shia'.

In May 2013, a Nur member of parliament, Tharwat Attallah, said that Shia 'pose a danger to Egypt's national security' and called for an end of tourism from Iran. Tourism is a major component in the national income of Egypt. At this stage, tourism had not even picked up between Egypt and Iran. But this demonstrates intolerance of this Salafi political party of Egypt against Iran despite the fact that there was a potential benefit for the country's economy in boosting tourism. An article titled

---

33 AhlulBayt News Agency, http://abna.ir/data.asp?lang=3&Id=434882, 29 June 2013.

'Cooperation between the Da'wah Salafiyyah, Nour, and the Police to Remove Husayniyyat' was posted on the Nur website. It discussed the need to strengthen coordination between the missionary activities of the Salafis and their Nur political party with the police to ban the Shia places of worship in Egypt. This is the background of one of the most horrible crimes committed in Cairo, which violated the very dignity of humanity, not to mention the Islamic religion, under whose garb these pretenders and hypocrites take refuge.

The deposed President Morsi himself called for jihad in Syria. For the Egyptian Army, the Syria rally had crossed a national security red line by encouraging Egyptians to fight abroad and by creating a new generation of jihadists, according to Yasser El-Shimy, analyst with the International Crisis Group. The sectarian bitterness was on the rise, and the Egyptian people were shocked to see their own countrymen, in the name of sectarianism, rejoicing in the scenes of disfiguring the dead, which the Prophet of Islam had strictly forbidden, but the Umayyads had revived and encouraged and which continue to this day.

After committing a heinous and inhuman crime, the Salafi extremists congratulated each other and shouted, 'You sons of dogs!' as they dragged the bodies of their victims in the streets. If these paranoid people were worried that in the heartland of Egypt, the Shia faith is spreading, then all they had to do was to look at their own barbaric actions and ask themselves how many people who would have seen these nauseating scenes on television would be attracted to their interpretation and brand of Islam.

Salafism itself is a new phenomenon in Egyptian society. It has spread since the 1970s by the Wahhabi educated clerics, after the oil price boom and flow of petro dollars. It succeeded in creating a wedge between Muslims. It made representations in the name of Sunnis without any mandate from them. Yet there is no denial that the Salafi militants and terrorists have a strong support in mosques, in clerical circles, and in the popular Arab media.

Within ten days of the publicly displayed crime against humanity in Giza Province, the elected President Morsi was toppled by military takeover. There are lessons to be learnt from the shameful saga of mutilating a dead body, which was condemned by all the political parties in Egypt. It was highly inappropriate for the president of seventy million people to succumb to the influence of a few Salafi opportunist clerics. They misled the president by politicising sectarian bigotry and discriminating against religious minorities in the country.

Throughout the year in which the ex-president Morsi was in power, he could not grow out of sectarian bigotry. To be a chairman of a movement or a group is different from being president of a major state in the Arab world. He should have behaved in the interest of his nation. He should have upheld freedom of people to practise their faith and religion as they liked, especially since Egyptian society, like Syrian and Turkish societies, is secular in nature. The people of Egypt had not elected him to act as the deputy of God. Only God has the power of reckoning, not the extremist thugs of the *takfiri*s, who brought the end to Morsi's presidency on its first anniversary. To rub salt into wounds, Morsi remained apathetic as his partners in the government, the Salafis, embarked upon a campaign against the tiny religious minority. They publicly declared that there was no place for the Shias in Egypt, although all of them were of Egyptian origin, and the constitution of the state gives the citizens the right to practice their faith as they like without intimidation.

Sometimes the opportunity of learning from past mistakes is lost forever; and this is what happened in this case. Since the military takeover, violence intensified in Egypt, with attacks on public buildings, military personnel, and police. The unofficial casualty figure was more than a thousand. The new administration, the transitional government, declared the Muslim Brotherhood party as a terrorist party, banned its activities, and nationalised its assets. This was the end of one of the principal Islamic political parties in the Arab world, which espoused the aim of Islamizing the society.

In a rally in Qatar on 1 June, 2013, Al-Qaradawi appealed to the Sunnis around the world to go to Syria to fight the Shias, following their bad defeat in the battle of Qusayr. Rallies are not normally permitted in Qatar, but this one was. According to his rant, the Shias were bent on 'exterminating the Sunnis'. Unsurprisingly, his comments were welcomed by the grand mufti of the Wahhabis, Shaykh Abd al-Aziz Aal al-Shaykh in Saudi Arabia.

Al-Qaradawi's dubious role in the Gaddafi crisis is worth mentioning. In his zeal to get him toppled, Al-Qaradawi went as far as misusing the name of the Prophet by claiming that if the Prophet Muhammad were there, he would have supported NATO's airstrikes on Libya. The problem with these types of clerics, who are influenced by politics and are playing into the hands of politicians, is that they give themselves the authority of reading the mind of God and His Prophet. In a letter addressed to Al-Qaradawi in July 2013, the secretary general of the Ahlul Bayt (AS) World Assembly wrote from Iran, 'He who supports *takfiri* terrorists will stand responsible for each drop of blood that is shed in Islamic countries'.

Upon the fall of President Morsi, once again Al-Qaradawi issued one of his controversial fatwas, urging the Egyptian people that it is incumbent upon them to support the deposed president and that he should be restored to power. But the tone used in his fatwa invited the wrath of the shaykh of Azhar, the highest authority in the Sunni world, who said that the words and expression used by Al-Qaradawi in his fatwa are an indication that he is involved in the *fitnah* (sedition). It also criticised Al-Qaradawi's disrespect for the Muslim *ummah* and Islamic scholars.

The popular media in the Arab world provides a fortress for defending and preserving Salafi thought. In this context, a critical review of some TV programmes would demonstrate how the viewers in the Arabic-speaking wider community are fed with biased perspectives on Shia Muslims. These programmes are run not by villagers of Giza in Cairo but by very educated opinion makers.

The Al Jazeera Arabic channel, in the popular programmes of Dr Faysal Qasim, adopted a very hostile attitude against the Shias after the battle of Qusayr. The Shia community and their faith were demonised because they perceived them as their political rivals. All the suicide bombings that have taken place since then in the south of Beirut in the Shia civilian areas are known to be in revenge for Hizbollah, the Shia militia in south Lebanon, joining forces with the Syrian Army to flush out the insurgents from this key Syrian town. Otherwise, the strong presence of the terrorists would have posed a direct threat to the security of south Lebanon. But the supporters of the *takfiris* are not the least interested in viewing and weighing the matter from the perspectives of their opponents.

Some other media outlets also provide a platform for promoting propaganda against the Shias. They provoke Shia–Sunni disputes for political motives. For instance, if the choice were theirs, even in this enlightened century, they would have prohibited the Shias from entering Islam's holy cities of Makkah and Madinah. Their spiteful attitude goes back to centuries, of which this study will provide evidence. Their media and clerical circles still hold the Shias responsible for murdering the second caliph, Umar, fourteen centuries ago. If they had done their homework, they would have found out that Caliph Umar had forbidden any Persian Muslim from entering Madinah. The Persian slave who murdered him was brought to Madinah under the protection of one of the chieftains of the Umayyads. But they hid this historic fact from the public lest it implicate some influential figures of the Umayyads for murdering the caliph, as the Lebanese Sunni author Abdullah al-Alayli discusses at length in his celebrated book *Al-Imam al-Husayn*.

A popular programme is hosted weekly on Al Jazeera Arabic TV by Dr Faysal Qasim. It is called *Al-Ittijah al-Mu'akis* (*The Opposite Direction*). The two episodes of 28 May, 2013 and 4 June, 2013, both of which were repeated the next day, are referred to hereinafter.

On 28 May, a militant leader from Syria was a guest on this programme. The host personally joined him in the tirade against the Shias. Being a moderator, Dr Qasim is expected to be neutral. But how can he have a sense of fairness and justice, which their progenitors never had? The militant referred to the Shias several times as 'products of *mutah*' (contract of marriage where the period is predetermined by mutual agreement by the couple, with strict conditions, which is permissible in Shia jurisprudence). He called them *safyunis*, a derogatory term for Shias coined on this programme. At one point, the militant leader even used the term *daharah* (brothel) while describing the Shias. The militant leader on Al Jazeera Arabic channel was defaming the faith of the ethnic community of hundreds of millions around the world and using them as scapegoats to vent his malice and hatred, which he had inherited from his progenitors. Only a couple of days later, on 7 June, 2013, the same militant leader appeared in a discussion programme on BBC Arabic TV. All the talks about *mutah* and *safyunis* simply evaporated in the air, and no mention of these terms was made. This means that two different standards of decency and manners were displayed and maintained in the programmes on two different channels.

On the defensive side, on the programme of 28 May, a Christian from Lebanon defended the Shia militia from south Lebanon. Dr Qasim had the audacity of asking him, being a Christian, why does he have to interfere in this matter, forgetting that he himself had invited him on the programme. Dr Qasim kept on yelling that Syria is the state of the

Umayyads and is going to remain as such, forgetting that more than a thousand years have passed since the first Abbasid caliph, Abu al-Abbas al-Saffah (d. 754 CE), had left the Umayyads no room on the surface of the earth in Syria. They had to go underground, wherever it led them.

It has now become customary in the circle of the extremists and militants that when referring to Shias, they call them 'products of *mutah*'. They believe that by doing so, they are offending them. They believe that the marriage of *mutah* is tantamount to committing adultery, no matter that the Islamic theology does not look at it in this manner. That is why when the *takfiris* make pretensions about Islam, it does not go beyond empty words simply because they do not care less about the true traditions of the Prophet. All they care about are their caprices and imagination that they impose on Islam.

The history of Islam records testimonies of some of the prominent companions of the Prophet that this mode of marriage contract was quite permitted at the time of the Prophet. It was prohibited later on by the second caliph, but the Shias do not recognise anybody else's authority over that of the Prophet.[34] This is the point that the mischievous elements among the clerics and broadcasters do not clarify to their public. Consequently, the ruffians among the extremists and their supporters go on passing lose remarks against the marriage of *mutah*, forgetting that a wide variety of marriages have emerged in their own society in recent years called 'summer marriages', *misyar* and *munakahah*, the latter of which is tantamount to raping the women of their opponents. The first uproar against this abuse came from Tunisia, where a minister disclosed in public that a group of women had gone to Syria to do 'jihad of *munakahah*' and had returned back pregnant. An appeal was made to the government that it should take stern measures to stop women going to Syria.

---

34 http://www.al-islam.org/shiite-encyclopedia-ahlul-bayt-dilp-team/temporary-marriage-islampart-7-necessities-and-advantages, accessed 5 March 2014.

In his June 4, 2013 programme, Dr Qasim hosted a Saddamite and introduced him as a Shia. Then he embarked upon his usual tirade. The Saddamite acted on the programme exactly as his Umayyad ancestor Ziyad ibn Abih (Ziyad, the son of his father, as he was known in history) had done in the time of Mu'awiyah, accusing the Shias of every evil under the sun. There is a striking correlation between the mind-sets of the *takfiri*s and of the Saddamites. If they had confidence in their own convictions, they would not have felt the necessity to hide behind somebody else's identity. If they had any confidence in what they were claiming, they would not have resorted to cunningness and blunt lies.

Hundreds of examples can be presented from history of this type of hypocritical mind-set. Whenever these extremists are cornered for committing certain offences, they simply put the blame on their adversaries.

The Shias could never refer to Saddam as a 'martyr' like this man on the programme did. He produced pictures of mass killings committed by his despot, as recognised internationally, but had the audacity of blaming the Shias for these crimes. He produced other pictures of civilians being hanged on lampposts by the Baathists after the execution of the tyrant Saddam but blamed the Shias for that. Then he presented another picture of a man and a woman representing an outlaw organisation. He branded the organisation as 'peaceful', disregarding the fact that until yesteryear, the same organisation was categorised by the European Union and the United States as a terrorist organisation.

Dr Qasim angrily proclaimed that some groups gathered in the Sunni town of Aleppo were chanting the Shia slogans of '*labbayk ya Husayn!*' He asked what the Shias were doing in a Sunni town. Fourteen centuries have passed since the massacre of Karbala, which their caliph Yazid, the son of Mu'awiyah, had committed against the holy household and family of the Prophet of Islam. But his devotees cannot bear hearing mere chants which remind people of the great tragedy that no other previous communities on the face of the earth had committed against the progeny of their own Prophet, except the Umayyads and their devotees.

As Aleppo is a Sunni town, the weird logic of the bigots says that no Shia had the right to be born and grow up in that town, and there could not have been any Shia communities living in Aleppo, which is utter nonsense. At the beginning and end of his programmes, Dr Qasim produced the results of votes taken online on the resolution that the pro-Syrian Lebanese militia and Iran are the enemies of Arabs and Islam. In his 28 May programme, he came up with a 74 per cent majority; in his June 4 programme, he came up with a 94 per cent majority, and in his June 18 programme, he came up with a 95 per cent majority in favour of the resolution that Shias are the real enemies.

He, therefore, concluded that a vast majority of 1.3 billion Muslims (the total Muslim population in the world) believe that the Shia militia from south Lebanon, which fought in Syria, and Iran, are the enemies of Islam and Arabs. It did not occur to Dr Qasim that the biggest Muslim communities, in countries like Indonesia, India, Pakistan, Bangladesh, Iran, Turkey, China, Russia, and other non-Arab nations, which represent more than 80 per cent of the total Muslim population, would not have even heard about his programme and his bigoted and fabricated poll.

This poll was commissioned just because the *takfiris*, the terrorists, and the rebels had suffered a very bad defeat in Qusayr. If the situation had been the other way round, the bigots would have celebrated, and no concern for the defeated would have been expressed. The insurgents released videos on YouTube, showing that they were proudly setting the houses of the Shia residents of Hatla on fire, beheading the defence-less Shia clerics, and kidnapping women. They even killed the male breadwinners in front of their children. They resorted to grotesque acts of terrorism and crimes, for which no poll was undertaken by such disgraceful media sympathetic to the terrorists. However, in subsequent programmes, the confession came from the horse's mouth that certain groups, notably the Salafis, tend to vote in these polls en bloc, thus changing the result of the poll overnight, which means that a database of voters is maintained by this programme to defame the opponents in the name of the global Muslim population. This explains how much trust can be placed in these phony polls.

In the episode on 11 June, 2013, Dr Qasim came up with a story that in Qusayr, the Shias gathered all the people named Umar and massacred them. So in a war zone where the entire town had been reduced to rubble, it was possible to take an accurate census of how many people by the name of Umar lived in the vast town of Qusayr, to check their identities, and then to transport them to a particular place and prepare them for the slaughter as if they were sacrificial goats. No news agency in the world picked up this witchhunting story. Only the news agency of the *takfiri*s, who, a few days before, had executed a boy of fifteen in front of his parents in Syria for allegedly abusing the Prophet, was the sole source of this fable. Later, there was another story whereby a reporter from the Muslim Brotherhood, of which Qatar is a great fan, alleged that Iran has sent revolutionary guards to fight in Syria. What was the evidence? That the reporter personally overheard the conversation on the telephone!

On 12 June 2013, BBC Arabic TV hosted a debate in which all the debating parties were given a fair chance to express their opinions. No party was shouted at by another. Each one debated in a civilised manner. The moderators expressed a sense of fairness. No party resorted to yelling to subdue the voice of the other. There was no attempt at demonising anybody. Irrespective of who was in favour of whom and who was against whom, this was a debate for fair-minded people to make up their minds for themselves and not under duress, which characterises the mentality of the *takfiri*s and their establishment.

In the 18 June, 2013, episode of his weekly programme, Dr Qasim hosted Habib Salih, a Syrian opposition figure who has appeared previously on Dr Qasim's programmes. Mr Salih took off his shoe during the debate and compared it with a Shia leader. This is the type of manners they learn in their schools and at home. While debating with an Iraqi Shia, he kept on yelling, 'Are you Muslims?' He justified the influx of thousands of terrorists into Syria and called them 'freedom fighters'— the type of freedom that they themselves display in their videos posted on YouTube. They take pride in and congratulate each other for beheading people, eating human organs, torturing their captives to death, mutilating bodies of their opponents, looting their properties, beheading their victims, and playing football with their severed heads. All this is officially recognised as jihad against infidels by their terrorists and clerics, who are making a mockery of Islam and human values. When it comes to demonising the Shias, according to the duty assigned to them by their barbaric and unrepresentative leaders, they have no hesitation in making false and exaggerated claims even at the cost of their own credibility in public.

In the same programme, the *takfiri* guest displayed his profound ignorance by claiming that Imam Husayn is the imam of the Sunnis, not of the Shias. It took him a few minutes to contradict himself. He had a strong objection to the use of the slogan 'Ya Husayn' by the Shias in Qusayr. The reason for his hysteria against the chanting of 'Ya Husayn' (the call O Husayn) is an age-old phenomenon. The uprising of Imam Husayn (the third imam of the Shias), even after fourteen centuries, is the biggest threat that the *takfiris* and their clerics are facing. This uprising was against oppression, injustice, and tyranny, which are embodied in them even today.

In the aforesaid programme, the host came up with the most ludicrous story ever heard. He said that the Shias do not commemorate the martyrdom of Imam Ali ibn Abi Talib because he is the imam of the Sunnis and the Shias had killed him. He forgot that on the same programme, he had said that the Shia sect has started only recently during the time of the Safavids in Iran. As if this tirade was not enough, he then went on to accuse the Shias of Iran, Iraq, and south Lebanon of being Israeli agents and working for Israel to implement the American agenda in the area. But when he was reminded about the 2006 war between Israel and the militia in south Lebanon, he turned a deaf ear as if he did not hear anything.

Then Dr Qasim joined Mr Salih in claiming that as the G8 conference held in Belfast (at that time) condemned only Al-Nusra Front, it meant that Al-Nusra are working against the Israeli and US interests. Anybody fighting Al-Nusra, therefore, has to be the ally of Israel and the United States, according to Dr Qasim. This implied that the Syrian regime and the Iranians, Iraqis, and south Lebanese, who fought Al-Nusra Front, were all allied with Israel, the United States, and NATO, according to his political analysis. Notwithstanding the fact that Al-Nusra openly paid allegiance to Al-Qaeda and has been classified as a terrorist organisation by the United States, there was an attempt to legitimise its existence by cunningly turning the tables against the adversaries of Al-Nusra. In Iraq and Syria, Al-Nusra has been heavily involved in torturing and killing civilians and in suicide bombings, which, in the last quarter of 2013, resulted on average in one hundred casualties a day.

But according to Dr Qasim's philosophy, those who fought Al-Nusra are the real terrorists. Indeed, since the fatwa of Al-Qaradawi, their media have been using the term 'terrorists' for the Shia militias but never for Al-Qaeda or Al-Nusra or the Taliban or even ISIL. After displaying double standards, they have the courage to scream their heads off in front of their congregation in the mosques, claiming that people are increasingly converting to the Shia faith. Before expressing their paranoia in public, they should have critically reviewed their own self-contradictions.

People have brains of their own, and they can think for themselves. The masses notice the contradictions and brutalities being practised in the name of religion by their state-sponsored terrorists for no other reason than sectarian malice. Their establishment endeavours to impress the masses with false propaganda against their opponents. When the masses find out the truth and start leaving the beliefs of their forefathers, the establishment starts searching for scapegoats. They think that the best solution is to distort the image of their adversaries and to defeat their opponents through polemics, for which they get away with 95 per cent votes in their favour, 5 per cent less than what the tyrants Saddam and Gaddafi used to get in their polls.

Muslims are disgusted and tired that their faith and beliefs are being hijacked by the extremist *takfiris* on the one hand and their biased media on the other, although both of them complement each other. The absolute vast majority of Muslims are not interested in hate mongering, which has now become the principal strategy of the *takfiris* and their clerics. Shouting at each other instead of discussing, arguing for the sake of arguments, polemics for the sake of subduing the views of others, and war mongering in the name of jihad—all these may well be the second nature of the *takfiris*, but Muslims have nothing to do with these deceptive tactics. The majority of Muslims are too busy in their daily lives to make ends meet. They may not even be interested in politics at all. Therefore, the agent provocateurs who are actively involved in dividing the Muslims on sectarian grounds are bound to expose themselves sooner or later. Indeed, the respectable Sunni scholars and masses have already started voicing their concerns that their school of thought is being hijacked by the *takfiris*. But as long as the oil powers in the Middle East are their godfathers, there is nothing much the helpless masses can do.

PAKISTAN: INVASION BY THE ALIEN IDEOLOGY

In the game of power politics, several terrorist groups in Pakistan and Afghanistan were financed and supported from 1980 onwards. A string of target killings followed, which continue until today. Hundreds of Shias, especially from the Hazara ethnic minority, were, and are, being killed in cold blood by their ideologues. The mayhem caused by the terrorist groups has reached a phenomenal level. There have been several occasions where buses carrying Shia pilgrims returning from the pilgrimage of holy sites in Iran were stopped and the passengers were lined up and machine gunned with their children.

The dictator of Pakistan, President Zia-ul-Haq (1978–1988), was a very close ally of Saudi Arabia, as much as Nawaz Sharif, the current prime minister, is. Ever since the religious extremists set their foothold in Pakistan during the reign of Zia-ul-Haq, the country has not enjoyed a day of peace. The country has been dragged into the culture of guns, drugs, and bomb attacks on Shia mosques and their religious gatherings. His absolute reign robbed the people of Pakistan of peace and security. Thousands of innocent citizens of Pakistan were subjected to genocide for no other reason except that they were from the rival ethnic communities.

Several terrorist groups were established in the time of Zia-ul-Haq like, Sipah-e Sahaba (Soldiers of the Companions, now calling themselves 'Ahl al-Sunnah wa al-Jama'ah' after they were officially banned in Pakistan), and Lashkar-e Jhangvi (which broke away from Sipah-e Sahaba in 1996). Their objective was to form a front in Pakistan against the Islamic Republic of Iran. Almost all their atrocities were directed at the Shia community together with targeted killings of Shia intellectuals and professionals.

The motive of the extremist groups was and still is to kindle trouble between Sunnis and Shias so as to qualify for handsome stipends from their paymasters. Sectarian tension is fuelled by fanatical clerics, who are bankrupt of any Islamic etiquette and credentials. They are easily manipulated under the complicated domestic political manipulations.

In 1981, US President Ronald Reagan gave billions of dollars of aid to General Zia-ul-Haq. In return, he became the main recruiter for the CIA–Saudi propelled jihad in Afghanistan.[35] Simultaneously, in order to create a barrier against the influence of the Islamic Revolution in Iran, the Deobandi–Wahhabi *tablighi*s (missionaries) were financed heavily by the Saudi Wahhabis to proselytise other Muslims to their cause. The Taliban, who were their agents on the ground, acted with extreme brutality against the recalcitrant groups, as Ibn Saud's Ikhwan had shown in the early days of the Wahhabi movement. True to their indoctrination, they viewed all Muslims except the Salafis/Wahhabis/Deobandis as infidels.

The emergence of malignant extremist groups in Pakistan was noticeable in the slogans that appeared on the walls around the city of Karachi, especially in areas where the Shias and Sunnis lived together peacefully. The unemployed street boys were given the task of painting on the walls of the city, in wall-length letters, offensive slogans like 'Shia *kafir*'. This spiteful task involved cost of labour for street boys and the cost of wall paintings, which could not have been undertaken without generous funding coming from elsewhere. This is only a small example of extremism in Pakistan. At a much more advanced level, its true effect was transparent when the country was facing the worst natural catastrophe in its history in 2010. One third of the country was under flood waters with millions of people displaced from their homes. But even in such a catastrophic situation, it did not deter suicide bombers from

---

35 A declassified documentary, http://www.youtube.com/watch?v=J6O5V8wwjU4, discloses that the US aid of millions of dollars was given to Afghan mujahidin through the Pakistani Intelligence Service under President Zia ul-Haq.

carrying out their mission of terror on their fellow citizens and on the mosques of their opponents.

The terrorist leaders are only the by-products of deformities inherent in extremism. The gangs that have been engaged in target killing of Shias in Karachi, Parachinar, Gilgit-Baltistan, Peshawar, Quetta, Baluchistan, and other regions have adopted atrocious measures. In Gilgit-Baltistan, on 3 April, 2012, a fleet of buses was stopped by Al-Qaeda and the banned Sipah-e Sahaba in order to carry out ruthless genocide of the Shia passengers, including their women and children.

On this occasion, the terrorists checked the identity and names of the passengers, segregating the Shias from the rest, and shot and mutilated bodies of their victims. They threw acid at their faces so that they could not be identified. This type of massacre was also carried out in the past against the Hazara Shias of Afghani origin. The young boys of school age, who did the killings on the Gilgit-Baltistan highway, were Deobandi 'jihadis' who had the backing of the extremist elements in Pakistan Intelligence Service (ISI). The criminals were promised seventy virgins in paradise for killing Shias.[36]

For facilitating the gangsters, the Pakistani officials at that time jammed all the means of communication with Gilgit-Baltistan and instructed the print and electronic media to refrain from using words such as 'Shia killing' or 'Shia genocide' and instead to use a false neutral term like 'sectarian violence between Sunnis and Shias'. The aim was to cover up the crime.[37] It has been observed time and again that when international media outlets report violence and ethnic cleansing in which Shia Muslims are the sole victims, they, too, use neutral terminology like 'sectarian violence'. In this way, the identity of the

---

36 http://aut.abis.org.nz/the-ongoing-ethnic-cleansing-of-pakistan, accessed 17 May 2012.
37 'Eyewitness accounts of Shia genocide in Gilgit and Chilas', http://www.aimislam.com/eyewitness-accounts-of-shia-genocide-in-gilgit-and-chilas, 12 April 2012.

victims is totally lost, and they never receive justice. When a sit-in was organised outside the Pakistan Embassy in London in protest against the genocide of Hazara Shias in January 2014, the Pakistani Embassy personnel denied any knowledge of Shia killings although widows and children of the victims sat in freezing cold and heavy snow in that region, refusing to bury their dead until the government undertook an operation against the killers.

The website Hazara.net claims that the terrorists involved in the ethnic cleansing of Hazara Shias are trained by the Pakistan Frontier Corp., protected by the army's intelligence outfit. They claim that the annual aid of $100 million flows from Saudi Arabia and Persian Gulf states to the Deobandi and Ahl-e Hadith, the close affiliates of the Wahhabis.

In the present time, the manifestation and reappearance of the kharijis (secessionists) of the early Islamic history is noticeable in several terrorist groups in Pakistan. They are involved in kidnapping and murdering and giving ultimatums to the Shias in poor areas that either they change their faith or be prepared for grim consequences, exactly as they did in the early days of the Wahhabi movement in Arabia. If one watches video clips of their barbarism in massacring children and the elderly in Gilgit-Baltistan, one would deduce that the era of ignorance (*jahiliyyah*) is represented in their merciless slaughter, irrespective of their pretensions in the name of Islam and jihad. The Pakistani government forces failed to bring the leaders of these terror gangsters to justice. But they were quick to arrest the doctor who disclosed the whereabouts of Bin Laden to the CIA and, in return, was sentenced to a thirty-year prison term in a court of law. This explains how precious the life of Bin Laden and other militants must have been in the eyes of their fellow ideologues.

When it comes to the rights of children, no acts of brutality could be justified, whether the children are of Hindu, Christian, Muslim, or other origin. The Prophet considered all children to be innocent, whether their parents had any faith or not. But the extremists, who misuse the name of Islam to justify their violence, have not spared even the lives of children and infants.

Since 1980, hundreds of attacks have been carried out on Shia religious gatherings, mosques, professionals, and intellectuals, especially doctors, lawyers, teachers, religious preachers, and community workers, through assassinations, bombings, arson, kidnappings, and suicide attacks.

In one of the massacres inside a Shia mosque in Karachi, on the holiest night of the holiest Islamic month of Ramadan in 1995, well-known philanthropists and devoted community workers were lined up and shot dead. On the same night, a coordinated massacre was carried out in another Shia mosque by the same murderers after having completed their first operation. Many people believe that if there were no collaborators, providing logistics and intelligence to the terrorist gangs for undertaking their evil mission and walking away free, many terrorist attacks would have been contained decades ago.

In total contrast, top Shia religious jurists (grand ayatollahs) totally prohibit meeting violence with violence so that the lives of innocent people are not endangered. If this deterrent did not exist, then revenge killings and tit-for-tat attacks would have started a spiral of vicious cycle of violence in Pakistan and elsewhere. Because of the shackles around their necks, anybody contemplating violence to avenge the killing of their loved ones is restrained.

History proves that killings have been going on for the last three centuries on ideological grounds. This phenomenon has now been exported from Arabia to Pakistan, Iraq, Syria, Bahrain, Somalia, Yemen, some North African countries, and lately to Europe and the United

States. As the financial reward with the package is too lucrative to be missed, those who have been instigating ideological offensives are sparing no efforts to pull others into the spiral of coercion and violence.

The violent extremists have gone further by permitting, in the name of Islam, the shedding of blood and the violation of the life, property, and honour of their opponents. Bin Laden might have been only a tiny product of institutionalised radicalisation. If he had restricted himself to killing the Shias only in Afghanistan, Pakistan, and Iraq, they would have had no qualms against him. Hundreds of indiscriminate terror attacks on Shia civilians in several countries failed to attract any meaningful condemnation from the Saudi-Wahhabi official media and their clerics. But when terrorism started threatening their own back garden, they moaned and groaned, and the congregation leaders started shedding tears in the course of their sermons delivered from the Grand Mosque in Makkah.

The mind of the extremists has been moulded on the absolute falsity that the Shias have a different Quran and that they are unbelievers. On this basis, the extremists advocate shedding their blood. In any case, many extremists can't even read the Quran because of sheer illiteracy. If this factor is the main reason for labelling the Shias 'unbelievers', then the problem can be solved very easily. They should be able to present a copy of a different Quran which they insist the Shias believe in. If they can't, then it means that Muslim masses are being deceived for some ulterior political and ideological motives.

Two case studies are cited here to illustrate how, in recent months, to quench their thirst for the blood of the Shia Muslims, the terrorists and their sponsors in Pakistan, as in Iraq, have been killing Sunni Muslims too. As long as they are able to get at the Shia targets, the casualties of the Sunnis are taken as an acceptable allowance.

In Abbas Town in Karachi, Sunnis and Shias lived together as good neighbours, without any sectarian problems. On March 3, 2013, a blast left forty-eight killed and 140 injured, with many houses of the residents burnt down. The Lashkar-e Jhangvi terrorist gang proudly claimed responsibility.

Their real nature is perceptible in their armed attacks on 15 June, 2013 in Quetta, where a civilian bus was targeted. Dozens were injured and twenty-nine killed, including fourteen female university students. What they did ninety minutes later demonstrates the evil nature of the ideology they espouse. They carried out a massacre in the hospital which was treating the injured. Earlier, on 16 February, they killed ninety and injured two hundred Shia Hazara Muslims. A Pakistani minister said that Lashkar-e Jhangvi were involved in 80 per cent of terrorist activities in the country. Yet the government failed to protect their Shia citizens.

SCANDAL MONGERING AND CREDIBILITY CRISIS

In the wake of the invasion of Bahrain by the Saudi-Wahhabi troopers on 14 March, 2011, two TV channels based in Egypt emitted their spite and malevolence against the Shias without any action taken by the Egyptian governments of Mubarak and, later, the Muslim Brotherhood. On the contrary, the old and the new regimes remained quite indifferent to incitement of commotion and hate mongering.

A case study would give an idea of what type of rotten mind-set works behind sectarian-motivated propaganda. Al-Mustakilla TV, now defunct and off the air, in one of its programmes gathered a panel of four, three of them anti-Shia and one of them a Shia. Each one was given quarter of the time available. The gang of three had the task of attacking the Shia faith. Those on the offensive side were allotted threefold the time of the lone Shia. The Shia scholar was given quarter of the time to defend his beliefs. Ironically, this explains their level of confidence.

The programme presented someone who posed as a Shia scholar and claimed that he attained his level of *ijtihad* (high scholarly status of independent reasoning) after completing his higher studies in the renowned Shia seminary of Najaf in Iraq. He claimed that he abandoned the Shia faith after attaining the highest educational level in the seminary. Yet he retained his attire of black turban and black cloak, which is the traditional dress that the Shia religious scholars from the descendants of the Prophet (sing. *sayyid*; pl. *sadaat*) wear. Although this type of attire is considered *makruh* (detestable) by his fellow Wahhabis, the converted cleric did not see any contradiction in his word and deed by retaining his preconversion dress.

These cheap tactics are meant to impress the viewers that the Shia faith is being attacked by somebody who looks like them. Lately, this cleric with his black turban and black cloak appeared on the Saudi-financed Al Arabiya TV channel for promoting Shiaphobia and misrepresenting their faith. The cleric did not realise that he was making a fool of himself. Any conscientious cleric has to look back at the past twenty years when some Wahhabi TV channels had commissioned their services to attack the Shia beliefs, posing as Shias. As soon as they outlived their usefulness, they were thrashed. Nobody remembers them anymore.

When calls were received on the air, other clerics from Riyadh, the capital of Saudi Arabia, joined the chorus to vent their tirades. But if a Shia scholar happened to be online and wished to defend his beliefs, he was cut off by the moderator under the pretext that there was no more time left. This happened more often than not. It was observed many times by the regular viewers that the guests on this TV were engaged in generating bias by naming the Shia Arabs of Iraq 'the remnants of Safavids'. The Safavid ruling dynasty in Iran (1502–1736) had officially embraced the Shia school of jurisprudence of the Jafari faith. The undertones aired on this channel tended to classify the majority of Iraq's population of Arabs as non-Arabs just because they subscribe to the Shia school.

The moderator focused on certain quotations he had picked up from the website of the internationally respected Grand Ayatollah Sistani, the religious leader to the vast majority of Shias in the world. He found an article in which an independent writer had expressed his personal opinion that those who do not believe in the imamate (leadership) of Imam Ali ibn Abi Talib and the eleven imams from his progeny have breached the fundaments of faith. The moderator capitalised on this statement and publicised it on the moving text of his TV screen for several weeks in succession, provoking the sentiments of the Sunnis by claiming that the Shias believe that all Sunnis will burn in hell because they do not accept the imamate of the twelve imams.

Then the programme convener picked up certain sermons of Imam Ali found in the *Nahj al-Balaghah* (*The Peak of Eloquence*), a compiled work which contains his historic sermons, letters, and sayings. The Shias believe that this book is a treasure of knowledge and has inspired even non-Muslim scholars and thinkers, whose testimonies are well documented in the foreword to the book. But just because the knowledge had been bequeathed by Imam Ali, the first imam of the Shias, the opponents insist that the book has been made up, although ancient sources available prove otherwise. Any sources that do not succumb to the whims of the Wahhabi and Salafi ideologues are written off as unreliable.

The moderator targeted a sermon from this book, which he did not even consider authentic, according to his sectarian bigotry. Yet he asked his Eritrean colleague on the panel about his thoughts on the contents. The Eritrean 'intellectual', grasping the opportunity of discrediting the Shias, reiterated his preconceived conclusion, saying that the path and teachings of Imam Ali are quite different from the path and teachings of the Shias. This means that whenever it suits their sectarian interest, they pose as the spokesmen for the Imam of the Shias, and then they take about-turns in the opposite direction and adopt the malicious political strategy of his archenemy.

On December 26, 2006, in the midst of the pilgrimage (hajj) season, which is the season meant to promote love, fraternity, patience, and tolerance, the moderator on the now-defunct Al-Mustakilla TV interrupted a programme halfway through and read seven pages of what he called a 'very important' document which, he claimed, was brought to his attention. He alleged that the Shias, especially members of a very respectable Al-Hakim family in Iraq, having blown up the Shia shrine in Samarra, were now plotting to blow up the holy Ka'bah by using pilgrims to smuggle weapons into Makkah. Again, in line with the political interest of his establishment, these allegations were meant to derail the political process in Iraq just because the Shias were in the lead in a free and fair election. They thought that this was an opportune time to sow the seeds of *fitnah* (sedition), although, according to the Quran, *fitnah* is worse than committing manslaughter. But when it comes to politics, the exhortations of the Quran are thrown behind the back and forgotten.

Any responsible individual would have critically assessed the seven pages of tripe before wasting the time of his viewers. There are some elements in the wider Muslim community who take these allegations at face value and build a pile of malice against their rival sects. Later, some British Shia pilgrims were beaten up in Makkah by the religious police. Had the British Embassy in Riyadh not intervened, this group would have remained in detention indefinitely.

The late Sayyid Abd al-Aziz al-Hakim, the former head of a major Islamic political party, led the political process in Iraq, which the extremists were determined to derail. The moderator should have asked himself that if the Shias were plotting to blow up the Ka'bah, then why did King Abdullah of Saudi Arabia take the pain of inviting Sayyid Ammar al-Hakim, the present chairman of the party, to his palace prior to the general election of 2010 in Iraq, long after the alleged conspiracy was uncovered on this Wahhabi channel?

The presenter hosted a programme on 23 November, 2010, using sarcasm against the Shias. This style had been the bread and butter of this channel, despite the fact that the moderator kept on talking about the need for Muslim unity and tolerance. In his boring rant, which had been going on for more than a decade, he talked about the so-called *shirk* (polytheism) in which the Shias are said to have fallen. He, therefore, obliged himself to offer free advice for their 'guidance', as he claimed. As usual, he targeted the website of Grand Ayatollah Sistani.

On one occasion, the presenter was supported by his Eritrean col-league. The Eritrean gentleman on the panel came up with a story that he met a Christian on Edgware Road underground tube station in London. The latter praised him that he was very much impressed by their method of defending monotheism (unicity of God), notwithstand-ing the fact that the fundamental faith of the Christians is essentially based on the trinity.

The Wahhabi intellectuals on this channel were only interested in mudslinging. The moderator was told time and again by the viewers that if he wanted to be a participant in the debates, then the least he could do was to give up his position of chairing these debates because he was unlikely to abandon his prejudice against the Shias. The person chair-ing or moderating the programmes should be impartial, allocating time among the debating parties justly and equitably. But the lame excuse that the moderator kept on giving was that, as the Shias are only 10 per cent of the total Muslim population, they qualified for 10 per cent rep-resentation on the panel. Simple logic would have required that if the debate was between two different belief systems, then equal representation should have been given to each side.

Most of the advertisements this channel got was from Saudi Arabia to keep it buoyant. Its style was to invite Shia scholars under the slogan of Islamic unity, and at the end of the day, almost all of them ended up getting insulted and ridiculed. The Wahhabi presenters and anti-Shia guests lost credibility in the eyes of many Shia viewers who stopped watching this channel. Some respectable Shia scholars in the United Kingdom were publicly insulted by the presenter and his guests.

Some cronies were introduced on the TV, calling them 'ayatollahs'. These homebred ayatollahs were engaged in misrepresenting the faith of other Muslims. They read passages from the Quran in the middle of the programmes. When they were tired of reading the Quran and ridiculing the Shias, they sang classical songs on tambourine, which would have caused nauseating effects even on the devil.

Dr Abd al-Rahim al-Baluchi had been appearing for more than twelve years on Al-Mustakilla TV. He brought with him enormous hostility against the Shias in general and against Iran in particular. He was an asset to this Wahhabi channel because he, too, claimed that he was a Shia once upon a time and converted to become a Sunni. Yet nobody in the Shia world bothered to raise an alarm that Shias were getting converted to the Sunni sect, as Al-Qaradawi had done, by creating phobia and alarm against the spread of Shia faith in Sunni countries. Those who have confidence in themselves and in their faith will not make a show out of trivial issues. People have minds of their own, and they do not need to fall at the feet of their clerics to permit them for bidding farewell to the beliefs of their great-grandfathers.

On 14 April, 2009, Dr Baluchi claimed on this TV channel that the Iranian regime has the support of Israel and America (!), whereas

Saudi Arabia, the 'only Islamic state' in the world, according to his diatribe, is on its own and does not have the support of anybody. This was meant for the consumption of ignorant public opinion in Saudi Arabia.

On April 14, 2009, Al-Mustakilla channel hosted an anti-Shia programme, in which Dr Baluchi, who is more Wahhabi than most Wahhabis, was on the panel. A member of the royal family was given a clear telephone line without any interruptions to air some hilarious stories about the Shias of Iran.

Dr Baluchi claimed on the programme that in Iran, the Shias say, '*La ilaha illa Zahra; la ilaha illa Ali; la ilaha illa Fatimah*' (meaning, 'There is no God but Zahra; there is no God but Ali; there is no God but Fatimah'!). Neither the moderator nor anyone on the panel objected to this impromptu and blatant lie, which any ordinary individual could have verified for himself. The radicals did not have any hesitation in trampling over the exhortations of the Quran which require Muslims to proclaim truth in all circumstances. The Quran curses the liars in several of its admonitions. If the Iranian Shias were pronouncing such words of polytheism and disbelief in the unicity of God, how come the Saudis permit them to enter the holy land and perform pilgrimage when non-Muslims are prohibited in Saudi Arabia from entering the holy land? But they did not have that much common sense to vet their own claims critically.

Even the prince did not give the matter any thought before joining the chorus of Iran bashing. He had the audacity of claiming that he had received a confidential letter passed to him from a Shia lady from Iran, which, as he put it, was authentic because it was passed through the management of the hotel where she had been staying in Makkah. She allegedly claimed in the letter that a number of Shia young menthe had accompanied her from Iran on pilgrimage and raped her one time after another in the sacred precincts of Makkah, to the extent that she was not able to perform the pilgrimage.

First of all, it is the Saudi visa condition and requirement that a lady cannot travel without a *mahram* (a close relative whom she cannot marry, except her husband). Second, a pilgrim could only go for pilgrimage from Iran with a caravan of pilgrims or through a tour operator, which is required to check that the *mahram* condition is fulfilled. Third, how did the hotel management permit a lady to be booked in a room or suite with a group of young men who were strangers? It is said that a liar has a forgetful memory and exposes himself through his words and expressions.

The prince swore by Almighty God that apart from this 'authentic letter' that he received from the lady (whom he had not even met), he possessed other proof, but he did not want to reveal them on the TV lest the life of the lady be put in danger. After sometime on the same programme, Dr Baluchi swore by the Almighty God that he had personally received the letter and passed it on to the prince and that the letter was 100 per cent genuine. According to him, it carried 'instructions from Iran on how to perform *mutah* [temporary marriage] in Makkah'. So Dr Baluchi suddenly emerged as part of the hotel management team; otherwise, in what capacity did he receive the letter and pass it on to the Saudi Prince?

As if this tirade was not enough, Dr Baluchi claimed that the lady was contacting him 'day and night' from Iran, as he put it, and that he was not even able to come out from his house except for Friday prayers. Through gross exaggeration and incredible stories, they were determined to insult the common sense of the viewers. The prince claimed that Iran wants to create instability in Saudi Arabia. How? By encouraging the Iranians to perform temporary marriage in Makkah? These types of allegations had already been made in a TV programme in 2009, and similar claims were made in a programme in October 2011.

The prince alleged on the aforesaid Wahhabi channel that Iran was responsible for the Soviet occupation of Afghanistan and for supporting Al-Qaeda and for terrorism in Iraq. It seems that the prince may have been late in catching up with international news. It is known globally that Al-Qaeda and Taliban are twin babies who have come out from the womb of Wahhabism. Both the Wahhabis and Al-Qaeda consider Iran their archenemy and religiously believe that all Shias are heretics and should be fought against.

Dr Baluchi claimed that Ayatollah Khomeini was supported by the British. He knew that he could never substantiate such allegations, except through concocted documents and distorted facts. Said K. Aburish has discussed in his book *The House of Saud* the increasing influence that the international oil companies exercise on the oil-producing countries of the Middle East. Yet, according to their religious beliefs, obedience to their rulers is tantamount to obeying God and His Prophet; whether the rulers themselves obey God and His Prophets is immaterial to them.

Dr Baluchi alleged that Iran wants to take over Saudi Arabia, the 'only Islamic nation' in the world, according to him. This claim was aired in the said programme on Al-Mustakilla TV in 2009. It was repeated with striking harmony three years later. In October 2011, the king, the foreign minister, the top clerics in the Holy Land, and the media blamed Iran for instigating demonstrations in the eastern region of the country by the Shia Saudi citizens, who were demanding their basic rights of citizenry. The foreign minister of Saudi Arabia, Saud al-Faisal, who remained in his position for thirty-nine years before he died in office, threatened that if further protests came out in the eastern region, this would indicate Iranian interference into the internal affairs of his country. The Saudi policy, therefore, was shaping itself to find a scapegoat for its own total failure. On this occasion, too, the mantra was played time and again that Iran wants to take over Saudi Arabia. Dr Baluchi alleged on the programme that the Shias are the murderers of the caliph Umar, Uthman, Ali, and Husayn and that Iran with the support of the United States and Israel wants to act as Mongols against the Sunnis.

In one of the programmes on this channel, a Saddamite racist was included in the panel for Shia bashing. He claimed that no Arabs could possibly have participated in killing Imam Husayn, the son of Imam Ali and the grandson of the Prophet. He implied that the Persians were involved in the massacre of Karbala. But he did not give any thought to a dilemma he was creating for himself. The tragedy of Karbala was a link in the string of tragic events which will always remain reprehensible against the Umayyad dynasty and their followers. The claim of the Saddamite racist was tantamount to saying that the people who persecuted the Prophet at the dawn of Islam for thirteen years in Makkah and who rained stones on him in the streets of Ta'if (the town to the southeast of Makkah), and those who conspired to kill him on his way back from Tabuk (at present, in northwestern Saudi Arabia) were all Iranians, not Arabs, even though the Persian Empire had not even been conquered in those days.

In relation to the veracity of the event of Fadak (the land gifted by the Prophet to his daughter, Lady Fatimah), the Saddamite claimed that the entire Shia *madhhab* (school of law) falls down like a domino because of the concept of imamate (leadership after the Prophet) and because of the claims of the usurpation of Fadak and the burning of the house of Lady Fatimah. To illustrate this point further, he questioned why the Prophet only remembered Fatimah and forgot his other three daughters in bequeathing Fadak? Neither the Saddamite nor other members on the panel had the flimsiest idea that Lady Fatimah was the only surviving offspring of the Prophet at his death and that the deceased cannot be named heirs.

Besides, Fadak was the private property of the Prophet, and he had gifted it to Lady Fatimah in his lifetime. This speaks volumes about the knowledge of Islamic history that these ideologues have blessed themselves with. A radical Bahraini salafi on the panel kept on expressing his gibes on this channel and insulting the top Shia religious scholars. He later appeared on other Wahhabi channels based in Egypt because it is there that he could realise his full potential of venting Shia-phobic outbursts.

IDEOLOGY BASED ON SYSTEMATIC INDOCTRINATION

One of the most provocative messages of Al-Qaeda's late mercenary in Iraq, Abu Ayyub al-Masri, was picked up by Al Jazeera Arabic TV from one of the Internet sites of the terrorists and was given coverage in several of its news bulletins on 10 November, 2006. What was so attractive in Al-Masri's message that warranted such importance? It carried all the prejudices that pan-Arab nationalists could possibly emit against their opponents. It conveyed hatred of the Americans, not for occupying Iraq but for 'assisting Iran', as he put it, to widen its influence in Iraq, Afghanistan, and the Levant (Syria). The terrorist leader was worried that President Bush's 'obstinate policies', as he called them, aided Iran to establish the 'old Persian Empire' (of the pre-Islamic pagan era). To stress this point further, Al-Masri described the Iranian Muslims as 'Zionists' in southern Iraq and called them *'al-furs al-majus'*—a derogatory term used against the ancient Persian fire worshippers. In line with the policy of his establishment, the terrorist leader did not accept that the Shia Muslims of Iraq were Arabs. He called them the remnants of Persian Magians or pagans.

Al-Masri also claimed that he had an armed force of twelve thousand with ten thousand reservists. The vital point in his message was that he inferred that the United States was conspiring with Iran in realising its ambition of 'empire building' over the Arab land. This is the type of indoctrination which is institutionally fed into the subconscious of terrorists. If it is successfully sold to illiterate men in the streets, as some channels are doing, then they could succeed in provoking racial prejudice and old rivalries of the pre-Islamic era between Arab and non-Arab regional powers. Hence, the pan-Arab nationalists have some common grounds with the violent extremists in banking on Iranophobia.

Violence against civilians has not sprung in vacuum overnight. The mudslinging has become the official policy of this establishment, even at the cost of staking its own credibility. The radicals neither have any mandate from the renowned scholars of Al-Azhar in Cairo nor from the Barelvi establishment in the Indo-Pak subcontinent to act as their representatives and spokesmen. They could never ever get such a mandate from the Shias. They are aware of the impediments facing them in imposing their ideology on other Muslims. They have geared their policy, therefore, to demonise the Shias to impress upon the Sunnis that they are facing a common enemy.

To illustrate how the psychology of the militant extremists works, an additional case study is presented. It shows a striking similarity in their thinking in whichever country they may be.

SHIAPHOBIA IN YEMEN

A report in the Yemeni newspaper *Al-Watan* covers a message from the late second-in-command of Al-Qaeda in the Arabian peninsula, a Saudi national, Sa'id al-Shahri, who chose the title Abu Sufyan for himself.

According to the statement issued by Al-Qaeda on 17 July, 2013, he was killed in the fourth American drone attack.

Abu Sufyan of history, from the dawn of the Prophet's mission, had fought against the Prophet and against Islam in every major battle before the final conquest of Makkah. He opposed the Prophet willingly but accepted Islam unwillingly, according to historic accounts.

The recorded message of Al-Qaeda's Abu Sufyan, like that of Abu Ayyub al-Masri, was filled with garbage to the brim. In the name of defending the Sunnis, he used the same sectarian rant which is persistently perpetuated by the extremist Wahhabi clerics against the Shias. He also used the same rallying cry that Umar ibn Sa'd, the commander-in-chief of Yazid's forces, had used in Karbala when launching his attack against the nearest members of the Prophet's family. The published picture of Al-Qaeda's Saudi second-in-command shows that he had a striking resemblance in face and features with his late leader Bin Laden. In the light of the obnoxious message of Abu Sufyan of Al-Qaeda, it is clear that their slogans and rallying cries were that of the avowed enemies of the Prophet's household.

Abu Sufyan of Al-Qaeda attacked the Saudi royal family for not doing enough to fight what he called the Iranian *rafidi* invasion, stretching from the eastern region of Saudi Arabia to the northern region of Yemen. He appealed for recruitment of youths from the Persian Gulf countries for his style of 'jihad'. Apart from being ignorant of history, he had no idea of the geopolitics of the region. He claimed in his message that Iran had already invaded Syria, Bahrain, eastern Saudi Arabia, and now northern Yemen. He turned a blind eye to the declared policy of Qatar and Saudi Arabia in financing and arming to the teeth the Salafi insurgents and terrorists in Syria and elsewhere. In Egypt, the Salafi faction was involved in triggering sectarian violence since the downfall of Mubarak. In Tunisia and Libya, the Salafis created political crisis through violence and political assassinations of their opponents, for which they faced public outcry. Yet Libya acts as one of the largest recruits of jihadists for Syria, in addition to eighty-two other nationalities.

In an attempt at throwing mud in the eyes of Muslim masses, the terrorist leader simply ignored violence, murder, invasion, occupation of foreign land, destruction of mosques, and burning of the copies of the Quran, which his fellow extremists had carried out in a number of countries. All these crimes were committed not by Iranians but by his fellow extremist forces nurtured from petro dollars. Human-rights records in Saudi Arabia have been heavily criticised by Human Rights Watch, Amnesty International, and the Foreign Office.[38]

Abu Sufyan of Al-Qaeda paid tribute to the Muslim Brotherhood movement in Yemen for fighting the so-called Iranian incursion, referring to the Huthis (the Shias from the tribe of Huth in the north of Yemen). The fact remains that Huthis have been the natives of Yemen and have inhabited that region centuries before the ancestors of Abu Sufyan of Al-Qaeda were even conceived and invaded and occupied the Arabian Peninsula.

Paradoxically, the Muslim Brotherhood movement had been under the tutelage of Al-Ahmars tribe, which was the closest ally of the Saudis in Yemen and looked after their interest in Yemen, whereas the Muslim Brotherhood movement in Egypt turned into bad books of the Saudi regime, who had put all its weight behind their rival political factions. This is the grim reality of contradictions and countercontradictions in Middle Eastern politics.

---

38 http://www.guardian.co.uk/world/2004/nov/11/humanrights.politics, 11 November, 2004.

The case studies referred to illustrate how the mentality of the militant extremists has been geared and groomed to spread lies and malicious messages and to expect others to believe them blindly, no matter how irrational and ill-conceived the messages might be. Thanks to the revolution in the means of communications, Muslim masses refuse to be treated as herds of cattle, like they had been by the despots and their offshoots in the past.

Chapter 4

THE NEGATIVE ROLE
OF THE MEDIA

The administration of Husni Mubarak in Egypt granted facilities and licences to two TV channels, Wesal and Safa, to engage in a sectarian propaganda war. A cleric from Hama in Syria, Shaykh Adnan Arur, was a regular guest on one of these channels, and his job was to express his gibes and insults and to defame and vilify the Shias and attribute to them unknown traditions and narrations. He was hired to carry out mudslinging on every aspect of Shia faith as well as their revered religious personalities. The role played by this cleric was not free from malicious political motives. The militants in Hama in Syria consider him as their religious guru and take his guidance. Since the last few months of 2013 and the beginning of 2014, interfighting between the *takfiri* terrorist groups in Syria exploded because of power struggle between them. Until then, as long as they were fighting the Syrian regime, these two branches of Al-Qaeda were richly supported from petro dollars. Since they started killing each other, the cleric from Hama, settled in Saudi Arabia, and the media of the *takfiri*s branded the other side, fighting their allies, as the creation of the Iranian and '*rafidi* Shias'.

Amazingly, they conveniently forgot that both of these terrorist factions were conceived in the first place by the oil rich supporters of the militants to treat the Shias, especially the Iranians, as their avowed enemies. But now, when the allegiance of the terrorist group changed, the dejected leaders saw the need for an easy exit by labelling this faction as the product of the Iranian Shias.

In the beginning of February 2014, Ayman al-Zawahiri, the leader of Al-Qaeda, disowned Abu Bakr al-Baghdadi, the commander of the faction calling itself the Islamic State of Iraq and Sham (Levant) (ISIL) because he had rebelled against the leader of Al-Qaeda and declared himself 'commander of the believers'. In order to stop interfighting between the two factions in Syria, the clerics of the insurgents wanted ISIL to get out of Syria so that it could concentrate all its efforts in spreading the reign of terror in Iraq, which it did with initial successes.

Adnan Arur, a religious mentor, addressing the ISIL in a state of hysteria, shouted his head off in one of his talks, ordering it to leave Syria immediately and urged that its duty of jihad lies in Iraq. As ISIL was not in the mood to listen to anybody except its commander, it was labelled a 'misguided group' and a 'crony of the Syrian regime'. But as soon as it shifted many of its militants from Syria to Iraq in mid-June 2014, the same group suddenly became 'freedom fighters'. Without a flicker of shame, the bigoted popular Arabic media seemed to be redefining their paradigm in relation to the militants that were now hell-bent on unleashing havoc and yet were being called 'revolutionaries' and elements of 'uprising' and 'freedom fighters' in Iraq.

When ISIL terrorists took over Mosul and Takrit in Northern Iraq with the support of the Saddamites, they unleashed their propensity for mass killings and summary executions. They declared that they would not tolerate the presence of any Shias in the Sunni regions.

They robbed the Central Bank in Mosul and overnight became one of the richest terrorist groups in the world. They went on a rampage in destroying the holy sites and caused mass exodus of civilians. They armed children and involved them in their killing spree. Yet they were portrayed as liberators of the Sunnis from the control of the Shia government.

With this sense of twisted justice and total disregard for humanitarian tragedy affecting thousands of innocent civilians, most of whom were Sunnis anyway, the biased popular media reflected the policies of the countries that have a vested interest in the balkanisation of Iraq. If Iraq is broken up into different regions, then it would not be able to compete with them anymore as the second-largest producer of oil in the Middle East, the first being Saudi Arabia. Therefore, it was the duty of the media to dramatise and exaggerate the conflict as 'Sunni versus Shia', whereas this was not a sectarian conflict, but it was a core conflict for the survival of Iraq as a united country. The Iraqi and Iranian media covered the scenes of the Sunni clerics joining the Shia clerics in appealing for a united and joint defence in the face of the terrorist onslaught threatening the country as a whole. This was a crucial development. But unsurprisingly it was totally ignored by the media sympathetic to the insurgents and terrorists.

After a few weeks of this tumultuous development in northern Iraq, the terrorist group started blowing up and destroying the churches of the Christians, who had lived as a peaceful minority for many decades in that region. Then they started destroying the shrines of Sunni Sufi Sheikhs, razing their tombs. This attracted condemnation and protests from Sunni religious figures in Iraq and Egypt, where prominent clerics declared that the new Islamic State (global Islamic caliphate) that ISIL declared has nothing to do with Islam. On the contrary, all their actions are in direct violation and breach of Islam and its values.

They appealed to the global Muslim community to pay allegiance to Abu Bakr al-Baghdadi, the newly installed caliph of the Islamic State. They threatened the Sunni tribes in Iraq that if they do not oblige, then they will be treated harshly. It seemed certain that the honeymoon of portraying ISIL as 'deliverers' and 'liberators' of Iraq was short-lived. The Sunni tribes started forming alliances with the military to flush these elements out but at what cost? The well-trained and well-financed IS were already widely entrenched to remain there for months if not years to come.

WHEN FICTION IS ADOPTED AS FACT

In one of the TV channels of Egypt called Safa, supporting the anti-Shia radical ideologues, the guest cleric fires allegations upon allegations from the script prepared for him, claiming that what he says is written in the Shia books. But his intelligence does not require him to name the books he quotes from and to name the publishers and the year of publication. It is taken for granted that the viewers would simply accept whatever trash he throws at them. The Egyptian moderator intervenes to strengthen the allegations of the cleric. He tells his viewers that normally he does not interfere in discussions but acts only as moderator. The regular viewers could vouch that this is simply not true.

The facilitator continues to say that he would start the discussion on the agreed premise (agreed between him and his cleric on the programme) that the 'fundamental beliefs' of the Shias is 'abusing the *sahabah*' (companions of the Prophet), 'believing that the Quran is fabricated', 'performing *mutah*', and believing in the imamate of Al-Mahdi. With the exception of the last statement, all the other statements are sheer misrepresentation of facts, which anybody having any idea about the Shia faith could tell. But nowadays ignorance is deemed to be the only requirement for participating in these types of polemics and mudslinging.

Taking these allegations as a case study, these need to be analysed because a fiction that is repeated often in the media is most likely to be adopted as a fact by the viewers. Most viewers do not have time and capability to verify these claims independently. The Shias have been arguing that they do not have problems with all the companions of the Prophet. On the contrary, they respect the devoted, loyal, truthful, and sincere companions. They only have problems with the unjust who committed treacheries, betrayal of trust, breach of covenants, and caused divisions in the Muslim community, resulting in bloodbaths. They only curse those who are cursed in the Quran and in the traditions of the Prophet. The Shias believe that in the matter of accountability, there is no immunity granted in Islam to anybody, companions or no companions; otherwise, it would mean that the law does not treat everybody fairly and justly, which is absurd.

But the extremist Wahhabis and Salafis have succeeded in indoctrinating people of their own ilk against the Shias by portraying them as enemies and abusers of the companions of the Prophet, whereas this establishment itself has committed the worst abuse against the Prophet's companions by desecrating, destroying, and razing to the ground their burial places in the historic cemeteries of Jannat al-Baqi' in Madinah and Jannat al-Mu'alla in Makkah. They have been engaged in a war against Islamic sanctities and history, violating the honour of the companions and that of the nearest family members of the Prophet. This war continues until today. When the terrorists of Al-Nusra Front, the branch of Al-Qaeda entered the Adhra region in Syria, they destroyed the shrine of the veteran, and one of the most sincere, loyal, and devoted companions of Imam Ali, named Hujr ibn Adi. They hold malicious gibes against this companion because he, his young son, and his entire entourage were slain on the orders of their leader, Mu'awiyah, the archenemy of Imam Ali.

The malevolence of fourteen centuries against Imam Ali and his companions was revived. The criminal gangsters of Al-Nusra not only desecrated the burial place of Hujr ibn Adi but even dug his grave to exhume his body. This barbaric act was condemned unanimously by the Shias and by many sincere religious scholars at Al-Azhar, the renowned seminary of the Sunnis. But the Wahhabi and Salafi religious scholars hid their faces in the sand and remained deaf, dumb, and blind to the sacrilegious act against this honourable companion. This adds to the long list of self-contradictions of this establishment. Ironically, the Salafi cleric Shaykh al-Qaradawi did not remain silent at the destruction of the idols of Buddha by the Taliban in Afghanistan. In this case, he did not show any respect previously shown for the idols of Buddha. Forgetting their own disrespect for the companions of the Prophet, they passed the edict permitting killing of Shias for allegedly abusing the companions of the Prophet.

To allege that the Shias believe in a different Quran or they believe that the Quran in the hands of the Muslims is distorted is a sheer hypocrisy. The book *Al-Itqan*, by Allamah Jalal al-Din al-Sayuti, the renowned Sunni exegete of the Quran, quotes narrations from authentic Sunni sources which claim that there are additions and deletions in the Quran. But the Shias do not build an argument over weak and fabricated narrations. They do not misuse the Quran to make political or sectarian gains. These weak narrations have been unanimously refuted and rejected by the Shia scholars of the classical era and present times. But the radicals have a habit of throwing the burden of their own guilt on others.

Al-Shaykh al-Saduq (306–381/919–991 AH/CE), among the most prominent classical Shia religious scholars, issued his verdict, more than a thousand years ago, in *I'tiqadat al-Imamiyyah* (*A Shiite Creed*), that, 'Our belief is that the Quran, which Allah revealed to His Prophet Muhammad, is [the same as] the one between the two boards (*daffatayn*). And it is that which is in the hands of the people, and is not greater in extent than that. The number of surahs [chapters] as generally accepted is one hundred and fourteen...And he who asserts that we say that it is greater in extent than this (the present text) is a liar...And that the extent of the Quran is no more than what is in the hands of the people'.[39]

This is one of many verdicts of the prominent Shia scholars emphasising that the Shias do not believe that the Quran has any distortions, additions, or deletions. Yet their opponents keep on insisting upon their unfounded and concocted allegations, based on weak traditions, for the purpose of earning some points in sectarian politics.

As to the performance of *mutah*, the facilitator on the TV and his guest did not bother to inform the viewers about the definition of *mutah*, which is 'a fixed-term marriage, where the period of time is predetermined by mutual agreement between the couple'. This is the type of marriage that was never prohibited by the Prophet. The facilitator and his cleric did not have the courage of disclosing that these days a weird concept of marriage has emerged in the oil-rich regions of the Middle East, called 'summer marriage', where a wife is taken for the period of the summer vacation only and then dumped without any rights. They did not disclose that in Egypt itself, the marriage of *misyar* is very popular, where the wife accepts a visiting husband and remains in the house of her parents by relinquishing some of her marital rights. In many Arab countries, there are hundreds of nightclubs, casinos, and other places of vice operating under the very nose of the clerical institutions. Even during the rule of the Islamic political party the Muslim Brotherhood, any attempt at containing brothels failed.

All these contradictions and abuses are the direct result of prohibiting what was permitted by the Prophet. They have replaced the marriage of *mutah* (under strict terms and conditions) with promiscuity, perversion, moral vice, and child abuse. A brief search on the Internet can reveal far more serious things happening in the Egyptian and other

---

39 Al-Saduq, p. 77.

Muslim societies, for which corruption and double standards are the main causes.

Mutah has nothing to do with the 'fundamental beliefs' of the Shias, as alleged on the said TV programme. Like permanent marriage, this is a facility which is permitted under solemn contracts. It does not mean that it is performed by all Shias. It does not mean either that it has to be performed for the sake of it. But the radicals give the impression that the Shias have nothing else to do in life but to perform *mutah*. The Salafi media have been branding all the Shias 'products of *mutah*' to cause offence, according to the standards they have set for themselves to satisfy their paranoid nature. Since the uprising in Bahrain, even the official media in that country have been naming the majority population in Bahrain as 'products of *mutah*'.

In regard to the imamate of Imam Ali and Imam Mahdi (the first and the twelfth imams, respectively), if the moderator and his cleric had done their homework, they would have discovered that there are not few but many traditions of the Prophet in their own sources, with authentic chains of narrations, talking about the advent of the mahdi (the awaited imam who would restore justice in the world after it would have been filled with injustice and oppression, as foretold by the Prophet). But if they were to accept this genre of authentic hadiths, then they would be sharing the essential faith of the Shias. Instead, they have chosen to censure the traditions or hadiths of the Prophet to follow their own caprice and wishes.

An Iraqi shaykh phones the open-line programme on this TV channel and asks for a few minutes to read some traditions from *Sahih al-Bukhari* (the most authentic book of traditions in Sunni schools) to make the viewers aware of the wide disparity between the views expressed on this TV channel and the sources which they believe to be authentic. But the moderator smells a rat, so he does not permit him. At this point, the moderator intervenes and addresses the viewers, alleging that all the proof which the Sunnis have been presenting is based only on the Quran and Sunnah, whereas, all the arguments that the Shias have been presenting are based on their dogmas, which they impose on the Quran and Sunnah. Having arrived at their preconceived conclusion, they hail themselves as victorious over the Shias without realising that theirs is a style that betrays scholarship and rational thinking. At times, when a Shia viewer calls, he is bluntly told that Shias are not allowed on this programme. With this type of juvenile behaviour, they purport to act as the sole representatives of the noble Sunni communities, who are not even aware of how their school of thought is being misrepresented.

A lady, like many other hired characters, phones up and says that she was a Shia at one time and has now left the faith to become a Sunni. The moderator seeks to make the story spicy and sensational. So he appeals to her in the name of God the Almighty to tell the viewers whether the message they have been putting across on their TV or the one that the Shias have been putting across is clear. The answer does not need any imagination. Again, they end up congratulating each other that they have won the day. The aim of these TV channels is to provoke the emotions of their fanatics and extremists on sectarian grounds by replacing facts with fiction.

In the documentaries screened on one of these TV channels, the Iranian people are portrayed as *majus* (Magians, or fire worshippers), in compliance with the rant initiated by the doomed tyrant of Iraq, Saddam, during his eight-year war against Iran. It warns the Lebanese to be aware of the invasion of their country by *majus*. The propaganda on paranoid TV channels and the venom that their clerics emit have the objective of demonising the Shias, whom they do not even consider Muslims, as if the Shias are desperate to get their faith authenticated by psychopaths.

The assassinated religiopolitical leader of Iraq, Sayyid Muhammad Baqir al-Hakim, is portrayed as a paedophile through some manipulated photos screened on one of the channels. Their dirty minds did not even exempt an internationally renowned figure from character assassination. If Danish and Swedish cartoonists and Dutch filmmakers had indulged in portraying the Prophet of Islam in similar derogatory manner, they got their lead from these psychotic extremists.

After viewing the manipulated photos against their political and religious leaders, the Shias could have retaliated by targeting their religious figures like Ibn Taymiyyah and Ibn Abd al-Wahhab with similar expressions. The Shias could have made gains out of the celibacy of their top religious gurus, like Ibn Taymiyyah, Al-Ghazali, and Al-Nawawi, who never got married despite advising and preaching others to get married in compliance with the established tradition of the Prophet. But despite admonishing the public that the Prophet has said that whoever turns away from his traditions and practices is not his follower, these scholars contradicted his traditions in practice.

In another instance on the TV channel, the guest cleric then addresses his viewers in Sham (the Levant, historically comprising Syria, Lebanon, Jordan, and Palestine). He appeals to them, saying, 'O people of Sham! Open your eyes. They [the Shias] will spread *fitnah* [discord or mischief] in your country by cursing the caliphs and the mother of the believers!' The phobia he generates against the Shias is a classic provocation in which the extremist Salafis and Wahhabis have demonstrated their expertise. But if an individual was to conduct a research from his own sources, he could prove the extent to which they themselves have abused the caliphs and the wife of the Prophet.

The Shias are the largest ethnic community that visits the holy places and shrines in Syria. But the said cleric gave an impression that the

Iranian visitors were arriving to invade Syria. Many of his cosectarians believed him because he commands influence among the extremists in Hama, the epicentre of the militant Salafis and Muslim Brotherhood movements in Syria. In one of the totally fabricated news items, the cleric claimed that the Sunnis were being besieged by the Shias in Sayyidah Zaynab, on the outskirts of Damascus. This town houses the shrine of the granddaughter of the Prophet. Although the overwhelming majority of visitors to this town are Shias from around the world, the majority of its residents are Sunnis, who are the main beneficiaries of the tourist trade. But the cleric's objective was to foment trouble between Sunnis and Shias.

This TV channel showed scenes from the Ashura commemorations and gave itself the right to mock at the traditional practices of the Shias. Within Sunni Islam itself, there are hundreds of practices that the radical fanatics do not approve of. But they dare not devote TV programmes to making a mockery of the Sunnis. This shows that they are only interested in unleashing their malice and hatred against the Shias.

In the month of Ramadan in 2008, the same cleric expressed his wish on Al-Mustakilla TV to perform *mutah* (temporary marriage) with Shia women. The people of his perverted ilk have always accused the Shias of committing a prohibited act. But by expressing his wish to perform temporary marriage with Shia women, this double-faced cleric was stripping the veil of hypocrisy from his own face because he was publicly confessing that he wished to perform an act that is *haram* (prohibited) according to his own belief and commitment.

The Muslim community is facing umpteen gigantic social problems in many countries. Poverty, unemployment, lack of amenities, lack of clean drinking water, overflowing sewage in towns, piles of garbage collected on the street corners, child abuse in the form of child labour and child beggars, endemic official corruption (even among members of parliament), lack of education, and substandard health facilities in many Arab and Muslim countries are pushing a large segment of the population below the poverty line. This is the main reason for public frustration and revolt against the corrupt regimes. Starvation in Somalia and other North African countries has been nightmarish by any human standards. But the extremists either do not understand these issues or are totally divorced from the basic needs of the public. Instead of involving themselves with real-life issues, they waste their time, energy, and money on matters which do not concern them and which are not likely to benefit the Muslims in any way.

Throughout the holy month of Ramadan 2009 (1430 AH), one of the TV channels hosted the same cleric who hurled abuse at the faith and belief in the awaited Imam Mahdi and insulted and vilified the Shias who believe in his existence and reappearance. This cleric was awarded by certain religious authorities in Saudi Arabia a half million rials for allegedly rendering the Shias 'speechless'. In fact, he debated nobody but himself, judged himself to be the winner, and passed the verdict of victory in favour of himself, seconded by his facilitator and rubber stamped by his fellow fanatics. This is the type of sense of proportion that prevails in their establishment.

A cleric wearing the attire of an Egyptian cleric posted a video on YouTube in which he prays to God to make all Shias suffer from cancer and starvation to death and to destroy them and burn them in the fire of hell. Then all of a sudden he becomes immersed in emotions and starts crying. He implores God in desperation as if to convince God by saying, 'Please, please, God, destroy the *rawafid*' (derogatory name given to Shias). After having condemned all the Shias to hell, then he prays for their guidance.

These types of schizophrenics work on the assumption that they are rightly guided, that they are at the apex of perfection, that they are the only righteous creatures in the universe, and that they have the exclusive right to decide who goes to paradise and who ends up in hell. Hence, there is no scope for improving their psychotic thinking. They fail to perceive their own faults. The phenomenal spite they spread on YouTube, after making loud noises about Islamic unity and Islamic brotherhood, brings into question their sincerity, reliability, stability, and trustworthiness.

When millions of Egyptian youths held vigil in Liberty Square in Cairo, the court clerics loyal to Mubarak did not support the masses. Many of them implored the people not to rise against the oppressive ruler. One of the TV channels operating from Egypt blamed Iran for fomenting trouble in Liberty Square and for standing behind the youth revolution in Egypt. As the voices against unrepresentative regimes started to rise on the streets of the Arab capitals, the bigoted media kept on pointing fingers at Iran at every crisis. The most common tirade spread by them was that Iran wants to convert all Sunnis to become Shias. Little did they ponder that if Iran musters such a vast influence in the Arab world that people are not even capable of demanding their basic rights or defending their school of thought without Iranian support, then this is an insult to the honour and dignity of the Arab people as the overwhelming majority are Sunnis.

There are many respectable and noble Sunni scholars who do not concur with this venomous style of sectarian witchhunting. But their silence is encouraging the propagandists to spread untrue views that the Shias are on the march with a ghastly plan to invade Egypt and the holy lands of Makkah and Madinah.

At times, they choose passages from the scripts of papers in their hands, alleging that these are the beliefs of the Shias, which the Shias may not even have heard of. The Shias abide by certain etiquettes and principles without stooping to their level of polemics and spurious and malicious claims. Otherwise, there are hundreds of books written by their radical scholars which could be capitalised upon to demonstrate stark contradictions therein.

Chapter 5

THE LEGACY OF COURT JURISTS

In the last two decades, the emergence of Arabic and Muslim TV satellite channels provides prospects for bringing communities closer to one another and spreading beneficial knowledge and information among the masses. Despite a great potential for constructive and positive change, a large segment of the media is misused to implant animosity and lies and in disturbing peaceful coexistence among nations, communities, and races.

This is the age in which all means of communications have developed to a level where the globe has become a small village. With a few clicks of a button, it is possible to transmit large files, books, and even contents of a library across cyberspace. The Internet is leading the media revolution. Humankind certainly benefits from this development and change. But when the media are misused to spread filth, mischief, lies, and evil goals, then what is apparently advantageous turns into a disadvantage.

A movement exists among the right-wing Christians in Europe and the United States claiming that these continents are traditionally

Christian and should remain Christian. They claim that the Muslims are aliens in their countries and do not have the right to spread Islam among the indigenous people of the region. They consider the growing presence of Muslims a security threat to Europe and the United States.

Fanatical individuals and extremist groups are not in need of any empirical evidence, facts, or rational arguments to justify their conjectural beliefs. Whether the extremists are Christians, Jews, or Muslims, they are unlikely to study the issues in their proper contexts and with unbiased and balanced thinking because their judgment is based on prejudices.

BETWEEN PHOBIA AND OBSESSION

Shaykh Yusuf al-Qaradawi seems to have adopted the rationale of the right-wing Christians by claiming that only the four schools of the Sunnis have a place in the Sunni world and that the Shias should stop preaching their teachings in the Sunni countries. But he readily exempts his own sect, that of Salafism, which has embarked on a globalised proselytising mission. It is well known that the Salafis differ from all the four Sunni traditional schools of law by adopting *in toto* Ibn Taymiyyah's ideology, which was vehemently rejected by the jurists of the Sunni traditional schools. It was they who had complained to the authorities against his offensive writings and got him imprisoned in Damascus, where he died two years later.

The biased attitude of Al-Qaradawi is comparable with the phobia that the right-wing Christians promote. He himself is actively involved in missionary activities in the Christian and non-Christian world. But he sets different standards for Islamic teachings of the Shia denomination.

In this era of technological revolution and the fast speed at which information travels across the globe, it is irrational for Al-Qaradawi to warn of the rising Shia threat to the predominantly Sunni countries. In order to realise what is happening in the world of communications, one only needs a laptop in front of him rather than to indulge in unnecessary outbursts.

Al-Qaradawi was banned since 1981 in his own country, Egypt. He became exiled and was adopted by the rulers of Qatar, where he had a free reign in preaching the Salafi ideology; later, he became a popular icon on Qatar-based Al Jazeera Arabic TV. He does not seem to be bothered that some heterodox missionaries have a free hand in spreading their beliefs among the Sunnis, despite the fact that the latter consider them misguided. He does not object at the spread of many Sufi orders in Egypt and other North African countries, although the Salafis accuse them of spreading innovations in Islamic practices. This is because these religious groups do not pose any political threat to their interests. But the spread of Shia thought is a direct challenge to the political hegemony they have enjoyed for several centuries. Therefore, from their viewpoint, the spread of Shia beliefs has to be fought with vigour.

Al-Qaradawi does not seem to sense any threat to the religious life of Sunnis as a result of widespread secularisation in predominantly Sunni countries. He does not seem to be bothered that many people are giving only lip service to religious teachings and are increasingly adopting secular life. He is not concerned that Islam merely has a ritualistic place in the life of many Muslims in the Muslim world, where wine, prohibited by Islam, is consumed openly and the places of vices function under the very noses of these clerics and lawmakers.

The court clerics, who make loud noises about the need to implement the shariah, remain blind in the face of the booming business of nightclubs and casinos in their own cities, where indecency, nudity, and promiscuity are widespread. It does not take a keen observer to notice that Islamic moral teachings are breached left, right, and centre in most Muslim countries. But the court clerics become worried only when their political and sectarian monopoly is under threat.

Al-Qaradawi carefully chose the time for his outburst on Al Jazeera Arabic TV against the Shias of Iran. He took undue advantage of the Iranian nation coming under international pressure for its peaceful nuclear programme. Although more than eight years had passed since his last personal visit to Iran, he warned of the imminent danger of the Shia faith. His phobia against the Shias would have been justified if they had converted anybody at the point of a gun, had spread their beliefs under the threat of a sword, had coerced their beliefs onto others, or had bribed any officials or clerics to permit them to distribute their literature. If they did nothing of the sort, from which it could be deduced that the Shias are forcing their beliefs on the Sunnis, then Al-Qaradawi's motives remained mysterious. The respectable Sunni traditionalists oppose the Salafi and Wahhabi attempts at hijacking their jurisprudential schools. This is the main cause of concern and worry for them that they are being disowned by their own masses.

Al-Qaradawi chose the platform of Al Jazeera Arabic TV for his warning as this channel has made a hero out of him through his weekly programme *Al-Shariah wa al-Hayat* (*The Shariah and Life*), in as much as it had made a hero out of Bin Laden by broadcasting his video messages regularly.

Al-Qaradawi himself confessed that he was given a very warm welcome in Iran, where top government officials received him. Thousands of people prayed under his lead. Yet he reacted with ingratitude after more than eight long years to all the hospitality, favours, and valuable gifts lavished upon him. He was treated as a dignitary by the administration of the past president Khatami.

On Sunday, 18 February, 2007, in his interview on Al Jazeera Arabic TV, Al-Qaradawi expressed his deep concern that the Shias are proselytising the Sunnis. This was repeated on the *Al-Shariah wa al-Hayat* programme, and the channel itself reiterated it on a number of occasions.

A simple question would have solved the dilemma. If the Shia students attend any Sunni institutes or seminaries, will they be taught and trained according to the Sunni faith or according to Shia faith? Likewise, the learning in the Shia institutes is based on the Shia teachings, irrespective of the sect to which the students belong. If after graduating from the Shia institutes, the Sunni students decide to embrace the Shia faith, would this be construed as proselytising the Sunnis? When the Sunni missionaries convert people to Islam, don't they take for granted that Islam encompasses only Sunni denomination? This method is quite acceptable to Al-Qaradawi provided the new reverts do not become Shias, but if they do, then it is not acceptable. There is a limit to multifaceted attitude but not with this type of clerics.

The Shias have a right to ask: Why didn't Al-Qaradawi have a single word of objection against aggressive proselytising process adopted by the Wahhabis in the Sunni world since the influx of petro dollars? Why didn't he object to the Salafi jihadists openly venting their malice against the Shias by calling them 'infidels'? Lately, he himself has joined the chorus with the *takfiri*s, branding all Shias as 'heretics' and as members of the 'party of Satan' and openly appealing to everybody in the Sunni world capable of fighting to fight the Shias.

In the wake of a very bad defeat that the insurgents suffered in the Battle of Qusayr in Syria, where Shia militia from Lebanon fought the insurgents alongside the Syrian force, Al-Qaradawi unleashed his tirade in his Friday sermon in Doha. He said, 'How could one hundred million Shias defeat one-point-seven billion (Sunnis)?' So, according to his rationale, all people (Sunnis and Shias) were at the opposing end of the conflict. The most naïve analyst could have vouched that the overwhelming majority of Muslims do not have anything whatsoever to do with armed conflicts and with acts of terrorism being sponsored and practised in the name of Islam, thanks to the psychotic provocateurs. But he laid down the foundation of *fitnah* (dissention) in the places of worship. He continued, 'Only because (Sunni) Muslims are weak'. The conflict, therefore, was projected to the misguided masses as Sunnis versus Shias, as simple as this.

Only a few days before, Dr Faysal Qasim had disclosed on Al Jazeera TV that the total population of Muslims worldwide is 1.3 billion. Within a few days, the population of only the Sunni Muslims jumped to 1.7 billion. This type of exaggeration, presenting false figures and twisting the facts purely for political motives, has no place in Islam, which requires men of religion to be straightforward and to speak the truth in all circumstances.

The propensity of distorting the truth is a dangerous politics. It banks on the ignorance of the masses. This type of ignorance, unfortunately, is not only prevalent among the ideologues and the people under their influence but even in some Western circles. Trofimov writes that the Wahhabi uprising of Juhayman and the takeover of the Grand Mosque in Makkah in 1979 was depicted as a 'Shia uprising' in the memoirs of some French and American politicians. This indicates that they were 'obsessed with Iran',[40] Trofimov claims. Whatever the motives might have been, when supposedly well-informed politicians cover up or twist facts, their objectivity and credibility become questionable.

THE UNTOLD STORY
Shaykh Yusuf al-Qaradawi was refused entry visa to the United Kingdom in 2008 and to France in 2012, although he enjoys unqualified support

---

40 Trofimov, pp. 243–244.

from the Salafi establishment and Qatari government as a popular jurist. Despite the fact that Qatar enjoys friendly trade relations with Israel, ironically, Al-Qaradawi had supported suicide bombings and believed that all targets in the Palestinian occupied territories were military targets. In the wake of the assassination of the Hamas leader, Shaykh Ahmad Yasin, he paid tribute to him in his Friday sermon from Doha and said that the Israelis were not worth the shoe insole of Shaykh Yasin.

In the present turmoil in Syria, Al-Qaradawi and another Syrian cleric, Adnan Arur from Hama, were instrumental in declaring jihad in that country, together with radical Saudi Wahhabi clerics. Although the Shias are merely 2 per cent of the population in Syria, the extremists made them scapegoats to quench the thirst of their sectarian campaign. This resulted in the militants and terrorists targeting the Shia civilians, with indiscriminate killings, burning of their houses, looting of their properties, and forcing them out of their homes, as happened in Hujayrah in the surroundings of the town of Sayyidah Zaynab in Syria.

After the assassination of the defence minister of the Syrian government on 17 July, 2012 in Damascus, the armed groups unleashed their sectarian violence, calling for jihad from the minarets of Sunni mosques in the town, which houses the sacred shrine of the granddaughter of the Prophet, revered by all the Shias and many Sunnis. Violence continued for several days. Many people were killed in cold blood. According to eyewitness reports, there was no military presence in the area. There was no policing, and the Shia civilians were left on their own undefended. They were not prepared for a sudden turn of events. The terror groups that were heavily armed showed their 'bravery' by targeting the unarmed. A Shia pupil of sixteen was beheaded, and several were kidnapped. But there was a tight-lipped silence from the clerics and the media of *fitnah* (discord). Some Shia youths, therefore, were forced out of necessity to take up arms for defending the holy shrine and the civilians living in that area, otherwise the brutes would have carried out massacres.

It remained an unfulfilled wish of the prominent Wahhabi cleric, the late Abdullah ibn Jibrin, that his fellow sectarians must take an initiative of destroying the holy shrine of Sayyidah Zaynab. Indeed, as soon as the militants succeeded in creating havoc in the town, the first attempt was made at the shrine itself after burning down a large charity hospital built by the Iranians in the town. The threat continues to this day, although it has received minimal news coverage in the popular Arabic media.

The militants succeeded in displacing Afghani refugees from the neighbourhood of the shrine by stabbing helpless people when they showed resistance to vacate their homes. They displaced Iraqi refugees from their houses by looting and burning their properties. They displaced Syrian Shias who were evicted from major towns of Homs and Aleppo and had taken refuge in the town of Sayyidah Zaynab. They turned thousands of families homeless overnight. As months passed by, it became clear that there was a correlation and coordination between the terrorists in Syria and Iraq. All these facts were observed and monitored by eyewitnesses in Sayyidah Zaynab town and other remote towns of Al-Nubbal and Al-Zahra. The foreign-backed insurgents had besieged the Shia civilians for many months in these towns. But these facts were suppressed and, three years later, simply denied by the Opposition Alliance attending the Geneva II Conference in early 2014.

The so-called Opposition Alliance denied existence of any insurgency and terrorism in the country. Western intelligence reports, and confessions of foreign personnel on international forums, proved otherwise. They put all the blame of destruction and carnage and the killings of more than 150,000 security personnel and civilians solely on the shoulders of the Syrian regime, Iranian Revolutionary Guards, and Shia militias from south Lebanon and Iraq. Under their bigoted and psychotic vision, they simply shifted the blame and underplayed the key role of Al-Nusra Front and ISIL or any one of a dozen other insurgent groups which had carried out large-scale brutal massacres, destruction, and bloodbaths in the country with advanced weapons and finance coming from oil-rich countries.

If the Opposition Alliance were to accept the existence of foreign-backed insurgent and terrorist groups, which had crossed the borders illegally with the connivance of the neighbouring countries, then the government delegation was bound to raise the question of rebuilding, which might take decades with ensuing costs which might run into billions of dollars because the scale of destruction had affected almost the entire country. They, therefore, found a soft corner of putting the entire blame on others as if they themselves were merely playing the roles of Mother Teresa and Nelson Mandela.

TURNING OF THE TIDE

The Salafi-sponsored TV channels had conducted flattering interviews with the would-be 'martyrs' who, as in Afghanistan in the 1980s, were joining the ranks of their jihadists in Syria. It seemed that this was the most expedient and effective way of solving unemployment problems in Saudi Arabia and other Persian Gulf states. But this type of economic philosophy started to backfire on them.

An outspoken Saudi reporter and writer, Dawud al-Shiryan, sparked off a public debate and openly challenged and criticised the radical clerics in his interviews screened on MBC Arabic channel. He alleged that these clerics misled and brainwashed the Saudi youths since the Afghan war and that they are responsible for getting them killed in Afghanistan, Iraq, and now in Syria, while their own youths are quite safe at home.

From January 2014, a heated debate raged between this reporter and the clerics involved in motivating and recruiting the jihadists. Conversely, they demanded the authorities to arrest the renegade reporter. But he and his supporters named and shamed a few prominent clerics responsible for getting 'our children', as they put it, killed for a wrong cause.

The financiers of insurgents in both Iraq and Syria were facing multiple setbacks. The enormous Saudi and Qatari pressure on the United States to carry out military action in Syria had already failed as the United States sought to protect its own national interest first rather than jump into another unending war. The Saudis were hoping for Western military action against Iran over its nuclear issue. But this hope was in tatters, too, over which the Saudis publicly expressed their disillusionment. Many Western media outlets reported the Saudi dismay over the US policies and spoke about strained relations with their closest ally.

In early February 2014, when the Geneva II Conference over Syria was being convened, the late King Abdullah of Saudi Arabia issued a royal decree that any Saudi national going abroad to fight and anybody recruiting the jihadists and supporting the extremist organisations will be liable to imprisonment for between three and twenty years. These corrective measures were meant to appease the mounting criticism at home against the Wahhabi clerics for their roles in pushing the Saudi youths into the mouth of imminent danger. But the Wahhabi clerics had historically enjoyed moral and financial support of the royal family, though there was hardly any record of any member of the royal family getting killed among thousands of insurgents abroad.

Under the pretext of the royal decree, the authorities sought to kill two birds with one stone. They subdued any protests against their policies by classifying peaceful demonstrations in the country as acts of terrorism. The king's decree, however, was an implied confession that there had been Saudi nationals fighting in Afghanistan, Chechnya, Lebanon,

Yemen, Iraq, Syria, Bahrain, and Pakistan, to name only a few countries, parallel with the incursion of Al-Qaeda.

At times, these militants fought pitched battles against regular armies. None of these battles were legal. None of them had the consent of the international community or the United Nations. But the proponents might argue that they were fighting jihad, and the mujahidin do not need anybody's approval to fulfil their obligation. If so, then the king's decree banning Saudi nationals from fighting abroad was expressly an ant jihad measure. This was in contravention with the Wahhabi doctrines, which vehemently promoted jihad for the last three hundred years to spread their ideology, ever since their founding fathers spread the reign of terror in the Arabian Peninsula and the neighbouring countries.

The king's decree, therefore, either contradicted the Wahhabi values and faith, or else all the battles fought on somebody else's territories by the insurgents had never been jihad in the first place. When the highest religious authority in Saudi Arabia, the grand mufti, at long last came up with a religious ruling that suicide bombings are against the shariah and that the suicide bombers will end up in the fire of hell, the fatwa was too late. Even after the issuance of this fatwa, suicide bombings continued in Iraq, Syria, Lebanon, and Pakistan, where the ideologues were averse to any changes.

But in the first week of February 2014, after the new royal decree had been issued, the Saudi government went ahead in facilitating the return of the Saudi mujahidin from Syria through Turkey and of bearing all their expenses. The insurgents had left their own country legally with the full knowledge of the country's security apparatus and intelligence agency but entered into the territory of others illegally to perform criminal acts. In the end, they enjoyed an honourable repatriation back home legally, without any action or accountability for acts of terrorism and mass murder committed abroad. This was a stab in the backs of other insurgents who were lured from eighty-three countries to join the *takfiri* Salafis and Wahhabis in Iraq and Syria.

The king must have become worried that if the kingdom keeps on trying to decide the fate of other nations at an enormous cost in human life, then it would be difficult to stop the winds of change when they start blowing in its direction. But the kingdom had gone too far in pouring billions of dollars into supporting insurgency in Syria and Iraq to be able to give up its exercise in futility so easily. By the end of February 2014, the Russian government protested against the supply of advanced rockets and missiles from Saudi Arabia to the militant groups getting military training in Jordan for attacking Syria. It seemed, therefore, that after suffering multiple defeats on the northern and central fronts, there was a plan of igniting the southern borders of Syria through Jordan.

It was amazing how the moderate states like Jordan were getting entangled into this crisis. Johnlee Varghese writes in *International Business Times*, 'As the American government is contemplating on whether or not to launch an airstrike on ISIL that is threatening to destroy Iraq, reports have now surfaced that way back in 2012, the US Army had trained members of the same terrorist group in Jordan'.[41]

There are several newspaper reports that claim that even the arms to the rebels were channelled through Jordanian borders into Syria.

This emboldened ISIL and their supporters to demonstrate publicly inside Jordan by displaying their black flags and shouting sectarian slogans, cursing the Shias, and chanting, 'Shias are enemies of Allah!' One may ask if the country's security would have permitted the same chanting against the king or against the Sunni community. No question

---

41 International Business Times website, http://www.ibtimes.co.in/iraq-crisis-isis-terrorists-were-trained-by-us-2012-syria-conflict-602594, 19 June 2014.

arises. But in this case, the country's security did not bother to intervene or take any action. During the demonstration, they even used core Shia slogans addressing Imam Ali, which people of their own ilk consider to be *kufr*. But in this case, as they were using these slogans in their favour, double standards were quite permissible. Full coverage of this hypocritical show was filmed and posted on the Internet.

Hitherto, Malaysia and Indonesia had maintained their status quo. Although the latter is the largest Muslim-populated country in the world, there were hardly any reports that militants from these countries had joined others in acts of violence against Iraq or Syria. But the agent provocateurs sought to involve them in sectarian strife to break their status quo. In Malaysia, the extremist elements attacked the places of worship and religious gatherings of the Shias. The residential quarters of the Shias were set on fire in Indonesia under the pretext that they espoused what they called heretical beliefs. This has been a typical approach of the *takfiri*s who seem to have penetrated the Southeast Asian society.

Malaysia tolerates one of the worst cultures of nudity in the world. But this does not seem to bother the fanatical clerics and agent provocateurs, who, for ideological reasons, are intolerant towards people having a different belief system.

The *takfiri*s made their presence felt in Indonesia, too, where the religious extremists held in Jakarta their first-ever Anti-Shia Alliance convention in March 2014 in a huge conference hall amidst pomposity. It called for jihad against the Shias. It called upon the Indonesian government to follow the example of Malaysia in sectarian purging. The apartheid convention, in gross violation of the international accords, sought to take the Far Eastern countries also back to the Middle-Ages by advocating violence against fellow citizens. The government did not take any action.

In the aftermath of successive defeats of the *takfiris* in several countries, it seems that provoking the uninformed masses and creating imaginary demons out of political adversaries was the alternative they could bank on as a face-saving devise. This could be the shortest cut to camouflage their humiliation and loss of credibility. The victims will be the innocent public, irrespective of which sects, schools of thought, races, or colour they belong to. All this could change only if those who exercise influence over the opinions of the masses stop treating them as herds of sheep. If neutral countries like Malaysia and Indonesia are not vigilant of the contagious politics that the *takfiris* and their oil-rich establishment have been playing with innocent people and their faith, then they may get drawn into sectarian strife, which is what the *takfiri* extremists want. The lives, faith, beliefs, and sanctities of other people have to be respected. Gone are the days when treachery and cunningness were considered the art of politics and religious values used to be treated as subservient to political manoeuvring.

INCITEMENT AND FLARE-UPS

This is a case study that proves the extent to which the faith and sanctities of others are exploited and abused.

In his interview on 24 December, 2006, on the Al Jazeera Arabic channel, Shaykh Al-Qaradawi made serious accusations directed against the Grand Ayatollah Sistani and other top Shia religious scholars in Iraq, alleging that they do not prohibit the shedding of blood of the Sunnis, whereas, in dozens of his pronouncements, Ayatollah Sistani had forbidden any revenge attacks provoked by the agent provocateurs and called for calm in the face of suicide bombings, targeting the Shia civilians and their sacred places across the country.

Following the destruction of one of the holiest Shia shrines in Samarra, had it not been for the fatwas of Grand Ayatollah Sistani prohibiting any retaliation, there would have been a bloodbath in the country. It is not possible that Al-Qaradawi was unaware of these well-publicised fatwas. But by taking undue advantage of the unawareness of his listeners and viewers, he ignored the crucial role that Ayatollah Sistani played in preventing flare-ups.

The *maraja* (jurists who are followed in jurisprudential matters) in the Shia seminary of Najaf issued joint fatwas declaring that it is *haram* (forbidden in the shariah) to attack anybody else's mosques or properties. Instead of thanking these *maraja* and expressing his gratitude for the active role they played in containing violence, Al-Qaradawi adopted a very negative stance in condemning them in his Friday sermon and on Al Jazeera TV, misguiding his listeners in the process.

Al-Qaradawi did not bother to raise his voice against the Wahhabis for issuing irresponsible fatwas declaring that it is 'obligatory' to destroy all shrines, as the late Abdullah ibn Jibrin had done. These mischievous fatwas were used as ammunition by the fanatical *takfiri*s to escalate violence.

When suicide bombers blow up innocent people, the expression used in the popular Arab media is the 'so-called terrorists'. In Iraq, when security personnel kill armed insurgents in confrontation, the expression used is 'the Shia police' against the Sunnis.

At the height of the Israeli Lebanese war in 2006, Abdullah ibn Jibrin, a prominent Wahhabi cleric, declared that people of south Lebanon are '*kuffar*' (pl. of *kafir*), forbidding any assistance to them or even praying for them. His fatwa found its way onto several Israeli websites. They found a valuable ally in the form of a Wahhabi cleric. Then he issued another fatwa that all the sacred shrines of the Shias must be destroyed. These types of clerics are void of any insight and foresight and do not care that due to their evil rulings, their fanatics end up killing thousands of innocent Muslims because of their religious beliefs. The overwhelming victims of the Muslim extremists are Muslims. In order to motivate the psychotic extremists to blow themselves up in crowded market places and mosques of the Shias, they promise them that the heavenly brides (houris) are waiting to welcome them at the gates of paradise. According to this psychopathic mind-set, the heavenly angels have no other job but to wait for these thugs and criminal elements at the gates of paradise.

Jamal Ma'ash, in his voluminous book *Al-Husayn wa al-Wahhabiyyah* (*Husayn and Wahhbism*), analyses the *takfiri* edicts issued by Abdullah ibn Jibrin and his fellow radical clerics. A question was posed to him that there are many *rafidah* (referring to Shias) with whom his cosectarians have to interact in workplace. What is the best way of dealing with them? He replied that when the Shias salute you, do not answer back their salutations; when they try to shake hands, pull back your hands; show resentment towards them through facial expressions, and make it clear to them that you hate them.

This cleric provided a sample of how the rotten mentality of the fanatics works. Through his replies, he violated the commandments of the Quran and the practices of the Prophet. He continued that his cosectarians should call the Shias towards the 'right path' (that is, towards Wahhabism or Salafism). If they are nonresponsive, and where the Sunnis are in majority, they should declare jihad against them. If this is what Abdullah ibn Jibrin called the 'right path', then his morals and methods were no better than the pre-Islamic Arabs who lived in the Dark Ages of ignorance.

He had also issued a fatwa forbidding the Shias from praying in the mosques of the Muslims, which means that he did not consider the Shias to be Muslims. But non-Muslims are not permitted to enter Makkah and Madinah in any case. But he was dead sure that the Shia pilgrims do visit the holy land and pray in the Grand Mosques in Makkah and Madinah, which means, he was hypocritically contradicting himself.

This late cleric was favoured by the Saudi authorities because of his inflammatory pronouncements against the Shias. In 1991, he described them as 'idolaters deserved to be killed', exactly the same rant that IS uses in Iraq and Syria. Following his incitement to murder, twenty-six Shia religious leaders disappeared, together with the Shia inhabitants in some villages in eastern regions of the country. In 1992, two students were sentenced to face executioners for reading the Bible as part of their studies.[42] The sentence was not carried out due to mounting international pressure. A Shia woman, Zahra al-Nasir, died in detention for having in her possession a Shia prayer book. 'Ali Salman Al-Ammar, 16, was imprisoned for two years for the same reason, and a Shia religious student, Sadiq Al Illah, was executed for heresy'.[43] This is the type of extremism that has spoiled the name of Islam and Muslims in the perception of the international community. It has betrayed Islam, Quran, the Sunnah of the Prophet, and humanitarian values.

In the context of local communities, the radical clerics search for the flimsiest of excuses to vent their vitriolic gestures. A toy appeared on the market in mid-2012. The manufacturers, either intentionally or unintentionally, built a recorded voice inside the toy, sounding like 'kill Ayishah'. Ayishah was one of the wives of the Prophet and is very much revered by the Sunnis. Irrespective of the fact that this is one of the common names among the Sunnis, clerics in Egypt, Sudan, Pakistan, and other places picked up the story and raised it in their Friday sermons. They provoked their congregation, claiming that the Shias are advocating killing of the wife of the Prophet, notwithstanding the fact that she had died fourteen centuries ago.

---

42 Aburish, pp. 110–111.
43 Ibid., p. 74.

TREACHERY AGAINST HISTORY

In his programme on Al Jazeera Arabic channel on 24 December, 2006, Al-Qaradawi cited the example of Imam Hasan, who, according to him, gave up his right to the caliphate despite the fact that he was given oath of allegiance and was entitled to the caliphate. This was a blatant distortion of history. He should have known better than most that Imam Hasan did not give up his right. Al-Qaradawi did not disclose to his listeners that there was a solemn peace truce between Imam Hasan and Mu'awiyah, the first dynastic ruler of the Umayyad dynasty, who had accepted all the conditions of the truce and then breached all of them.

There is a world of difference between paying an oath of allegiance to somebody and entering into a truce under specific terms and conditions. In the historic truce of Al-Hudaybiyyah, the Prophet did not recognise the authority of the clan of Quraysh over Makkah. He entered into a peace truce with them. As long as they abided by its condition, there was peace. When they breached the truce, the agreement became null and void. But when it comes to Imam Hasan's truce under similar circumstances, the radicals are in the habit of hiding or distorting the truth and historical facts.

On 25 February, 2011, Al-Qaradawi issued a fatwa permitting the shedding of blood of Gaddafi, although once upon a time, he had enjoyed cordial relations with the dictator, who had been a dictator ever since he assumed power in 1969. He made friendly appearances with the tyrant long after the apostasy of Gaddafi was public knowledge and long after he had made weird claims against the Quran in an attempt to replace Islam's sacred book with his own green book.

Safwat Hijazi, one of the leaders of the Muslim Brotherhood movement in Egypt, supported Al-Qaradawi's fatwa for killing Gaddafi. No such fatwa was ever heard of from these influential and popular clerics when Saddam committed massacres and genocide of his countrymen, just because his victims were Shias. When the political shape of Iraq changed after the invasion in 2003, the biased clerics accused the victims of sectarianism. They realised that as the equation was changing, the power would soon shift to the Shia overwhelming majority, which was a very bitter pill for them to swallow.

On the night of 11 February, 2011, Al Jazeera TV played an interview with Al-Qaradawi. He was jubilant over the success of the youth revolution in the Liberty Square in Cairo and said that this is how every oppressor will meet his end, meaning Mubarak. But at the time of the execution of Saddam, he issued a statement that Saddam died a 'martyr'. He forgave all the crimes of Saddam on behalf of God and on behalf of his victims. Through his biased statement, he highly offended the souls of thousands who had been massacred in Halabja's chemical warfare in 1988. He totally disregarded the ethnic cleansing of millions in the north and the south of Iraq. He did not show any sympathy and compassion towards those who were dumped in mass graves.

There was a world of difference between the oppressive measures of Mubarak and that of Saddam. The former was not involved in massacring his people, whereas the latter was heavily involved in these crimes against humanity. Yet the reaction of Al-Qaradawi in regard to the downfall of these two dictators was completely different. Had the rape victims of Saddam's republican guards been women of his own sect, there would have been loud protests in the popular Arab media and in his Friday sermons.

The harsh reality is that, when it comes to gross violation of life, property, and honour of the Shia Muslims, one could hardly hear a word of sympathy in their media and from their clerics, who are supposed to be upholding the moral and humanitarian teachings of Islam. Al-Qaradawi may have an excuse that the ruler of Egypt was brought down by his own people, whereas the ruler of Iraq was brought down by foreigners. It would sound absurd if anybody were to think that if a despot or an oppressor in the Arab world is killed by foreign occupiers, then he dies the death of a martyr.

During most of the nineteenth and twentieth centuries, the Arab world was occupied either by the British, French, Dutch, or Italian colonialists. If Al-Qaradawi's rationale is applied to the criminals who were punished by death penalties meted down upon them under foreign occupation, then all the murderers, robbers, and rapists would have to be declared 'martyrs'. Saddam's barbaric reign and his brutal massacres were a human tragedy on a mammoth scale. If the media, clerics, and politicians remain insensitive to human sufferings, then they would be seen to be failing in their basic humanitarian duties or directly supporting crimes against humanity.

In order to divert the attention of their followers away from their duplicities, failures, and shortcomings, the Salafi and the Wahhabi clerics of Saudi Arabia approved the screening of a controversial TV serial in the holy month of Ramadan in August 2011 which carried distortions of the established facts of history. They did not care that the Quran warns the fabricators, 'It is those who believe not in the Signs of God that forge falsehood: it is they who lie' (16:105).

Despite worldwide protests from Sunnis and Shias, especially from the highest Sunni religious authority of Al-Azhar in Cairo and the Shia religious authorities, they decided to go ahead with their sacrilegious TV serial *Al-Hasan and Al-Husayn*. True to the teachings of their guru, Ibn Taymiyyah, who was unequivocally loyal to the Umayyads—the most brutal and oppressive dynasty in the entire history of Islam—they did not respect anybody's protests. The purpose was to whitewash the brutality of this dynasty which had indulged in ruthless and widespread bloodshed of the members of the Prophet's closest family members.

This dynasty had also caused carnage to Islam's holiest cities of Makkah and Madinah.

Millions of dollars were wasted in producing this TV serial, with the blessings of Al-Qaradawi and Salafi court clerics. History was distorted, and the status of the murderers was elevated on par with the murdered. Oppressors were equated with the oppressed. If there was any sense of responsibility, they would have spent this money on the starving people of Somalia and rescued them from the worst drought and starvation the country was facing at that time, and they would have rescued the undernourished and starving children in Yemen. But the irony of the situation is that the wealth of Muslims is not being used for the benefit of the poor, deprived, and downtrodden masses. The wealth belonging to Muslims is used for dividing the Muslims, sowing the seeds of enmity between them, creating theatres of war, and serving the interest of the arms-manufacturing industry, of which the Arab and Muslim elites are shareholders.

The sacrilegious TV serial, shown on dozens of Salafi/Wahhabi channels in the holy month of Ramadan, was aimed at implanting discord between Muslims. It projected the Shia faith as the one founded by Jews. In making such unfounded claims, the producers solely relied on the mythical figure of Abdullah ibn Saba, who was introduced in history by a tale teller and fabricator, Sayf ibn Umar al-Tamimi. Their own critiques of the narrators have testified that he was a liar and an unreliable narrator. But this was an opportunity not to be missed for making some cheap sectarian gains.

If Al-Qaradawi had cared to prioritise his concerns for the welfare of the Muslim community, then he could never have escaped noticing the condition of the migrant labourers in his country of residence and domicile. South Asian migrant workers, who form 90 per cent of the labour force in the tiny Emirate of Qatar, are deprived of their fair wages and enjoy no support or sympathy from these clerics. Being the representatives of God on earth, as they claim, it is their prime duty to guide the policymakers so that poor workers do not end up being exploited and deprived of their rights. Many people have been right in asking that if the Prophet were among us, would he have approved the clerics wasting their time on TV serials and other deceptive gimmicks, or would he have ensured that justice prevails in society? It is flabbergasting that noises and slogans for Islamic justice suddenly evaporate in the air when it comes to judging with justice, as required by the Quran.

A 146-page Human Rights Watch report warns the *Fédération Internationale de Football Association* (FIFA) that they need to make sure that their commitments to respect workers' rights are carried out in preparation for the 2022 World Cup. The report says, 'Hundreds of thousands of mostly South Asian migrant construction workers in Qatar risk serious exploitation and abuse, sometimes amounting to forced labor'.[44] This is the condition at home, although the emirate spends billions of dollars to buy political influence elsewhere.

Exploitation of poor workers is not a new phenomenon in that region. The Yemeni workers in Saudi Arabia have been expressing their grievances for the last half a century about gross exploitation, abuse, and humiliation they face in that country. After the second Persian Gulf War, millions of Yemeni labourers were evicted. They had to leave behind their possessions or liquidate them at knocked-down values.

Such are the prevailing tragic humanitarian conditions under which the migrant workers have to survive. Yet they do not warrant the slightest attention from the clerics because they are not likely to earn them dividends from the elites.

---

44 'Qatar: Migrant Construction Workers Face Abuse', http://www.hrw.org/node/107909, 12 June 2012.

Chapter 6

TRAMPLING OVER
HUMAN RIGHTS

During the Arab uprisings from early 2011 onwards, Bahrain's mass protests hardly got any coverage in the popular Arab TV channels as these protests were envisaged to have direct repercussions on the neighbouring countries. The slogan adopted by the street protesters in Manama was 'No Sunni, no Shia'. This signified a national and not sectarian or religious movement. The peaceful protesters intended to thwart the attempt of the neighbouring Arab states in portraying the popular movement as a sectarian one.

At the hub of the crisis in February 2011, the announcement by the crown prince of the Al-Khalifah dynasty calling for calm so that he could declare a mourning period for the martyrs was taken as a distasteful joke. Innocent people were being killed by no other than the state security forces. The Al-Khalifah dynasty has been ruling Bahrain for the last 250 years. The prime minister has held his post for more than forty years.

After two years of continuous and inexhaustible mass protests, there was an attempt to bring Bahrain in federation with Saudi Arabia. If this plan had succeeded, then it would have turned the majority Shia population of Bahrain overnight into a minority and would have turned the Salafis/Wahhabis into the absolute majority under the new political order. From the viewpoint of foreign powers, it would have been expedient and convenient to deal with one Parent Corporation of the House of Saud, who has been the West's strategic ally in the Muslim world for almost three centuries. From the viewpoint of the House of Al-Khalifah, their amalgamation with Saudi Arabia under federation or confederation would have given them a survival kit and a longer lease on life.

Following the invasion of Bahrain by the Saudis, it appeared that the purpose of invasion was not to defend the tiny kingdom from any non-existent and imaginary foreign incursion but to fight their battle on somebody else's land. They sought to pass a message to their own citizens that if they are capable of creating mayhem in a neighbouring country, they are quite capable of creating a stranglehold over their own citizens in the eastern regions.

The Salafi/Wahhabi media were involved in demonising the Arab-origin ethnic bloc of Bahrain's population, calling the Shias 'agents of Iran' and 'Safyunis' (a derogatory term used for the Safavids). As the world watched the Saudi tanks rolling into Bahrain to suppress unarmed protesters, the Salafi/Wahhabi media were accusing Iran, but not the repressive policies of the regime, for stirring up trouble in Bahrain.

BAHRAIN BETWEEN DOMESTIC REPRESSION AND FOREIGN OCCUPATION

Two different standards were applied in covering the news of Bahrain. The media and the court clerics sensed that power would have to be shared with the Shias if their demands were met, as in Iraq. This would encourage the Shias of Saudi Arabia to demand their rights of citizenship, which were being ruthlessly denied since the commence-ment of the Wahhabi movement in Arabia.

As the protests in Bahrain gained momentum, the two Salafi TV channels, Wesal and Safa from Egypt, were going berserk. Ignoring the popular uprisings in other Arab countries, they embarked upon coun-terpropaganda against the uprising in Bahrain. Under their rationale, it was not permitted for the Bahrainis to demonstrate against the authori-ties. But in the cases of Tunisia, Egypt, and Libya, they were not con-cerned because in these instances, there was no Shia threat, according to their sectarian-orientated thinking.

On 10 March, 2011, on one of these TV channels, a frantic caller swore almost twenty times in the name of God, saying that for the sake of 'His Majesty the king of Bahrain', they are prepared to teach an un-forgettable lesson to the 'traitors' and '*majus*' (Magians), referring to Bahrain's Arab Shia majority. Increasingly, the totalitarian regimes in the region relied on their fanatical supporters, who do not recognise that freedom is one of the most important gifts and bounties that God the Almighty has bestowed upon humankind.

On 15 March, 2011, a female caller from Bahrain took the presenter on the Wesal TV channel by surprise. She told him that he is spread-ing *fitnah* (mischief) through his lies and false propaganda. She said that his claims that in the hospitals, the Shia doctors were checking the identities of their patients before offering them treatment was nothing but malicious lies. She told him that she was speaking from the very hos-pital he was referring to, and she assured the listeners that no hospital staff or doctors were checking the identities of patients. She rebuked the presenter that if he and his like had any sense of self-respect, then they should speak against the moral infidelity, wine consumption, and immorality for which the Saudis travel across the borders to Bahrain through the bridge built for this purpose and have turned the country into a place of vices. The broadcaster faltered and could not reply. So he cut off her call.

Later on, the inquiries revealed that it was the invading Saudi forces themselves who stopped the Shia casualties from reaching hospitals for treatment. Some of the injured Shia demonstrators disappeared from hospital. The heavy-handed sentences passed against the arrested doctors and nurses in military courts for the 'crime' of giving medical treatment to the protesters prove that the House of Al-Khalifah openly trampled over internationally accepted standards and norms.

The suppressive measures adopted against peaceful protesters in Bahrain have been covered by the Human Rights Watch World Report of 2012 for all the events that took place in 2011. Hundreds were arrested and held without trial; public-sector employees were summarily dismissed; systematic torture was administered; birdshot bullets, rubber bullets, tear gas, and live ammunitions were used on unarmed protesters. According to the report, arbitrary raids were conducted; doctors, teachers, nurses, students, athletes, defence lawyers, human-rights activists, and opposition leaders were arrested and later tried in a military court. Some detainees were tortured to death. Children were arrested and held without trial.

The military court conducted phony trials. No pieces of evidence were presented. The equally phony appeals court upheld the atrocious sentences, thus making a mockery of the country's judicial system. Academics lost their jobs, and students lost their scholarships. According to the said Human Rights Watch report, the United States announced a proposal for selling armoured Humvees worth US $53 million, and US $15 million was offered in foreign military aid to the Bahraini regime.

On 6 March, 2011, the Wahhabi clerics issued a fatwa that coming out in demonstrations against the rulers and rising against them are prohibited in the shariah. It is the same old story of using Islam as a scapegoat to twist the law in order to suit the interests of the rulers.

By 8 March, 2011, gangs of youths with clubs, sticks, swords, and hammers in their hands, and holding the portrait of the king, shouted slogans in his favour on the streets of Manama. They threatened and attacked at random even ladies and children who were participating in peaceful demonstrations. These criminal gangs were not Bahrainis, nor did they have any semblance to Bahraini people. They were imported by the regime from across the borders and given Bahraini citizenship to tilt the balance of the population artificially against the majority.

On 16 March, 2011, the English service of Al Jazeera TV unrealistically portrayed the invasion of Bahrain as a 'power struggle' between Saudi Arabia and Iran. Since then, the English service of Al Jazeera has distanced itself from the policies of the Arabic service. On occasions, it has reported Bahrain's human-rights violations fairly, and its documentary *Shouting in the Dark*, posted on its website, is a masterpiece in its own right.

In its programme on 6 May, 2011, the Al Jazeera Arabic channel hosted the Palestinian Arab thinker Azmi Bisharah, who said that he did not consider the Saudi intervention in Bahrain a foreign intervention because it is an internal matter between Arab brothers. As Qatar is a new home to the Arab thinker, his thinking is tuned to Qatar's foreign policy. If invading a foreign country and intimidating its citizens is the prerogative of the invading country under the pretext of 'internal affairs', then this type of thinking makes a mockery of international law and the Geneva Convention.

On 22 April, 2011, after the Friday prayers, demonstrations had occurred in several cities of the world in solidarity with the ruthless clamping down on the youths in Bahrain, where many were killed, wounded, tortured, and arrested from their homes, and the injured were denied medical treatment by the Saudi and Bahraini forces. This was the first time that William Hague, the then-British foreign secretary, gave a statement to the media, saying that all the reports showed that there was violation of human rights in Bahrain. That Friday was named the Friday of the Quran to protest the desecration of the mosques, sanctity of the Quran, and religious symbols of the Shia Muslims. By then, more than thirty mosques had been destroyed and bulldozed by the Saudi Wahhabi ideologues, with not even a whisper of protest from the Saudi clergy.

When the Bahraini authorities sensed that the matter was attracting the limelight at the international level, they blamed the demonstrators. They could not have been more cunning in laying the blame on the unarmed youths who were being shot by the invaders. Their blurred logic did not take into consideration that the bulldozers with which mosques were being demolished were only available to the government and the Saudi occupation forces, not to the unequipped youths.

Those being killed and injured in Bahrain's uprising were Shias, and all the mosques desecrated belonged to the Shia majority. But this did not stop an influential figure like Shaykh Al-Qaradawi from falsely alleging in his Friday sermon of 18 March, 2011, that the Shias were attacking the Sunnis and their mosques. If such clerics wearing religious robes could speak lies publicly, then no wonder their youths are moving away from religion.

In its talk show *Ittijah al-Mu'akkis* (*The Opposite Direction*) on 25 October, 2011, Al Jazeera Arabic TV focused on Bahrain. The spokesman of the popular movement faced a female member of the National Assembly of Bahrain in a heated debate. The demands of the popular movement were simple and straightforward without any twists or double talk. The suppressed masses were demanding their democratic rights—as citizens of the country—and a free and fair election. Their spokesman said that these are the absolutely basic demands which are recognised by international law. The other demands were the immediate end of atrocities and the end of torture and imprisonment of peaceful demonstrators, teachers, doctors, and nurses. He produced pictures showing that the security forces had resorted to repressive measures by arresting ladies and forcing them to lie in the streets with their hands tied behind their backs. These types of measures were adopted by Bahraini security.

On the other hand, Samira Rajab, the female member of the national assembly and information minister of Bahrain, denied that there were any violations of human rights. She even falsified the reports of Human Rights Watch and said they were unreliable. She said that Bahrain was already democratic; the monarchy was already a constitutional monarchy, and people already enjoyed freedom. She alleged that the Shias were in the minority in Bahrain, contrary to the internationally recognised census that the Shias are an absolute majority. She said the purpose behind the protests and demonstrations was to impose by force the Iranian system and open the way for Iran to occupy the country. She accused the demonstrators of being agents of Iran.

Her counterpart in the debate, Khalil Marzuq, was the leading figure in Al-Wifaq National Islamic Party of Bahrain. He produced a picture which showed this very lady in a rally in support of the dictator Saddam, holding two portraits of the tyrant, who, in her view, was perhaps the exemplary model for democracy, freedom, and human rights. It was no more possible for her to hide her Saddamite orientation. She defended her inclinations by saying that Saddam was the only person who had cracked the head of Iran. This lady was obviously suffering from acute Iranophobia, similar to most of the ultranationalists. Iranophobia has afflicted them like a plague. If Saddam was victorious in cracking the head of the Iranian nation, then why did he end up seeking refuge underground in gutter pipes, from where he had to be pulled out by the Americans?

As mentioned earlier, in his polemical programmes, Dr Faysal Qasim coined the term *safyuniyyah* (safyunism), along the lines of *sahyuniyyah* (Zionism), for causing offence to Iran, solely on the basis of racial and sectarian prejudices. He warned that Iran, having already swallowed Iraq, Syria, and Lebanon, according to his gross exaggeration, was now preparing to swallow Bahrain.

Safyuniyyah is a derogatory term meant to insult the Safavid rulers of Iran's history for the mere reason that they had adopted the Shia Jafari faith as the state school of thought. The policy of the Safavids still pricks as a thorn in the eyes of the Shiaphobic extremists.

Dr Qasim enquired to the representative of the popular movement in Bahrain, Khalil Marzuq, that if the Americans, British, and Saudis, nor the Persian Gulf countries, would allow their demands (of democratisation) to be fulfilled, then what is the use of making such demands? This was tantamount to saying that although President Mahmud Abbas of the Palestinian Authority was well aware that the United States would use its power of veto against the full membership of the Palestinian State at the United Nations, then what was the use of undertaking such a futile exercise? It was also an implied confession that the rulers of Bahrain have no independent policies of their own but are subservient to the dictates of foreign powers.

Khalil Marzuq and Samirah Rajab again appeared on the BBC Arabic TV programme *Open Agenda* to mark the first anniversary of the uprising of the people of Bahrain on 14 February, 2012. By this time, Bahrain's Independent Commission had already issued its report to the king of Bahrain, who was to act as prosecutor, judge, and jury—three in one—and end up implementing nothing at all from the recommendations of the commission that he himself had personally appointed. The report stressed that there was ample evidence of detention without cause, forced confessions and systematic torture, the culture of unaccountability, and other human-rights abuses. This report 'clearly and categorically', according to the reporter on Al Jazeera English TV on *The Streams* programme (23 November, 2011), disclosed that no Iranian link whatsoever was found in Bahrain's protests.

The allegation of the involvement of Iran in the popular uprising in Bahrain was the deceptive tactic with which Bahraini authorities sought to justify Saudi military invasion to protect their dynastic and despotic reign. In light of the findings of the independent commission, one would have expected that the situation would improve. But in as much as there was no intention in the first place to make any changes or reforms, there was no intention to alter the premeditated mind-set of repressive policies. Since the report was issued and handed over to the king, imprisonment without trial, torture, arbitrary arrests, beating of female protesters on the street, frivolous use of tear gases, homicide of children, driving security vehicles into the protesters, and failure to re-instate workers who had been dismissed summarily from their jobs due to sectarian discrimination continued unabated.

The reports of Amnesty International and Human Rights Watch are replete with gross violations of human rights, including imprisonment of children and torture of human-rights activists, administered by the authorities in Bahrain amidst international apathy. It seems that the oil and investment interests of the Western powers weigh too heavily on their policies to abandon their total support of the totalitarian regimes in the region.

The flagrant double standards deployed by most Muslim countries and Islamic organisations in the face of desecration, burning, and destruction of hundreds of copies of the Quran by the Bahraini and Saudi occupation forces show the extent to which Muslims have strayed from the Islamic sense of justice. Muslim countries remained mute as more than thirty Shia mosques were destroyed in Bahrain. Just because the desecrators were Saudi forces, different standards were applied to them. This brings into question whether the violent protests witnessed in several Muslim countries, especially in Afghanistan and Pakistan against the burning of the copy of the Quran by the American troops in Afghanistan, were at all for the love of the Quran or hatred towards the Americans.

In Bahrain, the shrines to the veteran companion of the Prophet, Sasah ibn Suhan, and other companions were sabotaged by the Bahraini and Saudi troops. But the Islamic organisations under the tutelage of their clerics had no courage and honesty to condemn this blasphemous act which was meant to insult the companion of the Prophet in the worst possible manner. Ironically, they do not hesitate to hurl abuses against the Shias, accusing them of not respecting the sanctity of the companions of the Prophet. This proves that their garbled noise about the sanctity of the companions is nothing but a dishonest political ploy to make certain sectarian gains. The tragic part of this is that many people have fallen victims of their deception, and thousands of Shias have been massacred by terrorist groups like Sepahe Sahaba, now banned, in Pakistan.

The sort of 'respect' they have shown towards the companions of the Prophet can be noticed in their flagrant breaches such as in Syria in the region of Riqqah, where their 'mujahidin' attacked with missiles and damaged the shrine of one of the companions, Ammar ibn Yasir, very much respected by both Sunnis and Shias. The parents of Ammar, Yasir and Sumayyah, were the first martyrs in Islam. They were brutally tortured to death at the dawn of Islam by the foes of the Prophet in Makkah. Now, under the disguise of being the devotees of Islam, the insurgents and terrorists targeted the tomb of a personage who himself during the time of Imam Ali ibn Abi Talib had sacrificed his life while fighting the rebels and insurgents of that time. Perhaps this was the main fault of this aged and brave companion of the Prophet.

Another onslaught against the honour of the companions was that the terrorists operating in Iraq targeted the mosque and the shrine of Salman al-Farsi (Salman the Persian), the veteran companion of the Prophet, who is buried in Salman Pak, a city fifteen miles south of Baghdad. They converted his shrine into a storehouse for hiding weapons and for torturing their victims, who they held hostage. The shrine was badly damaged through continuous acts of terror.

All these breaches are committed while the Muslim world watches without any protests or condemnation. Because of this indifference, the militants get encouragement to continue with their blasphemous acts. It also gives them courage to hold women and children hostages, as human shields, to achieve their political ends, which they have been doing in Iraq and Syria.

RIGIDITY IN PERCEPTION

Certain radical groups have taken upon themselves the task of guiding humankind towards their style of perfectionist and self-righteous understanding of religion. From the discussion that follows, it seems that rigidity in perception has afflicted the mind-set of radical ideologues, and they do not seem to realise that they are increasingly emerging as the odd ones out in the world community. One group calls its endeavour 'revival of *aql*—an Islamic perspective'. *Aql* means mind or intellect. It is worth examining the bizarre ways in which this group would like the Muslims to use their minds. The message preaches, 'It has become quite common for Muslims to talk, write, and debate using the terms [and] the concepts of the *kuffar*...such as jihadist, ideology, terrorism, innocent, moderate, extremist, Islamic politics, and so on, and discussing whether Islam is "compatible with democracy", and whether Shariah can be, or should be, the basis, or a basis, for "law" in a modern "nation-state"', according to the harangue of this group.

Having condemned the use of some nouns and adjectives in common usage, the group does not propose any alternatives or whether a Muslim should just pretend that these descriptions, 'innocent, moderate, extremist', simply do not exist or risk being excommunicated for using them? The message continues to explode further bombshells: 'Such things are a modern extension of that particular imitation of the kuffar which began with the influence of Greek philosophical ideas upon [the] Deen [religion] Al-Islam and which is noticeable in the works of ibn Rushd [Averroes] and others…where kaffir powers such as Amerika [sic] dominate'.

If the use of these nouns and adjectives in everyday parlance is a sign of *kufr* (disbelief), then perhaps the use of the names of modern amenities and discoveries such as cyberspace, television, video, motor car, DVD, satellite, rocket, and aeroplane must also be a sign of *kufr* or infidelity. What happens when the extremists themselves use these amenities and discoveries in furtherance of their political objectives? According to the thinking of these extremist groups, a true Muslim should reject everything that is associated with the West. They preach that the West dare not compare its society with that which was established by the Taliban in the Islamic Emirate of Afghanistan, in which the shariah and not '*kafir* progress' or '*kafir* democracy' was applicable, according to their harangue.

If the carnage caused by the Taliban and Al-Qaeda had been compliant with the shariah, then Islam does not need any enemies at all. They have already done colossal damage to the reputation of Islam and Muslims. If the Taliban and Al-Qaeda had observed the limits of the Islamic shariah, then no innocent people would have ever been killed, which happened throughout their reign and since they have been deprived of the power to rule.

The sanctity of mosques was violated when the extremists chose their targets at the Friday prayers by detonating their explosives in the midst of congregational prayers. The fault of innocent worshippers was that they happened to be there at the time when the loathsome spirit of the Taliban and Al-Qaeda manifested itself.

LIFELINE OF DUPLICITIES

In the name of the Prophet, the radical elements preach that when a Muslim kills a Muslim, both the killer and the killed will burn in hell. But ever since the Umayyad and the Khariji (insurrectionist) revolted against the Caliphate of Imam Ali, up to this day, the Muslims have systematically engaged themselves in killing each other by revolting against the virtuous and righteous leadership and by colluding with the unjust and corrupt usurpers. To justify their insurrection, they claimed in those days in as much as they claim today that the Muslims who they kill are not Muslims but are *kuffar* (infidels). Under this pretext, they justify extrajudicial killings and outright terrorism in the name of Islam. They do not hesitate to practise deception to justify the bloodshed of innocent people.

The Salafis and Wahhabis strenuously believe that all and sundry in the era of the Prophet, the companions and the companions of the companions, will go to paradise, irrespective of the fact that the most harrowing crimes and bloodshed were committed in the early period of Islamic history against the nearest family members of the Prophet. They do not encourage any critical study of history for the first three generations because it shakes the very roots of their predetermined notions.

If they had weighed the veracity of their claims in the context of the Quran, then the verdict of the Quran unequivocally declares, 'So whoever does an atom's weight of good will see it, and whoever does an atom's weight of evil will see it' (99:7–8). Nobody, no matter how lofty his status may be, is promised any favouritism and exemption in the matter of reward for good and retribution for evil deeds. The Quran further declares, 'And that nothing belongs to man, except what he strives for, and that he will soon be shown his endeavour; then he will be rewarded for it with the fullest reward' (53:39–41). In the light of these verdicts, it is futile to attempt whitewashing the heinous crimes committed in the first three generations. The Quran is clear that people of all generations will be rewarded according to what they have strived to achieve and will be punished for their evil deeds.

Despite clear-cut rulings in the Quran, they abhor being asked about the bloodshed that had occurred between very close companions of the Prophet and between the companions of the companions (the second generation). Weren't Muslims fighting each other? But they skip over the issue altogether or react with evasive answers.

Without a shred of doubt, the first three generations of the Islamic era had produced the best and the most virtuous souls ever produced in Islamic history. But they had also produced the most atrocious and evil souls in human history. There is nothing in the Quran that suggests that if the oppressors are Muslims, they will be entitled to diplomatic immunity under God's justice.

Mu'awiyah ibn Abi Sufyan, the first Umayyad caliph, turned the Islamic governance into an imperial rule of the style of Caesar and Chosroes, adopting all their ostentations, arrogance, and injustices, precisely as the present hereditary dynasties do by imitating the precedents laid down for them in history. The biggest stumbling block against them was the household and the noble progeny of the Prophet. In as much as Mu'awiyah and his son Yazid adopted the strategy of removing their opponents out of their way, the present dynasties have adopted the same strategy. But little have they cared to learn from history. The Umayyad and Abbasid reigns crumbled despite the enormous power they mustered. The vicious crimes they committed had become a state policy.

They also made gibes against the dearest and nearest members of the Prophet's family and their followers.

The Umayyads had converted to Islam on the final conquest of Makkah against their will, when there was no other avenue open for them to continue their hostilities. It was no more possible to take revenge against the Prophet or his mission. The Prophet treated them with clemency and forgiveness despite being in a position of taking revenge for their hostilities. But their conspiracy against Islam never ceased. Immediately after the demise of the Prophet, the stars of these foes of Islam started shining on the horizon, when the caliphs appointed the governors of the largest provinces in the empire from the Umayyads. With no loyalty for Islam and with stark doubts about the prophet hood of the Prophet, Abu Sufyan, the chief of Quraysh, was honoured by getting his son Yazid appointed as the governor of the Sham (Levant) province.

After his death, his brother Mu'awiyah took over the governorship of Sham. When eventually he managed to grab the caliphate from Imam Ali through civil war, and until the collapse of the dynasty of the Umayyads, it became compulsory by the ruler's decree to curse Imam Ali on the pulpits in every Friday sermon. This un-Islamic and immoral tradition continued for almost seventy years until one of their caliphs, Umar ibn Abd al-Aziz, abolished the evil practice.

But even today, almost thirteen centuries after the vile practice of cursing and abusing the most virtuous and righteous souls was abolished, the grudges are being revived. In Egypt, an extremist Salafi *takfiri* cleric[45] expresses his spite by cursing in the most vitriolic and venomous manner all the Shias: the Iranians, the Iraqis, the Lebanese, and the Syrians; all Jews and all Christians; the Americans; and the Arab regimes

---

45 http://www.youtube.com/watch?v=gD9IYQXRE_o&feature=youtube_gdata_player, 17 July 2013.

who have abandoned the 'Sunnis of Syria', according to his illusionary outburst, hallucination, mental inhibition, and blatant lies, which he expresses in public in his congregation in the mosque. He desperately prays for the annihilation of the Shias and the Jews. It is precisely this type of spite which has produced in history and in this twenty-first century militants who take pride in chewing and eating human liver and then posting this ghastly scene on YouTube.

The video of the *takfiri* cleric referred to here substantiates in sound and picture that provocations continue in the mosques of the Salafi extremists in Egypt even after the toppling of President Morsi. It seems that as far as sectarian bigotry is concerned, nothing has changed, and there is no difference whatsoever among the dictatorships of Mubarak, Morsi, and Sisi. If there was the slightest respect and regard for law and order, these clerics would not have dared to act as agent provocateurs and as agents of seduction. But the fact they do proves that they feel they have full immunity from any accountability no matter how they misuse their positions of trust and the sanctity of prayers and religious teachings. They are confident that the authorities will fail to take any action against them, as much as they failed to take any action against the murderers who lynched the dead body of a respectable Egyptian Shia scholar, Shaykh Shihatah.

Hence, the *takfiri* clerics provide all the training ground for the violent extremists by trampling over the Islamic teachings and values of the Quran. The large congregation in the aforementioned video listens attentively as garbage is poured over their heads, chanting 'amen, amen'. By manipulating the name of religion, the *takfiri* clerics violate the basic principles and morals of Islam. Their malicious tirades and curses can be traced back in history to the Kharijis fourteen centuries ago. They prayed and recited the Quran in a melodious voice, as they do today, but massacred innocent people and violated the sanctity of Islam, as they do today. They deceive the masses through their rhetoric to the extent that their crowd has lost courage to object to the use of vitriolic language inside the mosques. They have turned their congregation into robots who cannot think for themselves. They have been moulded to accept any rubbish that their clerics choose to bombard them with, as the leaders of the Kharijis did in history.

An analogy needs to be drawn between the dictatorships of regimes and the dictatorships of *takfiri* clerics. Both aim at keeping the masses ignorant in order to enforce upon them their hegemony and ill-gotten authority. When people are brought up and nurtured under repressive regimes, this has destructive effects on their thinking and psyches. They are bombarded with propaganda, glorifying the despots and dictators. Despotism is based on nepotism and favouritism, where people are not rewarded and valued on the basis of merits but on the basis of their proximity to the ruling elites and their loyalty to them. In a nutshell, this is the type of worldview that the Umayyads promoted and bequeathed to their followers. The heritage of intimidation, coercion, torture, and corrupt political systems still prevails in many if not most Muslim countries. Similarly, the *takfiri* clerics resort to propaganda, which they use as weapons to cheat and deceive their congregations so that they may have the unchallenged say in religious matters.

The prevalent political systems cannot provide the unemployed with employment, they waste the wealth of the nation by interfering in the affairs of other countries, they cannot meet the basic aspirations of their citizens, and they rob the people of their livelihoods. This results in negative repercussions in the lives of the people. Their patience starts to wane, and the unemployed youths turn to extremism and militancy. Similarly, when the *takfiri* clerics do not preach the message of peace and spirituality in their mosques, they fail to generate hope and optimism in people and mould their congregation according to negativities and destructiveness. The misinformed and deceived youths turn to extremism and violence.

With the connivance of some countries in the region, terrorist organisations aim at breaking up Iraq and Syria to establish, according to their publicly declared plan, the Taliban-style 'Islamic emirate'. The countries which are providing safe haven to these militants and footing the huge cost of their maintenance and safe transit into Iraq and Syria are responsible for sponsoring international militancy and terrorism. These countries will never dream of getting a Taliban-style 'Islamic emirate' established on their own territories. But their 'Islamic' worldview permits them to contribute in creating instability in their neighbouring countries. But what goes around comes around, and already the effects of this conspiracy are quite manifest in some countries in the region like Turkey, where terrorism has struck blow upon blow on the national security of the country.

The *takfiri* clerics portray the sect they represent as a homogeneous unit united in outlook. Nothing can be more fallacious and further from the truth. They incite ill feelings in the mosques, provoking the congregation by claiming that the Sunnis in Syria and Iraq are being abandoned and massacred, their children and infants slaughtered, and their women raped by the Shias. They even raise sympathies for the terrorist organisations, implying that they are the only ones who have the interest of the Sunnis at heart. But they do not disclose to their congregation that, very often, their militants do not even spare the lives of the Sunnis.

Moreover, the Sunnis have never ever been a homogenous community. Under the umbrella of the Sunnis, there are leftists and rightists, there are Baathists and Nasserites, there are communists and socialists, and there are dozens of terrorist groups in the Arab world. Sometimes, these groups, vying for power, end up shedding each other's blood.

In Algeria, Sunnis fought Sunnis in a civil war that continued for a decade in the '90s, in which millions were killed. In Libya, Sunnis fought

Sunnis in a vicious and brutal civil war in which hundreds of thousands were killed. After ridding themselves of Gaddafi, a series of political assassinations, interviolence, and killings followed. There was no Shia element involved in Algeria or Libya. In Somalia, throughout the last decades, Sunnis have been killing Sunnis for political power. There are no Shias in the country. In Tunisia, after the departure of the dictator Zine El Abidine Ben Ali, political assassinations and violence between Sunnis have been increasing between the Islamic party and the secularists. There is no Shia element in these disputes either. In Egypt, in the country of Shaykh Al-Qaradawi and other *takfiri* clerics, Sunnis have been fighting Sunnis in Cairo, Alexandria, and other Egyptian towns. The crisis which is threatening the security of the nation as a whole is because of the power struggle between the Islamic and secularist parties. In the process, they do not seem to care that the country is drawn onto a self-destructive path. This is what a power struggle is all about. It dismantles and destroys all the achievements of the past. The supporters of the Muslim Brotherhood are staunch Sunni Islamists, and their opponents are secularist Sunnis. There is no Shia element involved.

People involved in clashes in the streets of Istanbul and Ankara in Turkey were all Sunnis. Who is fighting whom in Darfur in western Sudan? Sunnis are fighting Sunnis. There is no trace of any Shias there. Many more examples can be quoted to prove that there has never been any Shia interference in political disputes and violence in Sunni countries. Yet public opinion is being groomed and totally misled by the politicians and their dishonest clerics into believing that their enemies are the Shias.

In the holy month of Ramadan, considered the most sacred by all Muslims, no political wrangling, never mind vicious bloodshed, is permitted at all. But the sanctity and honour granted by the Almighty God to the holy month of Ramadan, according to the Islamic faith, was breached left, right, and centre by Muslims themselves. What is specifically prohibited in religion was practised in the name of religion as the Arab world was being torn apart. The month of Ramadan is supposed to be the best time to promote peace, love, fraternity, and tolerance, as well as to enhance spirituality. But because of political turmoil and rivalries, religious values and morals were totally shunned, even by the Islamic parties supposedly working to implement the shariah.

When the *takfiri* clerics, therefore, including some renowned international figures, raise an outcry in their mosques amidst their congregations and express their paranoia on TV shows that the Shias are fighting the Sunnis and are taking over the Sunni countries, this is nothing but fraudulent misrepresentation of facts. As a result of sectarian-motivated false propaganda, the conscience of Muslims has been demoralised and paralysed. Throughout the holy month of Ramadan, hundreds were killed, and thousands were injured in daily suicide bombings in Iraq, but the majority of Muslims were void of any humanitarian feelings towards senseless killing sprees of the victims of terrorism. Their apathy at the tragic plight of the Shia civilians in Iraq and Syria, in particular, demonstrates that they drastically failed to realise the dangers and threat that the *takfiri* political and religious establishment is posing against Islam and Muslims.

As the world is watching in shock and dismay the project of chaos and turmoil unfolding in a number of Sunni countries, the perceptible reality on the ground shows that the political upheavals in Sunni countries have nothing whatsoever to do with Shia–Sunni divisions. One would not have expected religious personalities to stoop to the level of twisting the facts to misguide Sunni masses for the sake of venting and promoting their sectarian prejudices.

The *takfiri* political establishment and their clerics do not even consider members of the splinter political groups among Sunnis as true Muslims. But when it comes to form a common front against the Shias, they lump them up together, and all these groups become one community, irrespective of their multifaceted political orientations and interenmities. The *takfiri* ideologues have done a great disservice even to their closest allies in the West.

Stephen Schwartz discusses how the extremist groups were financed with the Saudi money. He writes, '...until September 11 one of the most significant Wahhabi war fronts was located in the United States'.[46] In their campaign, they misled not only Muslims but their best allies too. Schwartz expresses these facts vividly: 'Saudis had sold the West a false depiction of the Shias everywhere as wild-eyed fanatics and of Wahhabis as trustworthy defendants of the traditional Islamic order. The truth was exactly the opposite'.[47]

We can refer to a number of cases to illustrate the duplicities inherent in the minds and characters of the *takfiri*s as they resort to intimidating others, believing that only they hold the solutions for the rest of mankind. In their minds, the best solution of solving differences in beliefs is to wipe out certain communities from the face of the earth. Al-Zarqawi, the Jordanian terrorist, was trained and indoctrinated on extremism and intimidation. In his very first video, shown on the websites of the militants and on Al Jazeera Arabic TV on 25 April, 2006, he used Islamic rhetoric by appealing to his fellow militants that jihad must continue against whom he saw as the avowed foes of the Muslims. He categorised them as 'the Jews', the 'cross-worshippers', 'the crusaders', the 'apostate Shias', and the 'zionised Kurds'.[48]

The late psychopathic terrorist, despite benefiting from all the facilities of the modern world, hypocritically claimed that accepting 'any measure' of manmade law is a denial of the belief in God. The impasse

---

46 Schwartz, p. 225.

47 Schwartz, pp. 166–167.

48 'Terrorism: Text of al-Zarqawi video in English', 28 April 2006, http://www.adnki. com/index_2Level_English.php?cat=Terrorism&loid=8.0.292490450&par=0.

between the *takfiris* and the majority of Muslims is quite manifest. There are many measures of manmade laws that are followed in the daily lives of Muslims in both Muslim and non-Muslim countries.

Even the suicide bombers of 9/11 and 7/7, who were arch-opponents of the system, had to abide by manmade law of purchasing airplane and train tickets and paying government taxes thereon, without which they would not have been able to embark on their deadly missions. A further proof of their obedience to manmade laws is the recorded message of the ring leader of the London suicide bombers of 7/7 urging the British Muslims not to work with the government and urging the Islamic scholars to disobey British laws.[49] He preached what he himself did not practice. He was an employee of a local school with a contract of employment drawn according to English law.

Historically, the *takfiri* extremists have exhibited in their actions regularity in praying, fasting, memorising the Quran, and performing other acts of worship ordained by Islam. They have been successful in impressing the masses with their semblance of piety. The videotaped messages of 9/11 hijackers, televised on Arabic channels, were exceptionally eloquent and emotionally appealing to the masses. Because of their ideological brainwashing, they gave themselves the right to decide who is a true believer and who is not and who is an infidel that needs to be annihilated from the face of the earth.

Conscientious people in the world communities were astounded when the affiliates of Al-Qaeda at that time, calling themselves the Islamic State, claimed responsibility for suicide bombings in which one of the two trucks loaded with explosives drove into a busload of young schoolchildren. Twenty-four nursery-school pupils were killed in cold blood, and the death toll reached 155. The statement from the terrorist organisation hailed the two suicide bombers as 'martyrs who had

---

49 http://www.channel4.com/news, 15 November 2005.

targeted the dens of infidelity'. Adding insult to injury, it described those who were killed, including innocent children, as the 'pillars of the Safavi and the Rejectionist State in the land of caliphate'.[50]

This type of harangue reveals the rotten mental condition of the extremist *takfiris*. They still consider Syria as the seat of the Umayyad caliphate and Iraq as the seat of Abbasid caliphate although both the dynasties had been confined to the garbage of history more than a thousand years ago. Yet there are militants who are prepared to kill and get killed for the sake of their illusions and daydreams of reviving these types of tyrannical caliphates.

The indoctrinated extremists accuse Iran of extending its influence in Iraq and other countries, notwithstanding the fact that the Shia school of thought did not start from Iran. It was started from Iraq by none other than the Arabs. The Shias take pride in learning and teaching historical facts to their children. They hold gatherings and commemorations on important Islamic events, especially the tragedies that had befallen the household of the Prophet after his demise. They do not conceal historical facts, no matter how unsavoury they are. They commemorate occasions based on narrations from popular sources. They do not commit treachery against the noble and holy personages of Islam by undermining their superior status in the eyes of God and the Prophet in light of the Quran and Sunnah. To accuse the Shias of sectarianism, therefore, expresses intolerance and shows the moral bankruptcy of the agent provocateurs, whose accusations pave the way for violent reaction and terrorism against them in several countries, as is happening now.

In the cyber world, most of the so-called Islamic websites remain totally oblivious to the cold-blooded killings by the *takfiris* in the name of jihad. They do not even consider this as double standards. A few instances

---

50 Richard Spencer, 'Al-Qaeda claims responsibility for Iraq's worst suicide bomb attack in two years', *Daily Telegraph*, 27 October 2009.

are worth reviewing to highlight the lifeline of duplicities prevalent in the Muslim world. Four members of the Jordanian Parliament had offered condolences on the death of Al-Zarqawi[51] although he had killed sixty-seven of their own fellow citizens in triple suicide attacks on hotels in Jordan.[52] But this was not considered a double standard.

Some Jordanian MPs declared that those killed in the Jordan suicide bombings (the victims, not the terrorists) will burn in hell. This was disclosed by King Abdullah of Jordan in his interview on CNN on 22 June, 2006. The insensitive MPs were jailed for the offence in this particular case; otherwise, Jordanian authorities were quite tolerant and accommodative when the so-called bridal parties were held in public by the families of the terrorists killed in Iraq as a symbol of getting them wedded to the heavenly brides.

In an academic paper presented at the Naval Postgraduate School in Monterey, California, the history of extremism in Jordan, like elsewhere in the Middle East, is traced back to the humiliating defeat of the Arab armies in the 1967 six-day Arab–Israeli war, followed by lavish contributions by the Saudis to prop up certain extremist groups in the wake of the soaring oil prices after the 1973 Arab–Israeli war. This was followed by the Soviet invasion of Afghanistan in 1979 and the influx of the jihadists. When the jihadists returned to their respective countries after the war, they brought a rigid ideology which visualised and saw nothing but 'infidels' around them in their society and in the world at large.

This is worrying the West today that when the jihadists return back home from Syria to different countries in Western Europe and America, they will bring all the military training and indoctrination they would

---

51 Mohamed Al-Du'ma, 'Jordan MPs in hot water for Zarqawi condolences', 11 June 2006,
http://aawsat.com/english/news.asp?section=1&id=5269.
52 'Suicide bombers kill 67 at Jordan hotels', 10 November 2005, http://english.people.com.cn/200511/10/eng20051110_220279.html.

have obtained in the camps of the insurgents. Hence, they would pose a security risk.

The said academic paper also analyses different layers among the Salafis, some of whom advocate nonviolent participation in the political process. Al-Zarqawi never advocated nonviolence, yet he was released from prison in 1999 under the amnesty granted by King Abdullah of Jordan. He believed in waging war against society, including Jordanian society. This fact was public knowledge in the wake of his rebellion in prison against his own mentor, Al-Maqdisi.[53] Jordan reacted in exasperation only when Al-Zarqawi sabotaged its national and internal security. But there were many extremists in Jordan who had a high regard for Al-Zarqawi.

The terrorists got nice coverage on the popular Arabic channels. The image of Bin Laden displayed on Al Jazeera Arabic TV as his audio message was being played on October 23, 2007, was impressive, with innocence overflowing from his eyes and the paleness of his face, portraying the supposed burden of responsibility he was carrying on his shoulders on behalf of the worldwide Muslim community. It, however, lacked one visual effect—that of encircling his face with a ray of light to turn him into a revered sacred figure.

The audio and videotapes of Bin Laden attracted headline news on Al Jazeera Arabic channel. After playing the audio tape, the newsreader said that Bin Laden calls for '*aam al-jama'ah*' (year of the community or reconciliation). This was after Al-Qaeda had suffered setbacks in Iraq. The newsreader continued that, historically, the year of reconciliation was declared when Hasan ibn Ali had sworn an oath of allegiance to the first Umayyad caliph, Mu'awiyah ibn Abi Sufyan. This claim was a gross misrepresentation of history.

---

53 Anouar Boukhars, 'The Challenge of Terrorism and Religious Extremism in Jordan', http://www.ccc.nps.navy.mil/si/2006/Apr/boukharsApr06.asp, 6 April 2006.

Aam al-jama'ah was declared by Mu'awiyah when he grabbed and usurped power through bloodshed, deception, and fraud. Under the pretext of uniting the Muslim community, which has never ever been united since then, he embarked on physically exterminating his opponents by poisoning them and by waging war against them, especially against the friends and followers of Imam Ali. The atrocities and massacres which followed the so-called *aam al-jama'ah* have been extensively documented in history, but they are being neglected and concealed by the loyalists of Mu'awiyah.

The news editor on Al Jazeera overlooked the fundamental fact of history that there was a peace treaty between Imam Hasan and Mu'awiyah, the terms and conditions of which were openly breached by Mu'awiyah. There is a world of difference between truce and allegiance. The Prophet had entered into a similar truce with the Quraysh in Hudaybiyyah, but he never accepted the authority of Quraysh. Abiding by agreement or covenant is obligatory, as commanded in the Quran, and any breach is considered a breach of covenant entered with God. It is not possible to neglect the Quranic injunctions when discussing the affairs of the Muslims to show how, at times, the management of the affairs of Muslims was, and is, divorced from the Quranic laws and regulations.

The Quran states, 'O you who have believed! Fulfil (all) obligations' (5:1) and 'fulfil your promise, for (every) promise will be enquired into (on the Day of Reckoning)' (17:34). The *Sahih*s of both Bukhari and Muslim, the two most authentic books of hadiths of the Sunnis, have reported that the Prophet said, 'A person who has the following four [characteristics] is a pure hypocrite and he who possesses one of them has a trait of hypocrisy until he abandons it: when he talks, he tells lies; when he is party to a covenant, he proves to be treacherous; when he makes a promise, he breaks it; and when he disagrees with others, he disputes violently'. But this is precisely what many Muslims have done historically and are doing in their zest to victimise their opponents. In the process, they do not hesitate to express their gibes in public to defame revered religious personages—something that Mu'awiyah encouraged his followers to do, of which history is replete with examples.

Expression of political and sectarian prejudice against the Shias reached its climax in the media in a programme called *Bila Hudud* (*Without Boundaries*), hosted by Ahmad Mansur on Al Jazeera Arabic TV on 2 May, 2007. The programme was filled with innuendos against the internationally respected Shia religious leader Grand Ayatollah Ali Husayni Sistani. In this programme, the so-called Sunni mujahidin were portrayed as single-handedly fighting the occupation forces in Iraq, and the Shias were depicted as collaborating with the Americans in 'murdering the Sunnis'.

Ahmad Mansur, the Egyptian interviewer, went overboard in insulting Ayatollah Sistani and stopped short of accusing him of conspiring with the American forces by not condemning the murder of Sunnis by the 'Shia militia', according to his rant. Extending his taunts against the Shia institutions and through his abnormal facial expressions, he even went along in suggesting that Ayatollah Sistani is in '*ghaybah*' (occultation) and that he might have already appointed his son to succeed him. He questioned whether the American occupation forces would have any say in appointing his successor and whether the government ministers will perform 'hajj' (pilgrimage) towards Ayatollah Sistani. With such malicious gibes, he continued his insults.

This is the type of diatribe the viewers of this al-Jazeera Arabic channel are accustomed to hearing. These innuendos were for the love of the so-called mujahidin, the most notorious criminals and suicide bombers, whose heads were dipped in the blood of children and babies.

In conclusion, it is common to hear rude and resentful comments on this channel against the Shias and their religious leadership but not against Al-Qaeda, Al-Nusra, ISIL, or Jundullah terror gangsters. The stark hypocrisy of making a show of resentment against the invasion of Iraq and against the US occupation is manifested in the fact that the reporters on Al Jazeera Arabic TV have never tried to criticise the existence of the largest US military base in Qatar, under the very nose of these reporters. The indiscriminate killings of civilians, which continue even after the withdrawal of the US troops from Iraq, have not received any rebuke or condemnation because this is considered a sacred duty for the militants who are afflicted with the worst Shiaphobia plague since the time of the Umayyads.

Chapter 7

SANCTIFYING THE DICTATORS

A Christian bishop and head of a diocese in England happened to visit Iraq after the fall of Saddam. He presented his chilling report to his congregation after his return. Although the victims of the reign of Saddam were predominantly Muslims, the stories of the bereaved victims moved this Christian clergyman. He reported that after hearing the harrowing experiences of the aggrieved, he could not help crying. This author shared a platform with him in the north of England in a seminar.

The bishop came across a family, all the male members of which were wiped out of existence. There was not a household he came across which had not been affected by the barbaric reign of Saddam. This was an impartial reporter whose judgement was not clouded by any racism, nationalism, sectarianism, or prejudice against Muslims. Rather, it was exclusively based on sympathy and compassion that humans share with each other. Whereas, there are Muslims who are reverting back to the stone-heartedness of the Age of Ignorance, where their sympathies lie not with the oppressed but with the oppressors; they do not side with the murdered but with the murderers; they do not stand by those whose rights are usurped but by the usurpers.

When a calamity befalls innocent people, it is observed that the church sends its clergymen to console the victims and provide them with shelters. At that time the aggrieved are in dire need of support, sympathy, and good counsel. Whether they are victims of an earthquake or a massacre, when they lose close family members, people normally sympathise with the victims and try to feel their agony. This is how the bereavement policy of the relief and charitable organisations should be geared.

SIDING WITH THE DEVIL

In the aftermath of the execution of Saddam, Shaykh Al-Qaradawi hailed in his Friday sermon, televised on Qatar state TV, his 'hero' and 'martyr', despite Saddam's ugly and excruciating record of crimes against humanity. He condemned his executioners for not respecting a human soul, as if Saddam had shown all the respect he could muster for human souls when he committed massacres of men, women, and children and dumped them in mass graves. The cleric used his position and authority as the president of the Association of Muslim Ulama (religious scholars) and the occupant of a pulpit in the mosque to defend and praise the tyrant, dictator, and mass murderer. This is precisely what they have done historically.

If Arab despots are found guilty after being tried in an open court and sentenced to death, the court clerics are in waiting to bless them with the status of martyrdom and wipe clean their record of atrocities. The tyrant of Iraq had used chemical weapons in his eight-year war against Iran, according to the UN reports as well as reports of US Congress and human-rights agencies. This was done for the sake of remaining in absolute power.

Al-Qaradawi showed sympathy for Saddam but had no word of sympathy for the feelings of four million human beings who were intimidated and persecuted during his reign for three decades. He kept on repeating in his Friday sermon the virtues of Saddam, saying that he stood like a mountain in front of his executioners, without bothering to ponder that this had everything to do with his big stature and not his deeds.

He praised Saddam for pronouncing, *'La ilaha ill allah'* ('There is no god but Allah') before being executed. According to Al-Qaradawi's rationale, the individual whose last words are the testimony of faith will go to paradise, disregarding the stern warnings in the Quran in many verses against the oppressors and unjust people. If a man of religion sides with the oppressors and looks at the affairs of the Muslims from the narrow prism of sectarian bigotry, then this type of thinking may deprive him of credibility in the eyes of the oppressed people. The Quran warns those who side with the oppressors: 'And incline not toward those who oppress lest the Fire (of Hell) touches you and you have no protectors other than Allah, nor shall you be helped' (11:113).

In his sermon on March 18, 2011, Al-Qaradawi branded the peaceful protests in Bahrain as 'the conspiracy of Shias against Sunnis'. Even though Bahraini protesters kept on reciting *'la ilaha ill Allah'*, not once but hundreds of times before being shot by the Saudi and Bahraini forces, they were not entitled to enter paradise simply because they did not have the credentials that Saddam had. In the same Friday congregation, Al-Qaradawi blamed the Shia opposition in Bahrain for not availing themselves of the chance offered by the crown prince for dialogue. He ignored the fact that as soon as the crown prince offered dialogue, the Bahraini authorities permitted the Saudi and army units from Qatar to invade the country. In their political parlance, dialogue means total surrender to the authority of the autocrats.

This court cleric and his unrepresentative organisation have played a very negative political game to promote his political party, Muslim

Brotherhood. When in mid-July 2016, a failed coup was uncovered against the Turkey president, Recep Tayyip Erdo an, this cleric issued a statement on behalf of his organisation that revolutions against established authorities are prohibited under Islamic laws and are considered a major sin, just because the Turkish president provided a backbone of support for his Muslim Brotherhood political party. But he never hesitated to act as the main agent provocateur against the established and elected president of Syria and had urged all Sunnis to proceed to Syria to fight a 'jihad' there. Therefore, in the aftermath of the failed coup in Turkey, with initially more than six thousand, reaching to more than fifteen thousand arrests of military, political, academic and legal personnel, many of them stood the chances of being tried for treason. Yet Al-Qaradawi was not bothered about their plight. Historically, whenever politically expedient, the court clerics have always used Islam as a political tool.

SHEDDING CROCODILE TEARS

The news coverage of the downfall of Husni Mubarak on popular Arabic TV channels completely differed from that of the downfall of Saddam, despite the fact that both were oppressors; both of them imprisoned their citizens without trial, both of them tortured political prisoners, both of them were totally unrepresentative, both of them rigged elections, both of them were sole candidates in most of the presidential elections, both of them prepared their sons as their heirs-apparent to inherit the presidency, both of them deprived their countrymen and -women of basic freedom and rights, and both of them were greedy for power. But the coverage of news and views on the biased channels remained highly in favour of the despot of Iraq, despite his bleak records on human rights and atrocious crimes. As long as the victims of the crimes of Saddam were not people of their own ilk, it did not matter what he did to others, especially the Shias and the Kurds.

The youth revolution in Egypt started on 25 January, 2011. Within a few weeks, several hundred youths were killed, and several thousand were injured by the military and militias; whereas, in Iraq, tens of thousands were massacred. The policies and measures of Husni Mubarak, but not Saddam, were referred to in some commentaries in the popular media as oppressive. The biased reporters found alibis for Saddam by blaming his aides rather than the dictator himself for his disastrous reign. When Saddam was executed, the female reporters on some ultranationalist Arabic channels dressed in black as a sign of mourning, which they have never done even on the death anniversary of the Prophet of Islam.

Al Jazeera Arabic TV showed many documentaries since the invasion of Iraq lamenting the casualty figures due to American bombings but hardly mentioning the casualties relating to the terror of Al-Qaeda and the Saddamites. Assuming that Al Jazeera's concern was quite genuine about the tragic plight of the Iraqi civilians who were caught up in the midst of violence, then for the sake of fair and impartial reporting, it should have commissioned an investigatory documentary on the direct role that Qatar and Saudi Arabia played in facilitating the occupation of Iraq by foreign forces. It is an open secret that these countries provided all the logistics to enable the American forces to fly bombing sorties over Iraq. But not a word of criticism could be heard against the Qatari and Saudi authorities for their roles in the calamity that befell Iraq and its people. Yet the media shed crocodile tears over the civilian casualties.

On July 1, 2006, in almost all of its news bulletins, Al Jazeera Arabic TV played the audiotaped message of Bin Laden, which was repeated in the next day's news bulletins. The objective of Bin Laden's recorded message was to derail any political process in Iraq and Somalia. He passed the customary fatwa of infidelity and apostasy against every soul that did not concur with his concept of jihad.

The worst-ever catastrophe that had befallen the people of Iraq was during Saddam's reign of terror. But despite being found guilty for crimes of mass massacre in an open court, the nationalist media portrayed the tyrant as a hero and martyr. When the media, therefore, lamented the occupation of Iraq, it was not because of casualties of innocent civilians; otherwise, they would have condemned the terror of Saddamites and *takfiri*s against civilians. The media reacted with resentment throughout Saddam's trial, as if pan-Arab nationalism itself was in the docks.

SADDAM: THE HERO AND SALAH AL-DIN OF ARAB NATIONALISM

Abdel Bari Atwan, editor-in-chief of the London Arabic newspaper *Al-Quds al-Arabi*, in his interview on Al-Hiwar TV on 10 April, 2009, said that Saddam makes the Arabs proud for many achievements such as fighting (non-Arab) Shia Iran with an army of Arab Shias, developing a nuclear arsenal with the brain of all Iraqis without sectarian discrimination, and winning to his side thirty-six of the most-wanted collaborators from the Arab Shias. If what he said was true, then why did such an exemplary 'achievement' come to an abrupt end when a well-fed, well-trained, well-armed, one-million strong army of Saddam withered away within a few days of the invasion by the coalition forces?

The repressive circumstances and the ensuing consequences of engaging the country in a series of destructive wars were the main factors that ruined the morale of the army. The dictator himself, the commander-in-chief of the armed forces, defected from the war to save his own skin. But the Arab nationalists may not appreciate the fact that it was a wrong sense of pride and hero worship that emboldened the despot to drag his country into confrontations with the international community to a point of no return.

Mr Atwan strongly defended the record of Saddam's reign, contrasting the tragic state of Iraq under the US occupation with that under Saddam. In their enthusiasm to defend the indefensible record of their dictator, some people cannot see beyond the vision of their ultranationalism.

The apologetics never mention the human sufferings and tragedy that befell the victims of terrorism and their families that lost their breadwinners. They do not mention how the dictator abandoned half a million children and infants of Iraq, without medicines and food, when he and his supporters were engaged in building super-luxurious palaces to live in extravagance. They turn a blind eye at the chemical warfare in which thousands of Iraqi children were killed or crippled for life. They do not mention the targeting of innocent people in the crowded marketplaces and mosques by the Saddamite and Al-Qaeda terrorists.

In their attempt at absolving their hero from dreadful crimes, they blame members of his administration for the excesses committed during his reign. But their excuses defy common sense. During the absolute dictatorship of Saddam, people lived in fear. His secret police used to spy on citizens by appointing informants from inside their family members. At the time of interrogation, his secret police and presidential guards used to kick the suspects on their faces with their boots and carry out brutal torture. They used to film their inhuman torturing techniques and preserve them for the Nero to enjoy the scenes in his spare time while smoking his big, imported cigar. The videos of savage torture administered by his equally savage presidential guards were shown on some Arab TVs after his downfall.

The torturing techniques extended to kicking his victims' heads and genitals. Summary killings, shooting of suspects in the heads, and dumping them in mass graves were rampant. Later, when the extremist ideologues formed a partnership with the Saddamites, the world witnessed the beheading of hostages and displaying the horrendous pictures of the victims on websites with sadistic pleasure, as happened with the Western hostages.

Under Saudi pressure, Bush the senior turned his face away as the disgraced and defeated Saddam's forces employed helicopter gunships and heavy artillery to quell the uprising in the south and north of Iraq. His bloodthirsty sons-in-law played a crucial role in this genocide. Later on, when they fell foul with the dictator, they were killed and dragged in the streets on the orders of their father-in-law. The mass graves are the heritage of Saddam's era, and they will torture the conscience of anybody who had consciously or unconsciously cooperated with him.

No matter how hard the sympathisers of Saddam try to whitewash the crimes committed by their Salah al-Din (known in English as Saladin), people cannot be duped anymore. If these people and their clerics believe that whatever emanates from human actions is in accordance with the will of God, as indeed they do, then why can't they accept that the execution of Saddam was also in compliance with the will of God?

The pride and arrogance of Saddam reached its apex when he decided to invade Kuwait, the country which was one of the main financial contributors in nurturing his arrogance during his eight-year war against Iran. He repaid the favour by causing untold damage to the country's infrastructure and by creating fear in the hearts of its people during his invasion of that country. But in his interview on Al-Hiwar TV on 3 July, 2009, Abdel Bari Atwan lamented that the Arab rulers had failed to stand by Saddam in his drive to develop nuclear weapons for the defence of the Arabs against Iran, as he put it.

The interviewer on Al-Hiwar TV called the attention of Mr Atwan to the fact that the neighbouring countries felt threatened by Saddam, and, therefore, they did not trust him. In reply, Mr Atwan said that Saddam had already faced punishment for entering Kuwait and had suffered the embargo for ten years, as if his own family and tribesmen were affected by the embargo. This means his slate of crimes and treacheries should have been wiped clean for the sake of forming a common front of Arab countries against Iran.

The fans of Saddam should have asked themselves some critical questions. Were their family members abducted by Saddam's forces? Were their daughters raped by his hedonistic and womanising sons? Were their sons summarily executed by his republican guards? Were their grandchildren dumped in mass graves? All these crimes were committed against others who were not cattle or sacrificial animals to be slaughtered and dumped in trenches. Under what right did they appoint themselves as the deputies of God to forgive him? Do they have any mandate to pass judgement on behalf of his victims? Or as long as their own loved ones were quite safe at home, it did not matter to them what agony his victims suffered.

When the terrorism of Al-Qaeda was at its peak in Iraq, the audio/ video messages of Bin Laden screened on Al Jazeera Arabic channel were immediately followed by the commentary of Abdel Bari Atwan. Often he referred to Bin Laden with reverential decorum of 'shaykh' (meaning 'religious mentor or tribal or political leader') on Arabic channels only. But when he appeared in interviews on English channels, he never referred to him as shaykh.

On another occasion, in a commentary that followed Bin Laden's videotape, Mr Atwan expressed his worry a number of times during the programme that Bin Laden did not move one of his arms even once, hoping that the shaykh was not injured or harmed in any way. What type of religious mentor or leader might a person be to advocate mass murder of innocent civilians and babies? As the issue of mass graves was the most discussed subject, the Arab nationalist media played down the crime against humanity committed in broad daylight and blamed what they called an 'international conspiracy' to defame Saddam.

CONDONING CRIMES AGAINST HUMANITY

On 23 October, 2007, the desperate and despondent tone in Bin Laden's speech addressing his devotees was quite reminiscent of the tone and wording used by Saddam when he was facing political collapse after the invasion of Iraq by the coalition forces. In order to save his own life, Saddam went into hiding, forgetting that he had appointed himself commander-in-chief of the armed forces and he should have been the last person to find himself a pigeonhole to hide in. Likewise, instead of fighting his war with his own life, Bin Laden played havoc with the lives of thousands from his hiding place by inciting young people with emotional religious slogans.

Not once did Saddam or Bin Laden express remorse and sympathy for innocent men, women, children, and babies who lost their lives as a result of their outrageous terrorism for several years in succession. Saddam and Bin Laden shared intense animosity against the Shias to the point of calling for their extermination. When Saddam invaded the sacred cities of Karbala and Najaf after the intifada (popular uprising) in the early 1990s, the slogan used by the tyrant's forces was 'No more Shias after this day'.

Harith al-Dari, the secretary general of the Association of (Sunni) Muslim Scholars in Iraq, promised to cleanse Iraq from Safavids (implying the Shia Arabs). He was quite apathetic that he was expressing sectarian and racial discrimination in the name of religion, which does not recognise any discrimination on the basis of ethnicity. Had these types of clerics shown any sensitivity for the sanctity of human life during the barbaric reign of Saddam, he would not have dared to embark on genocide.

In sharp contrast with these clerics, there are respectable and noble men among the Sunni community in Iraq who do not betray their country by seeking funds from foreign powers for breaking their country. At the instigation of court clerics, thirty-eight Saudi Wahhabi clerics issued a fatwa, declaring that it was a religious obligation to support the so-called mujahidin in Iraq. The only way of soliciting support of the Wahhabi clerics was to sell them the idea that the Shias were taking over the country. This provided sufficient incentive for the infamous fatwa that was issued in the aftermath of the Istanbul Conference, which was called by the Saddamites and the supporters of Al-Qaeda to form a common front against the Shia political parties, which they did.

Had this fatwa been sought to end the US occupation of Iraq, the Saudi political establishment would never have permitted the Saudi clerics to waste ink on paper. This means that the fatwa issued by their clerics was meant specifically against the Shias, fearing that they would retain power in Iraq after the departure of the US troops.

The sympathy with the oppressors is observed not only among the influential clerics who have cordial relations with the powerful politicians and oil-rich royal families but also among the so-called intellectuals. An Iraqi professor wrote a newspaper article from South Africa in the aftermath of the execution of Saddam, in which he claimed that his own mother was raped by Saddam's forces. Yet he believed that Saddam died a 'martyr' because, according to him, nobody had asked his opinion, in his capacity as the victim's heir, whether he wanted to forgive him or demand reprisal. What can be said about these intellectuals who could not see anyone else in existence except themselves, as if other victims whose lives were ruined by the tyrant were not human beings at all? If some people were willing to sacrifice the sanctity of their mothers at the feet of the despots, this does not mean that all other victims should disgrace their dignity and honour in a like manner.

THE TRIAL THAT SHOCKED THE TYRANTS

Removing Saddam, the tyrant of Iraq, by force was not only a moral but humanitarian duty because Saddam himself was a lethal weapon of mass destruction. The devotees of Saddam had the audacity of claiming that since Iraq was under foreign occupation and influence, Saddam's trial was unfair. Saddam had in fact attended some fifty sessions in the court. This author observed every single sitting of the court. This trial was one of many pending trials. He referred to himself as the 'elected president of Iraq', the election in which the number of votes cast under the surveillance of his co-tyrannical vice president, Izzat al-Duri, were no less than 100 per cent. He kept on shouting at the judge as if he were trying the judge for crimes and not the other way round. He was not tried in a secret military court. He received the fairest trial from which he had adamantly deprived his opponents throughout his reign.

All the settings of the court were televised so that people could see for themselves that he was given the full right of defence. All his life, he had waged war against his people and against Islam. He had persecuted men of religion and ridiculed Islamic teachings. In order to impress upon the irresponsible and naïve court clerics, he held a copy of the Quran in his hands. Hence, this was considered adequate proof for his cronies to conclude that he was a sincere Muslim, that he lived and died for Islam, and that he was a mujahid (fighter in the way of God).

In the *Open Dialogue* programme on Al Jazeera Arabic TV during the trial of Saddam, the viewers quoted verses upon verses from the Quran to plead that God is going to be the ultimate Judge. They, therefore, deduced that Saddam should not be undergoing the painful process of trial because he was, after all, a 'leader'. The same people would have had no qualms in putting ordinary criminals on trial without giving the matter a second thought that their plight, too, will be ultimately judged by God. So why put them at all through the ordeal of imprisonment or execution?

Conspicuously, in the wake of the first appearance of Saddam in the docks, a legal expert protested that international law does not declare the offences of invasion of Kuwait and mass graves as illegal. But no mention was made that the violation of territorial integrity of sovereign states and genocide are against international law, against the United Nations Charter on Human Rights, and against religious laws. Many elites believed that a head of state is above the law, even though he has committed serious crimes against humanity. This belief was reflected in the contribution of millions of dollars by the doomed Libyan dictator through his daughter Ayishah for Saddam's defence. Gaddafi's interest in Saddam's trial was quite understandable in light of his own atrocious records on human rights and his repressive domestic policies since he took power in 1969. In the trial and execution of Saddam, Gaddafi must have visualised his own ultimate plight at the hands of his nation and people. He and his daughter were the most arduous supporters of Saddam.

Qatar sent its ex-attorney general to defend the tyrant. Millions were spent in obstructing the trial and declaring it *ultra vires* because, according to their perverse logic, the head of a state in an Arab country cannot be put on trial. This means that the legal system in Arab dictatorships has to be based on double standards or outright hypocrisy. There have to be one set of laws for the poor and helpless and another set of laws for the rich and powerful. When a poor person steals or murders, the force of law is applied to ensure that he does not escape punishment. But if those in power steal millions and commit mass murders, they are exempted from any accountability and even glorified.

During the year in which Saddam faced justice and was executed, upheaval was created in the Arab world. In that year, on the day of the Islamic feast of sacrifice, Eid al-Adha, the Fatah and the Hamas factions of the Palestinians fought each other in bloody battles in which many people were killed. On the same day, twenty people were killed in

Tunisia, and violent clashes occurred in Bangladesh over the election procedure. In Somalia, violence between the party of the Islamic courts and the government forces claimed the lives of many fighters. All of them were Muslims, and the disputants commanded the support of the politicians and clerics on both sides. None of them bothered to appeal for cessation of hostilities and killings on the sacred day of Eid al-Adha.

But as soon as the news of the execution of Saddam hit the newswires, there was uproar in the Arab media and in the political circles. Overnight, one of the most brutal mass murderers of the century was turned into a martyr and hero of the Arab world. No stone remained unturned in the Arab media especially that run by the pan-Arab nationalists, to protest his execution on the day sacred to all Muslims. But even if he had been executed on some other day, his supporters would have considered the court to be illegal under foreign occupation and would have had many excuses to react with dismay at his execution. In this case, the sacredness of Eid al-Adha was used as a mere scapegoat.

Under the full light of history, Saddam neither respected the sanctity of human life nor the sanctity of any religious occasions. He killed his own sons-in-law in the Islamic sacred month of Ramadan. He invaded Kuwait and caused misery to the entire nation on the sacred day of Ashura. He killed his victims and tortured political prisoners throughout the sacred months, days, and nights, with unfair trials which were conducted by military courts. Ironically, the same media, politicians, and clerics raised no voice about the sanctity of the sacred months or days as the ruthless tyrant enjoyed a status above all sanctities. This explains that the media furore against his execution was politically and not religiously or morally motivated.

One of the historic achievements of the democratically elected Iraqi government was to subject a dictator like Saddam to the rule of law for standing trial according to the country's jurisdiction, granting him the fairest chance of defending himself. This was the first time in the modern Arab world that a brutal dictator had to face justice. But the poor Muslim people have been programmed by the court clerics of the unjust rulers to glorify the tyrants and autocrats, barring any uprising against them. They rely on certain weak and fabricated *hadith*s to suit the interests of the oppressive rulers.

In the Arab world, when the leader of a military junta grabs power, his first task is to wipe out his opponents. In Iraq, this process started ferociously ever since the Ba'ath Arab Socialist party assumed power in 1968. When Saddam took over in 1979 from the previous president, Ahmed Hassan al-Bakr, his personality was magnified as the 'father of the nation'. The schoolchildren were taught to hail the dictator. His statute as a liberator was erected in the centre of Baghdad although he had strangled all the liberties except indecencies in the cinemas and nightclubs. The cinemagoers were expected to clap and hail the dictator when he appeared on the screen. A budget was allocated from the national purse to nurture his ghost in the form of his protruding portraits that polluted every road, street, and alleyway in the country to impress upon the poor public that wherever they are, Saddam is watching over them.

On the state TV stations, the tyrant was portrayed as Salah al-Din (Saladin). This fake sense of heroism magnified his personality and led him to embark upon military adventurism against the neighbouring countries. He totally wiped out the communists from Iraq. His second targets were the Shia majority. Like the tyrants of Banu Umayyah and Banu Abbas a thousand years ago, the power maniac knew that if he was to realise his ambition of ruling over Iraq for life and bequeath the presidency to his hedonist sons, then the Shias would be the greatest hurdle he would face. At the behest of the Shiaphobic neighbouring countries, he embarked upon his campaign against the Shias in the south and the Kurds in the North. Some religious fanatics rejoiced at his anti-Shia policies. The extreme mental obsession that they carry against the Shias may be sensed from a call received on one of the Arab TV channels. While paying tribute to the despot, the caller said in clear words that his best contribution was that he succeeded in killing Shias.

In the aftermath of Saddam's execution, history was distorted, and the Arab world pretended as if there was nothing called the campaign of Anfal or the genocide of the Kurds in Halabjah and the mass graves in the south of Iraq. Perhaps for the first time, there was a consensus among the secular Arabs, the religious extremists, and the so-called moderate political leaders of giving a knee-jerk treatment to Saddam's crimes against humanity, including his torture chambers in the notorious Abu Ghurayb prison. When, ironically, similar torturing techniques were employed under the US occupation, the media did not turn a blind eye. Despite his brutal records, Saddam was glorified to an extent that one of his devotees declared on a popular Arabic TV channel that they will perform hajj (pilgrimage) to the burial site of Saddam, who, in his words, was the 'leader of the martyrs'.

Many people in the Arab world believed that deposing the de facto ruler of Iraq was unjustified. Deep inside the psyches of ordinary people, it has been implanted over the centuries that the standards of accountability which apply to the rulers have to be quite different from those applied to ordinary people. Two different standards have been enforced over the ages—one for the rich, influential, and powerful and the other for the poor, deprived, and downtrodden. When it became public knowledge that Saddam would face trial, Jordan's Bar Association raised the matter with the Arab Lawyers' Union in Cairo, and the lawyers opined that the head of state is immune from prosecution. This shows the extent to which many Muslims have divorced themselves from the Islamic concept of justice and accountability.

In July 2013, the prime minister of Bahrain for more than forty-two years was reported to have told a visiting delegation from the armed forces and police that they would not be made accountable for any act they commit, as much as the rulers are not accountable. Hence, the armed forces and police got a green light to commit whatever atrocities they wished against the recalcitrant, freedom-seeking members of the public.

The Prophet taught his followers that even he was not exempt from accountability. In an Islamic community where law is supposed to be applied to everybody justly and equally, the authorities and the protectors of law look for loopholes to exempt themselves.

Abdullah ibn Amr said, 'I heard the Prophet say, "If you see my *ummah* (community) fearing a tyrant so much that they dare not tell him that he is a tyrant, then there will be no hope for them"'.[54] But the elites and their court clerics in the Muslim world in general, and the Arab world in particular, are doing exactly the opposite. This duplicity, adopted over centuries, is backfiring on them. People have lost confidence in them as they violate the principles of justice, without which no society in the world can function in peace and harmony. Some Muslims have yet to go a long way to realise that there is something called justice in inter-human relations. When this principle was divorced from the system of governance in the Muslim world, they got stuck with the worst dictators and tyrants the history of humankind has ever produced.

The *takfiri* extremists and terrorists in Iraq have targeted mosques, religious gatherings, hospitals, schools, and universities; the poor labourers queuing up for daily work; the destitute living from hand to mouth; crowded marketplaces with women, children, and disabled inside; worshippers inside the mosques; funeral services and processions; the injured patients inside hospitals; and the dead in their graves.

---

54 Musnad Ahmad ibn Hanbal compendium of Hadiths.

For the grave phobic psycho maniacs, desecrating the grave sites, cemeteries, and shrines is an essential religious duty, which distinguishes their subnormality from the rest of the world communities. They operate with no mercy and human compassion in their hearts. The Prophet had declared all the places of worship to be under his protection. But the *takfiri*s and their new allies, the Saddamites, have breached all the Islamic values, moral teachings, injunctions of the Quran, and traditions of the Prophet. They have committed treachery against Islam and humanity.

BANKRUPT OF HOPE AND OPTIMISM
Throughout his eight-year war against Iran, the official media of the doomed Saddam's regime rained abuses at the Iranians, calling them '*al-furs al-majus,* and associating them with the pre-Islamic pagan religion of the Persian Magians or fire worshippers. This expression is now frequently used in the Arab media. It amply demonstrates that although Islam abolished discrimination on the basis of race or colour, racial discrimination and prejudice are, nevertheless, very much alive and have been institutionalised by the ultranationalists and partisans of the radical ideology.

If they had cared to study history, they would not have escaped finding out that Imam Abu Hanifah, the first imam of the Sunni school of law, was none other than Persian. Imam Tirmidhi, the compiler of one of the six most authentic voluminous compendiums of *hadith* in Sunni Islam, was none other than Persian. In addition, some of the most prominent and renowned Sunni scholars of *hadith* and other Sunni classical scholars like Abu Dawud, Al-Thalabi, and Al-Razi were none other than Persians. Yet the racists are engaged in deceiving the unaware members of the public through rhetoric, polemics, and half-knowledge. The traditions that the members of the public learn in their mosques are taken directly from the works of these imams, who were not Arabs but

Iranians. But because of their malice against Iran, they brand all the Shias—Arabs and non-Arabs—as '*majusi*', 'Safavi' or 'Farsi', without realising that these expressions equally apply to their topmost imams or religious leaders, whose jurisprudential rules and guidance they follow.

For centuries, the radical ideologues have accused the Shias of being heretics because, according to them, they are against who they call *awliya al-amr* (the ruling authorities). But their naïveté is obvious from their blanket accusation. People become disgruntled with the policies of the unrepresentative and ruthless regimes for a range of reasons. The futile attempt of the radicals at portraying the obedience to oppressive rulers as a religious duty has been thwarted by no other than the Sunni masses, in whose name they embark upon false allegations.

In international forums, Saudi Arabia claims to represent the Sunni world. But this false pretension did not stop it from committing genocide in Yemen even against the Sunni population. For over three decades, it has accused Iran of meddling in the affairs of the Sunni world. But this did not stop it from sending its former head of intelligence, Turki ibn Faisal, to the conference of the internationally recognised terrorists from among the Iranian opposition in Paris in July 2016, where Turki al- Faisal called for the forceful downfall of the Iranian regime and showed no etiquette and no respect for international relations by insulting in a derogatory manner, the revered Iranian religious figures. But this type of interference is quite permissible under their psychotic extremism. In Iraq, the army and the popular public movement have been making significant gains by kicking out IS terrorists from one town after another. When the terrorists get the beating, the trend is now established that top Saudi officials at the ministerial level moan and groan in public as if somebody has kicked them in the abdomen. But when the IS commits savage atrocities of civilians in Iraq, not even a word of condemnation is heard by the same officials. What does this mean? Unfortunately, it seems they still envisage the international community to be at the level of kindergarten as to not comprehend what is going on.

In some of the most prominent Sunni countries like Tunisia, Libya, Egypt, and Yemen, people have not only rejected their rulers but have succeeded in toppling them. Yet the ideologues would not dare to slur the Tunisians, Libyans, Egyptians, and Yemenis with defamatory remarks for not surrendering to the will of the dictators. If, according to them, people become heretics for opposing repressive and unrepresentative rulers, then all these countries which witnessed uprisings of the masses have to be heretical. It is exactly this type of passive mind-set that has cultivated extremism in the Muslim community.

In present times, when extremists and terrorists want to convey a strong political message, they resort to barbaric measures of indiscriminate serialised bombings and suicide attacks, as they have been doing in Iraq, Syria, Lebanon, Somalia, Yemen, and Pakistan, even by violating the sanctity of the sacred month of Ramadan. This means that the murderers and the political establishments that work for them are misusing the name of Islam solely for political motives to satiate their power hunger. Prior to the Arab League summit in March 2012 held in Baghdad, they embarked on serial bombings with the aim of derailing the summit. When negotiations between Iran and members of the Security Council were scheduled to be held in Baghdad in May 2012, the meeting was preceded by a series of deadly bomb attacks with the aim of obstructing the meeting and derailing any agreement between the big powers and Iran over the latter's nuclear programme. When the agreement was finally signed on 23 November, 2013, the top Saudi officials resorted to issuing threats.

The ideologues behind terrorism are only capable of communicating in one language, that of violence and destruction. Their messages are void of any hope, promise, or optimism. Their religious outlook, true to their indoctrination, is based on gloom and doom, sending most people to hell and reserving heaven for suicide bombers and their mentors. They like to see the rest of the Muslims become as despondent towards life as they are. Their pessimistic attitude towards life gives the impression that life is a curse rather than the greatest bounty the Almighty God has gifted to humanity.

TERROR AGAINST THE SANCTITIES

Whenever an opportunity permits, the clerics, the politicians, the diplomats, and the street boys of the *takfiris* talk in the same tone of destroying the tombs and shrines. Their noblemen and criminals alike consider the building of shrines as polytheism, even though no other deity than God is worshipped therein. Yet they dishonestly accuse the Shias of worshipping the graves. They seem to be suffering from acute grave phobia.

Egypt is the land of tombs and shrines, and it houses the ancient seminary of the Sunni world at Al-Azhar, where their religious authorities do not have any qualms in building and maintaining shrines. There is nothing in the Quran which suggests that building of structures over the graves is prohibited in Islam. But the ideologues act as if they need to teach the Quran its job.

They portray the Shias as 'grave worshippers'. They declare the Shias as 'accursed' because, according to their concocted narrations, the Shias violate the Prophetic prohibition of building shrines and mosques on the graves of saints. Their self-contradiction is manifested in the fact that they do not apply the same justifications against the Sunnis, who build shrines and mosques on the graves of companions of the Prophet and their Sufi saints in Egypt, India, Pakistan, Syria, Iraq, and many other Muslim countries. The entire history and heritage of the Sunnis are built around the graves of their religious personages.

It is the Sunnis, not the Shias, who built elaborate and flamboyant shrines, mosques, and tombs over the graves of Abu Hanifah, Shaykh Abd al-Qadir Jilani, Shafi'i, Ahmad ibn Hanbal, Khalid ibn al-Walid, Salah al-Din al-Ayyubi, Bukhari, and thousands of others. But the extremist Salafis and Wahhabis are aware that if they were to declare the Sunnis infidels and accursed, as they have been doing against the Shias, they will not be able to sustain the backlash from the Sunni world. They, therefore, do not act on the matter of principle because there is no principle involved here. They act solely on the matter of political expediency and sectarianism.

But so effective has been the propaganda emitted by the ideologues of this psychotic establishment that, today, militants in Iraq and Syria are vying to attack and destroy sacred shrines under the pretensions that their existence leads to polytheism. They do not have that much imagination that only God the Almighty, being the Creator and Giver of life, has the right and absolute authority to take life. To go on a rampage, depriving innocent people of their lives, is tantamount to giving oneself the authority of God on matters of life and death. To destroy human life at random is the worst imaginable *shirk* (polytheism) that these fanatics and their ideological mentors are committing.

The destruction of the thousand-year-old sacred Askariyayn shrine at Samarra in Iraq on 23 February, 2006, was a direct result of constant provocations and incitement at the highest echelon of the Wahhabi hierarchy, which brought Iraq overnight on the verge of civil war. But the very next day, in the Friday sermon from Makkah, which is heard by millions of listeners through the Saudi satellite channels, there was no condemnation of the heinous criminal act, which attracted worldwide condemnation even from non-Muslims. Instead, the imam of the congregation expressed emotional outbursts, regretting the acts of retaliation but not the original act of provocation that brought devastation to the holy shrine. He said in his sermon, 'In return for the destruction of a few graves, you have attacked the Houses of Allah (mosques). How do you judge?' What he did not mention in his sermon is that the shrine and the graves belonged to some of the most sacred personalities revered by the Shias, and it was a historic mosque in a region predominated by the Sunnis, who themselves used to pray regularly in that mosque. Such a biased reaction was an appeasement of the carnage caused by the terrorists, who were sent from across the borders.

This author monitored a joint interview of the minister of the interior and minister of defence of Iraq at that time. Both of them said that the crime was carefully planned. It would have taken a good twelve hours to transport all the explosives and to plant them inside the sacred shrine. The dilemma will always remain: what were the security and the occupation forces doing at that time? Daydreaming?

A wise and unbiased reaction from any responsible religious scholar worth his salt would have been to condemn the Samarra devastation unequivocally and simultaneously condemn any acts of retaliation on the mosques and properties of others. But these clerics were not bothered that their biased attitudes would trigger a vicious cycle of revenge and counter revenge. On the contrary, they sprinkled salt on wounds when the Wahhabi clerics mustered the support of the students from Muhammad ibn Saud University in Saudi Arabia, where the volunteers pledged to destroy all the shrines in Iraq because, according to them, they are the symbols of 'idol worship'.[55]

One can perceive the mental blockage with which these ideologues are afflicted. In Syria, for example, as they blew up Shia mosques and shrines with copies of the Quran stored inside, they shouted '*Allahu akbar*' ('God is great'). They did not ponder that by destroying the

---

55 http://www.nahrainnet.net/news/52/ARTICLE/10075/2007-07-19.html, 19 July 2007.

mosques, they were obstructing the worship of God, and by destroying copies of the Quran, they were desecrating the very source of the Islamic law, which they pretend to implement. They took their battle inside the oldest mosque in Aleppo, badly damaging the infrastructure of this historic mosque.

In Egypt, after the fall of Mubarak, the Salafi fanatics caused the destruction of one hundred shrines belonging to the Sufis. The individuals and nations that are religiously bent on marketing Ibn Taymiyyah's anti graves and anti tombs ideology have not shown any sincerity in applying their commitment consistently. They have hypocritically maintained and preserved the grave and tomb of Ibn Taymiyyah, who initiated this *fitnah* (dissention) and divided the Muslim community. They blew up and desecrated the Shia shrines in Iraq, Syria, and Bahrain but have not harmed the tomb of Ibn Taymiyyah in Syria. This shows that their ant tombs policy has nothing to do with Islam but is built on obscurity, mental obsession, and psychological inhibition. This disease does not seem to have any cure. It passes from one generation to another like a parasite, only because there is an oil power sponsoring it. In the process, their ruffians display ill manners even inside the sacred city of the Prophet, as their police force remains oblivious to the assault on the Shia pilgrims.

From a religious viewpoint, the Quran has not expressed a single word of disapproval against building a shrine over the Companions of the Cave as is quite clear in the chapter named 'The Cave' (Surat al-Kahf) in the Quran. Yet the despotism of this ideology seeks to overrule the Quran. Their ideologues start from the premise that only their way of thinking is the right way, and only they have been blessed with the acumen of judging what is right and what is wrong. But anybody having an iota of self-respect and integrity cannot compromise with such self-propelling and obstinate ideology, which has been pulling the wool over the eyes of the Muslims. Their pretension in the name of *tawhid* (oneness of God) against what they call grave worshipping is nothing but dishonest misrepresentation of facts.

Muslim masses are made to believe that the Shias are not Muslims that they do not pray, that they do not fast, and that the difference between Sunnis and Shias is that the Sunnis worship God and the Shias worship graves. This type of lunatic rant has appeared even in some documentaries televised on popular Arabic TV channels. Yet the innocent Sunni masses depend on these thugs and take them at face value. To make some sectarian gains, their clerics build the knowledge of their congregations merely on hearsay, knowing very well that rarely would anybody care to countercheck the veracity of the information conveyed from the pulpits to the congregation, often camouflaged in inaccuracies, prejudices, and emotional outbursts.

The last thing one could expect from thousands of people attending congregational prayers is to independently verify the facts and to trace the extent to which the speakers dress up the facts with their own conjectures. The danger lies when the matters of life and death are decided on hearsay and conjecture.

Chapter 8

IMPERIALISM OF IDEOLOGY

Since the oil-price boom of the 1970s, the Wahhabi establishment spent tens of billions of dollars to spread Wahhabi thought around the world. Research projects were undertaken, and generous scholarships were offered at the Saudi seminaries under the pretext of teaching 'pure' Islam—the type of Islam that was geared to condone every crime committed by the Muslim rulers of the past and present and to overlook every act of hedonism, extravagance, and debauchery committed by the Muslim ruling dynasties of the past and present.

From its inception, the Wahhabi movement adopted a very hostile attitude towards the Shias. History shows that Ibn Saud faced enormous pressure from his gang of Ikhwan, the offshoots of the Wahhabis who urged him to give an ultimatum to the Shia population in Hijaz: either adopt the Wahhabi ideology, or be exterminated from Arabia. But the Shias did not budge from their faith. In the face of extreme repression and compulsion, the overwhelming majority of the converts to the Wahhabi sect were non-Shias. The recalcitrant Shias in Arabia and elsewhere suffered massacres and displacement from their land, and until this day, they are not permitted to build their mosques and practise their faith in freedom in Saudi Arabia. These issues are amply covered in a number of reports from human-rights agencies.

From the time when Ibn Abd al-Wahhab, the founding father of Wahhabism, discovered that only his version of Islam was the right Islam, and that the Islam of the past one thousand years was Islam contaminated with impurity and polytheism, the Shias rejected these beliefs completely. Hence, they were seen as the main adversaries of the new ideology. Hostility against the Shias and propaganda war against their faith became an essential part of the curriculum in the Wahhabi seminaries. Simultaneously, thousands of *madrasah*s were sponsored around the world, especially in Saudi Arabia, Pakistan, and Afghanistan, where students were fed with wrong information against the Shia faith. As a direct consequence, some radical movements emerged in Pakistan, demanding that the Shia community be excommunicated or declared *kuffar* officially and legally. The purpose was to bar them from participating in public life, holding official posts, voting in elections, and even going for pilgrimages to Makkah and Madinah. The extremist political groups seek to apply to them the same jurisdiction that applies to non-Muslims.

NEW STRATEGY OF DIVIDE AND REJOICE

On a separate front, attempts were made to create divisions within the Shia community by making one group an enemy of another and diverting their attention away from real challenges facing them. The leaders and the followers of these splinter groups suffered a huge gap in knowledge, so this was considered the best cultivating ground on which they could sow the seeds of division. The groups that played into their hands were given enough incentives to get entangled over trivial issues which were magnified and presented as fundaments of faith. The poor members of the public were not even aware as to who was calling the shots by remote control and from where.

The opponents of the Shias had tried converting them through intimidation and mass killings but had failed badly. They, therefore, initiated a new campaign to fight the Shia faith from within. The naïve groups in the Shia community responded to this conspiracy because of their shallow knowledge. Through the leadership of the splinter groups, the adversaries of the Shia faith sought to achieve from within what they could not achieve from without by use of force and violence.

Among any religious community in the world, the teachings of the faith are preserved, protected, and defended by knowledgeable people, not common folk and the masses, who are too preoccupied in their daily lives to get involved in intellectual pursuits as they would have liked to. There are practical impediments like domestic responsibilities, circumstantial constraints, or simply total disinterest; whereas acquisition of knowledge requires deep interest, devotion, perseverance, and sacrifice of comfort and time in fulfilment of the objectives. Those who are half-literate and who tend to depend on sheer conjecture, imagination, abuses, and foul-mouthed rants cannot represent the faith. Only the top religious scholars, who have self-respect and respect for others and who have established their credibility by devoting themselves to acquiring knowledge from the original sources and by sacrificing their comfort, time, and energy for the faith can be the true representatives of the faith.

The adversaries of the Shias changed their strategy by killing two birds with one stone. A scenario of divide and dominate was taking shape by forming groups within the groups, each vying for control in shallow waters. The treachery was packaged in such a way that simple-minded members of the public did not even realise how they were being manipulated from within and how the rift in the community was engineered against the core teachings of the faith.

Under the new strategy, the adversaries of the Shias focused their attention on top religious scholars by making them targets of attacks and abuse. Their objective was to weaken the defence line of the faith. If the reputation of this frontline could be tarnished and the *ulama* (top religious scholars) could be subjected to defamation of character and disrepute, then the tasks of the opponents of the Shias became that much easier. The splinter groups were either completely sold out or could not see the overall picture and the depth of the conspiracy against the Shia community and its faith. They, therefore, became the facilitators for the opponents. The same evil manoeuvring that shaped the strategy of the Umayyads and the Abbasids was being applied once again, with new faces on the scene, to break the faith from within.

There are minor and major differences between various schools of law among Sunnis and Shias. But the propaganda against the Shias has intensified to an extent that on 4 May, 2009, a radical 'shaykh', Al-Kalbani, who leads prayers in the Grand Mosque in Makkah, made a shocking declaration on the Arabic service of BBC TV by claiming that all Shia *ulama* (religious scholars) are *kuffar*. He took his interviewer by surprise. He went further by suggesting that there is a need to repatriate all Shias out of his country, to where he did not say, notwithstanding the fact that the Shias in the oil-rich eastern region of Saudi Arabia are citizens of that country and have been living there centuries before the progeny of Saud came to power.

The highly discriminatory statements of Al-Kalbani in his interview on BBC TV attracted a storm of protests from Shias in many parts of the world but fell on the deaf ears of the authorities, which seemed to be quite comfortable with the bigoted outbursts of their cleric. The bond between Aal Saud (the progeny of Saud) and Aal al-Shaykh (the progeny of Ibn Abd al-Wahhab) is unbreakable. One without the other is like a body without a soul. Aal Saud is the political wing, and Aal al-Shaykh is the religious wing of the Wahhabi movement.

In the first week of January 2010, another 'shaykh', Muhammad al-Arifi, publicly mounted a vicious and malicious attack on the revered Grand Ayatollah Sistani, who is the religious leader to millions of Shias, by calling him insulting and derogatory names, and that, too, in a Friday sermon delivered in Riyadh, the capital of Saudi Arabia, where the contents of the sermons are heavily censored by the political authorities. Only if a green light is given can religious authorities open their mouths.

The religious leadership of Ayatollah Sistani is well recognised even among non-Shias. There were condemnations of Al-Arifi from around the world, including a statement from Shaykh al-Azhar and a strongly worded statement from President Jalal Talibani, the then-president of Iraq, denouncing such an attack on a highly respected religious authority. In a message sent to King Abdullah ibn Abd al-Aziz of Saudi Arabia, he said that had it not been for Ayatollah Sistani, Iraq would have drowned in sectarian bloodshed.

In his interview on one of the (Persian) Gulf TV channels of Dubai on 26 March, 2012, he claimed that the Prophet of Islam used to sell wine and gifted bottles of wine to his companions. He further stated that the companions of the Prophet went for prayers inside the Prophet's Mosque as their feet were washed with wine.

This was a blatant blasphemy against the Prophet. But the Wahhabi cleric was neither condemned nor disciplined by his religious or political establishment. Had these blasphemous testimonies emanated from any Shia individual, the Wahhabis would have made sure that on every pulpit in Friday sermons the matter was brought up with inflammatory speeches, and the Shia community *en mass* would have been accused of insulting and blaspheming the Prophet of Islam.

No question arose of demoting the Wahhabi blasphemer. On the contrary, this cleric took a leading role in assigning Wahhabi missionaries to the north of Yemen in the areas of the Huthis, the Yemeni Shias, to create sectarian tension in their area. The Huthis claimed that Yemeni children were being abducted and smuggled across the borders into Saudi territory to be indoctrinated from their childhood with Wahhabi teachings. This matter had attracted the attention of the Yemeni press.

In the wake of the recent publicity given by the British media to the recruitment of hundreds of British Muslims into the ranks of the jihadists fighting in Syria and Iraq, Muhammad al-Arifi's name featured in the Channel 4 main news bulletin. The programme compared and contrasted what he claimed in his interview with Paraic O'Brien of Channel 4 with what he said in his sermons in the mosques encouraging people to fight jihad.[56]

The rhetoric of the Wahhabi clerics extends to accusing the Shias of cooperating with *kuffar* against Muslims. If the claimants had a flicker of shame, they would have cared to study their own history. The entire history of the dictatorial regimes in the Muslim world is heavily dependent on the support and protection of the United States and European countries. At the inception of the Wahhabi movement in Arabia, had Ibn Saud and Ibn Abd al-Wahhab not remained loyal to the British imperial power, their very identity would have been lost in the desert of Najd. But the problem with these ideologues is that they are in the habit of fantasising history and like to mould historical facts to their liking. Neither Al-Kalbani nor Al-Arifi would have had the courage to question or object to the policies of their rulers for providing logistics and military facilities to the United States and the coalition forces for occupying Iraq. They would not have dared to express their disapproval by word or deed against the adamant opposition of the Saudi rulers to the withdrawal of the US forces from Iraq.

---

56 'No life without jihad', http://www.channel4.com/news/sheikh-mohamed-al-arifi-saudi-cleric-british-jihadis-cardiff, 25 June 2014.

The duplicity of this establishment can be demonstrated with further examples. The Salafis and Wahhabis consider the era of the companions of the Prophet as the best era to have passed in human history. If today, after fourteen centuries, any person was to enter an ordinary mosque with his feet washed with wine or alcohol, he would be considered a nuisance and would be reported to the police to get him evicted from the precincts of the mosque. Yet according to Al-Arifi, the companions lacked basic etiquette and cleanliness, having entered the Prophet's Mosque to offer prayers while wine was on their bodies and clothes.

This cleric wanted to prove that alcohol is not impure. So he chose the path of mudslinging against the Prophet and his companions. He tried to demean the status of the Prophet to bring it down to his level and standards. The only Muslim country that protested his blasphemy was Iran, whereas the passive attitude on the other side was tantamount to saying that as long as the Prophet is blasphemed by their own ilk, it is quite acceptable.

A few years ago, an infamous individual, in his personal capacity, insulted one of the wives of the Prophet. As a reaction, the Wahhabi clerics joined the chorus for blaming the entire Shia community for this offence despite the fact that it was condemned by top Shia scholars in the Shia seminaries. In sharp contrast, this top Wahhabi cleric insulted the Prophet, but there was no condemnation from the Wahhabi and Saudi establishment or from the Muslim masses in general. They have provided enough matter from their store of fables to the novelists and cartoonists in the West to follow in their footsteps in insulting the Prophet. The Shias adopt rock-solid stances in the face of any ill-mannered gesture in word or deed against the sacred personality of the Prophet and his household, whereas their opponents deal with sensitive matters of faith with laxity and apathy.

THE BRAINS BEHIND MILITANCY

The campaign of hate against the Shias has created an avalanche of violence. They have been subjected to massacres by the Taliban and Al-Qaeda and now by ISIL. In 1998, a dreadful massacre took place in Mazar-i-Sharif in Afghanistan. As many as twenty-four thousand Shia civilians were killed in cold blood. Amnesty International reported that the Taliban systematically killed civilians following their takeover of the city. After slaughtering men, children, the aged, disabled, and sick, this criminal gang left their bodies in the streets and took their women as slaves. The United Nations reported the frenzy of the Taliban in slaughtering thousands of civilians. But the Muslim world turned its face in the other direction as if as long as their victims were Shias, crimes against humanity could be branded as jihad.

The same evil mentality prevails across the board among the extremists, wherever they may be. In July 2013, the offshoot of Al-Qaeda, Al-Nusra Front in Syria, issued an edict in the name of the shariah that if Shias are caught, they should be killed outright, their properties confiscated, and their women taken as captives for the enjoyment of the terrorists posing as mujahidin.

Professor Abou El Fadl identifies a common feature between the Taliban and Al-Qaeda in that they are both heavily influenced by the Wahhabi thought, which labelled anything that did not originate from the Arabian Bedouin life as an innovation. They reacted in resentment against intellectualism, mysticism, and sectarianism. Despite the overwhelming evidence that the earliest Sufis were Arabs, they branded Sufism as a Persian innovation, considered intercession and visitation to the graves as a Turkish innovation, and accused rational philosophical discourse as originating from *kafir* Greek thought. The jurists who disagreed with such enigmatic assessments were branded infidels.[57]

---

57 Abou El Fadl (2005), pp. 45–50.

Ever since the Wahhabis took over Arabia, the Shias in the eastern region of the kingdom have faced systematic discrimination. The Wahhabi rule was established through bloodbaths in the name of Islam. Their founding fathers made a living out of attacking and looting caravans of pilgrims going to Makkah for pilgrimage. Many innocent Sunnis were also slaughtered alongside the Shias. The Wahhabi ideologues became too ambitious and started crossing the borders and invading Iraqi territories. Several incursions took place against the Shia sacred cities of Najaf and Karbala between 1801 and 1803. Their ambition remains unfulfilled to this very day, but they have not given up that their ultimate aim is to destroy the holy shrines of the Prophet's family members as they had done in Makkah and Madinah. Iraqi media reported on 28 June, 2014, that the Iraqi security forces intercepted twenty vehicles loaded with arms trying to enter the holy city of Karbala to cause massive bloodshed and mayhem. Back to the historic episode in Hijaz, Ibn Saud's power hunger led him to carry out raids from 1902 to 1925, with the ensuing mass killings of the recalcitrant tribesmen. According to Aburish, he employed an Egyptian cleric called Muhammad Tammimi 'to fabricate a family tree which showed him to be a direct descendant of the Prophet'.[58] At the dawn of the new Wahhabi/Saudi state, they claimed that the law of the country is the shariah. Yet the shariah was interpreted as it suited the interests and policies of Ibn Saud, his family, and the Wahhabis.[59]

At present, in the wake of the rising protests of their Shia citizens in the eastern regions, they have changed tactics and have adopted a different style to express Shiaphobia. They have attempted to draw the Sunni world to their side. They have succeeded at buying the allegiance of several violent splinter groups in the Indo-Pak subcontinent. At home, in the sacred land of Islam, where Muslims are supposed to be treated equally, the Shias face a barrage of offences from the Saudi

58 Aburish, p. 13.
59 Ibid., p. 28.

religious police called *Al-Amr bil-Maruf wa Nahi an al-Munkar* (enjoining good and forbidding evil), especially in Madinah. This type of surveillance on members of the public was later introduced by the Taliban in Afghanistan, where the offenders were whipped in public, similar to the policy adopted at the dawn of the Wahhabi movement in Arabia. Even today, the religious police pursue and harass the visitors visiting the graves of the religious personages. But they never involve themselves at all in very serious issues like bribes paid on arms deals in the kingdom to the foreign arms dealers and brokers.

In the pilgrimage season, when pilgrims from all over the world assemble to perform hajj, which is one of the pillars of Islam, the Shias are closely monitored. There have been many incidents in the past where the Shia pilgrims were beaten up by the security police. They bear this humiliation with patience because in the pilgrimage season, the believers are not supposed to resort to quarrels and fights or vain talks and arguments. The reputable Wahhabi clerics have given themselves the right to attack the beliefs of the Shias from the pulpits in Masjid al-Haram (the inviolable Grand Mosque) in Makkah and Masjid al-Nabawi (the Prophet's Mosque) in Madinah. The Wahhabi clerics read their Friday sermons from written scripts approved by the political authorities. This means that the religious wing of the Wahhabis is subservient to the surveillance of the political wing and not the other way round.

In the wake of peaceful protests by the Shia citizens in Al-Awwamiyyah in the eastern region in October 2011, a famous cleric, Abd al-Rahman al-Hudhayfi, who leads prayers in the Prophet's Mosque in Madinah, mounted an attack on the Shias, accusing them of being non-Saudis and foreign agents. As far back as Friday March 13, 1998, the same cleric had insulted the Shias in his Friday sermon. The ex-president of Iran, Shaykh Hashimi Rafsanjani, was the state guest and was attending the mosque when the cleric took undue advantage of his presence to unleash his malice against the faith and beliefs of the Shias. President Rafsanjani walked out of the mosque with his delegates.

This cleric was bankrupt of any sense of respect for the Prophet, who was the epitome of the highest moral character. The Prophet, in whose mosque he was embarking in vain and loose talk, was polite even to the polytheists and idol worshippers who used to visit him. The Prophet was the exemplary model of hospitality towards his guests. But then, if such clerics had followed the sublime character of the Prophet rather than their own wishes, the Muslims would not have ended up in a tragic plight as they are today.

Between 1998 and now, the world has changed, but Al-Hudhayfi and his fellow clerics have not changed. In a sermon in October 2011, this cleric called the Shias of Saudi Arabia *rawafid* (rejectionists) and said that if they believe in the *wilayah* (authority or guardianship) of their Imam Muhammad ibn Hasan al-Askari, the twelfth imam, then let them go to him. There is no place for them in Saudi Arabia, he continued. He accused the Shia citizens of Saudi Arabia of being non-nationals and called for their repatriation to Iraq. His accusations came as a re-action to the demonstrations held in Al-Awwamiyyah, demanding the release of political prisoners who, as usual, were being held without tri-al. The Shia citizens were demanding freedom of expression and the right to participate in the political life of the country. But in the view of Al-Hudhayfi and his ilk, this was a crime, as if they do not live in the twenty-first century but in the Middle-Ages.

Al-Hudhayfi added his voice to that of the Ministry of Home Affairs, under the late Prince Nayif ibn Abd al-Aziz, who was subsequently giv-en the oath of allegiance by members of the royal family as the next crown prince, in compliance with the king's directives. The ministry was quick to point fingers at Iran, accusing it of instigating trouble in Al-Awwamiyyah, but never confessing the fact that there is an official stranglehold over the freedom of Shia citizens in Saudi Arabia and that it was causing much frustration in the area.

THE NETWORK OF PLOTS

The negative stance adopted by al-Hudhayfi, in line with that adopted by the Ministry of Home Affairs, was in stark contradiction with the article written by the chief mufti of Saudi Arabia, Shaykh Abd al-Rahman Abd al-Aziz Aal al-Shaykh, in *Al-Riyadh* newspaper,[60] in which he wrongly claims that the Shias in Saudi Arabia enjoy equal rights and that they are employed in different organs of the state and participate in the social, economic, and cultural lives of the country without any discrimination. He further claims that they also serve in the armed forces and have been living in peace even before the establishment of the kingdom. Only the last part of his claim is quite true.

He writes that they have to be aware that they are different from Iran, which, according to his harangue, has political ambitions and a territorial expansion programme. He writes that there are many examples to prove this, but he fails to give a single one. He also conceals the fact that his country stood for eight years with Saddam, supporting him morally and financially in his expansionist invasion into the Iranian territories, despite being aware that he was heavily involved in using chemical weapons and crimes against humanity. There is an obvious contradiction between the line that the chief mufti promulgates in his article and the one that Al-Hudhayfi presented and promoted in his sermons.

If the faith and beliefs of the Shias were respected and they were treated equally, as the chief mufti claims, then there was no point for Al-Hudhayfi, one of the top clerics of the state, to mock and vilify the Shia faith in the imamate of Imam al-Mahdi. The officials of the state should have known that the pulpits of the Grand Mosques in Makkah

---

60 http://www.alriyadh.com/2011/04/08/article621509.html, 8 April 2011.

and Madinah are not meant for discussing divisive issues because there are thousands of Shias who perform pilgrimage and are part of the congregation. To attack them from the pulpit is, to say the least, tantamount to displaying the manners of street boys and ruffians, especially when they are not even in a position to answer back.

Both Al-Hudhayfi and the chief mufti were quite aware that the faith in Imam al-Mahdi is one of the integral, inseparable, and indivisible root beliefs of the Twelver Shias. Yet the Shia citizens continually face taunts, telling them that there is no place for them in their own country. The chief mufti calls these flagrant discriminations 'equality' and 'equal rights'.

The chief mufti could never have assured the world that there are no political prisoners in his country. He could never have denied that the Shia mosques have been forcefully closed down, because all these are well documented in the reports of human-rights agencies. He could never have denied that his country has been instrumental in invading neighbouring countries like Bahrain and Yemen and destroying their infrastructures through continuous aerial bombardments for almost two years and by violating the sanctity of the sacred months, where bloodshed was prohibited even in the pre-Islamic era of ignorance. Yet, in his view, it is Iran and not his own country that has territorial ambitions in the Arab world.

Anybody who follows the sermons that the chief mufti personally delivers from Masjid al-Namirah on the plains of Arafat on the very day of hajj would have noticed that he has been instrumental in promoting Shiaphobia by accusing them of being grave worshippers. This type of phobia has been heard time and time again from the tongue of the mufti himself. The Shias have been visiting the graves of the Prophet and the imams and saints, as their Sunni brothers have been doing.

If, as the chief mufti claims in the said article, Sunnis and Shias have lived together for decades and will keep on living that way forever, then why are their extremist clerics calling for the indigenous Shias in the country to be repatriated? The same Al-Hudhayfi and his colleagues have been appealing to Islamic organisations of *ulama* (religious scholars) to be aware that the threat to Islam comes from the Shia beliefs. The entire objective of these extremists is to get the Shias declared *kuffar* in order to stop them from performing their Islamic duty of hajj. In his article, the chief mufti says that we are all equal and enjoy the same rights and will 'live together forever, inshallah'. But does he mean it?

In the second half of February 2012, the Shias of Al-Awwamiyyah escalated their peaceful protests and demonstrations in the eastern region. Peaceful protests were the only measures they could adopt in the face of systematic discrimination, deprivation of rights, and their mistreatment as second-class citizens. In response to the demonstrations in Al-Awwamiyyah, their newspapers threatened that if demonstrations were not called off, there would be genocide and mass killings in Al-Awwamiyyah. Such are the concepts of 'freedom and equality' that they proclaim.

The extremists have morally and financially sponsored projects and satellite TV channels which target every aspect of Shia beliefs. They have published hundreds of books and magazines to promote these objectives and get them distributed free of charge. They have censored the new editions of books which were published decades ago by authors who are deceased. Huge amounts have been spent to spread propaganda against the Shia faith, portraying the Shias as 'products of the Jews'. Their scholars are directly involved in labelling the belief system of the Shias, which is built on the foundation of the Quran and the Sunnah, as being manufactured by the Jews. In this way, they misguide their followers and Muslims around the world against the Shias.

In the article under review, the chief mufti claims that the Iranian pilgrims, prior to the Islamic Revolution in Iran, were considered the best and most beloved of all pilgrims to visit Saudi Arabia. The people used to look forward to their arrival in hajj season for their buying of Iranian products, according to him. He further claims that the Saudis consider Iranian food to be the best. This at least proves that the prevailing discrimination does not emanate at the public level at all. The public is accommodative and innocent of the instigations originating from the highest echelon of the clerical hierarchy against the Shias in general and Iran in particular. Otherwise, if the Saudis prefer Iranian products over all other products and consider Iranian food the best in the world, and there is no problem with the Iranian people, then why did the Saudi religious police attack the Iranian pilgrims and shed the blood of four hundred innocent and disabled pilgrims who were in wheelchairs? The chief mufti forgot what had happened on July 31, 1987, during the reign of King Fahd. Why did the Saudi police carry out a massacre of the Iranian and non-Iranian pilgrims in Makkah in the last pilgrimage season and dump their corpses with bulldozers? These are all well-documented facts which nobody can deny.

The mufti concludes his article by trying to create a wedge within the Shia community, knowing well that by virtue of his position and status, there are many naïve people who would buy his story on face value, even though it is divorced from truth and reality. He writes that the political and religious leadership of Iran has no right to make the Shias enemies to all the nations of the world and especially their Sunni brothers and to make all the Arabs hate the Shias. He further writes that the Saudi Shias will remain Saudi nationals, and the Shias from all other countries of the world will remain the best of *hujjaj* (pilgrims). These expressions were gross exaggerations, filled to the brim with niceties and meant to appease the Iranian people that the Saudi regime distinguishes between the people of Iran and the government of Iran.

The chief mufti claims that the Iranian pilgrims will come back to be loved by the Saudi and the (Persian) Gulf people very soon, 'inshallah' ('God willing'), far from the hegemony of the leaders of the Iranian revolution, according to him. He further alleges that we have to distinguish between the Shias as peaceful nationals and Iran, the expansionist state in the Arab world. He continues that the Shias will remain and the revolution and its people will disappear sooner or later and that Saudi Arabia has more priority over its Shias than Iran. He advocates that the Islamic Revolution and its people will be liquidated, giving himself the right of passing a verdict on the destiny of a nation and its people.

If he were true to his words that the Shias enjoy equal rights with the other citizens in Saudi Arabia, then the Saudi and Bahraini Shias have the right to demand redress for the carnage and destruction the Wahhabis have caused to the holy sites and graves of the imams and the companions of the Prophet in Al-Baqi in Madinah and in the graveyard of Quraysh in Makkah. The Sunnis and Shias (except Salafis and Wahhabis) believe that the desecration of graves, tombstones, and shrines is in stark violation of the Quran and Sunnah.

Having acted as the mouthpiece of the foreign policy of the state, the chief mufti, in the interest of equal rights of the citizenry, could start an undertaking that the harassment by the religious police in Madinah against the Shia pilgrims will stop and everything will return back to normal as it used to be before the Wahhabis took over Makkah and Madinah. Not a single year passes by without harassment of Shia pilgrims. Either he is not up to date with the events, or he is deliberately trying to divert international opinion away from the unpleasant reality on the ground.

On one of the most auspicious days in Islam—the day of Arafat (which fell during the hajj rituals) on 9 Dhu al-Hijjah 1432 AH (5

November, 2011)—in the sermon delivered from the main mosque in Arafat, the same mufti propagated the virtues of his Salafi sect. This was an international gathering in which the majority of the congregation were not subscribers to his school of thought, but they subscribed to other schools. He could have kept himself impartial and talked in neutral terms. But even on this sacred and inviolable day, he was not to miss the opportunity of making sectarian and political gains. In regard to the establishment of the Kingdom of Saudi Arabia, he said that it was formed on the foundation of the Quran and Sunnah. If so, then where does it say in the Quran and Sunnah that when Muslims gain territorial control or conquer any land, they should give it the name of the conquering family? After Ibn Saud took control of the country, it was named after the family name of Aal Saud. Islam had conquered all of Arabia in the lifetime of the Prophet, but he did not give Arabia his family name, which he could have done. Giving the country the name of the family of Saud, therefore, was the biggest *bidah* (innovation) committed in modern history.

In his referred sermon, the chief mufti prayed for the success and long life of whom he called '*imam al-muslimin*' (leader of the Muslims), King Abdullah ibn Abd al-Aziz. Again, this was tantamount to taking undue advantage of the international gathering of hajj. In order to be blessed with this title, some fundamental requirements ingrained in the traditions of the Prophet have to be fulfilled. During his lifetime, the Prophet had explained unequivocally and in the clearest terms possible who is entitled to be the imam of the Muslims.

How can the Saudi monarchs call themselves leaders of the Muslims (?) when for more than two years in succession they are involved in aerial bombardment on the poor and starving country like, Yemen, mostly killing civilians, including women and children, according to several human rights agency reports.

There are reports on several websites which provide ample evidence of the negative role the extremist elements in Saudi Arabia have played in international affairs. The website A Second Look at the Saudis[61] presents a paper indicating that according to the '9/11 Commission Report', fifteen out of the nineteen hijackers (with the sixteenth hijacker missing) were Saudis; 80 per cent of Al-Qaeda members are Saudi nationals; 70 per cent of the trainees in Al-Qaeda camps are Saudis; 95 per cent of the respondents to *The New York Times* survey who approved of Bin Laden's agenda were Saudis; prior to 9/11, twenty-five thousand Saudi nationals had received paramilitary training; behind every major terrorist attack on US soil were Saudi nationals; and that the twenty most prominent donors to Al-Qaeda were Saudis. They were involved in blowing up and desecrating the historic mosque and sacred shrine of Samarra in Iraq. The vast majority of suicide bombers in Iraq were Saudis. Their involvement in Afghanistan and Pakistan goes far beyond mere financial aid.

The 9/11 terrorist attack was meticulously planned, and it was a crime against humanity and a humanitarian tragedy on a mammoth scale. One wonders what message these brutes sought to convey to their closest ally on this planet. Was this the way of repaying the favours to the nation whose leaders guarantee the security and the very existence of the absolute Saudi dynasty? It goes without saying that, never mind the sixteen hijackers, not a single Saudi soul could have possibly participated in this murderous venture without direct approval of the head of intelligence and the authorities. That is why when the American courts sought to try the Saudi government for their alleged involvement in the 9/11 crime, the Saudi government reacted by threatening that they would withdraw their funds from the United States. It must be noted that, since then, the American court has acquitted the Saudi

---

61 A second look at the Saudis website, http://www.asecondlookatthesaudis.com, 4 June 2008.

government from any involvement in the 9/11 terrorist attacks on the US soil.

Mass massacres of innocent civilians of this nature should not have been allowed to pass by in the first place without referring the perpetrators, financiers, and supporters of this horrendous crime, whoever they may be, to the international court of justice in Lahai so that they should spend the rest of their lives behind bars. Yet their politicians and top clerics, sympathising with Al-Qaeda and other militant groups, always make it a point to blame Iran for pursuing expansionist policies despite the fact that Iran has never invaded any sovereign state as they have done in the impoverished neighbouring Yemen. Throughout their war on Yemen, many reports have been issued by the United Nations and human-rights agencies, with warnings from the secretary general of the United Nations, that Saudi bombardment of civilian targets in Yemen[62] amounts to crimes against humanity. Amnesty International, Human Rights Watch, and other agencies reported that the Saudi coalition bombed hospitals[63], medical facilities, schools, orphanages, refugee camps, sources of food and medical supplies, and crowded marketplaces, carrying out massacres of women and children in the process. They responded by accusing the human-rights agencies and the secretary general of the United Nations of being biased. In response to Saudi bullying that it would stop contributing to the UN fund, the United Nations retracted its statement.[64]

---

62 "Yemen: Saudis Using US Cluster Munitions", Human Rights Watch website, https://www.hrw.org/news/2016/05/06/yemen-saudis-using-us-cluster-munitions, 6 May 2016.

63 "Atrocious attack": U.S.-backed Saudi coalition bombs 4th MSF hospital in Yemen, killing 11 people",
http://www.salon.com/2016/08/15/atrocious-attack-u-s-backed-saudi-coalition-bombs-4th-msf-hospital-in-yemen/, 15 August, 2016.

64 "UN: Shameful pandering to Saudi Arabia over Children killed in Yemen Conflict", Amnesty International website,
https://www.amnesty.org/en/latest/news/2016/06/un-shameful-pandering-to-saudi-arabia-over-children-killed-in-yemen-conflict/, 7 June 2016.

From the very beginning of what came to be known as the Arab Spring, Iran has been accused of instigating revolutions in Tunisia, Egypt, Libya, and Yemen; inciting protests in Morocco, Jordan, Muscat, and Oman; planning to occupy Bahrain, Iraq, Saudi Arabia, and the Persian Gulf states; provoking demonstrations outside Wall Street and across Europe; and encouraging Saudi women to commit the 'sin' of driving motor cars. They have stopped short of blaming Iran for triggering the global financial crisis and the collapse of the banking system. These paranoids have already accused Iran in their sermons and media of planning to conquer the Sunni world as a whole, as if the Sunni world is sucking its thumb and playing with dolls.

On May 4, 2012, in his Friday sermon from the Inviolable Grand Mosque in Makkah, Shaykh Abd al-Rahman al-Sudays, the imam of the congregation, used flowery and bombastic language which the overwhelming majority of his congregates could not have understood at all. He chose his vocabulary as if he were participating in a contest of poetry, oratory, and eloquence. The motive was not to advise and offer religious exhortations to tens of thousands of people listening to him around the world on satellite TVs, but to impress the ruling elites, his fellow clergymen, and the government censors responsible for censoring Friday sermons before they are delivered in public. His sermon was based on carefully thought-out symmetrical expressions and rhyme.

The important aspect of his sermon was the appalling political message he passed to impress the authorities, whose policies, in the views of the state clerics, are more perfect than perfection can ever be and whose endeavours are meant to promote peace around the galaxies.

Before making gross exaggerated claims of the peaceful role and wisdom of their highnesses, the imam of the congregation, at the most sacred spot on the face of the earth, according to the Islamic faith, should have shown a little bit of sensitivity to the catastrophe the policies of his country has brought on Afghanistan, Pakistan, Iraq, Syria, Somalia, and Yemen. The imam was not even bothered to study the harrowing human rights records of his country, presented in the United Nations, Human Rights Watch, and Amnesty International reports.

There are some excellent thoroughly researched papers published by think tank organisations, available on line, which discuss in detail the ongoing conflict in Syria, and the role that the foreign countries have played in fuelling the civil war, with $45 billion already spent from 2011 to 2015 in supporting and financing the violent militants, mainly from IS (formerly ISIL) and alNusra front.

The International Centre for the Study of Radicalisation and Political Violence presented its reports on foreign fighters participating in the Syrian conflict.[65] The report focused in particular on fighters from North America, Europe and Australasia. The Institute for Strategic Dialogue in London[66] also presented several papers on the subject (all available on line). The Syrian-German Centre that monitors the Syrian conlict presented startling statistics, discussed in the main news bulletin on al-Mayadeen independent Lebanese TV on 10 August, 2016 (https://www.youtube.com/watch?v=jDMUqYjpfls). It disclosed that between 2011 and 2015, the largest influx of foreign fighters in history, totalling 360,000 entered Syria, of whom, 95,000 were killed. Out of these, 25,800 were contributed by Turkey; 5,990 Saudi militants were killed out of a total of 24,500 that participated. The American and European fighters that participated totalled 21,500. Yet the Syrian army and regime against whom $45 billion were spent remain in tact and are the main forces on the ground fighting international terrorism; whereas, the neighbouring countries who financed insurgency, are left to make lots of garbled noises.

---

65 http://www.trackingterrorism.org/resource/international-center-study-radicalisation-icsr, accessed on 11 August, 2016.
66 Institute for strategic dialogue in London, http://www.strategicdialogue.org/, accessed on 11 August, 2016.

Within the Wahhabi establishment itself, for a long time now, there have been dissatisfactions and defections, which, at the extreme end, gave rise to clerics like Juhayman, who plotted to install his own mahdi (the awaited Messiah) in the precincts of the holy Ka'bah in 1979. This was the most evil plot since the inception of the Wahhabi movement. On the commencement of the new Islamic year of the new century, 1400 AH, this plot was implemented by Juhayman with the connivance of the influential Wahhabi muftis. Bin Baz, the then-chief mufti of Saudi Arabia, maintained his own contacts with the emissary of Juhayman.

This conspiracy resulted in butchery, carnage, and desecration of Islam's holiest sanctuary, with untold damage done to the Grand Mosque in Makkah and its minarets. Under the pretension of carrying out funerals, Juhayman's followers smuggled arms, ammunitions, and food items for his fighters into the Grand Mosque. The government brought French paratroopers inside the inviolable Grand Mosque to fight their homemade terrorists. Juhayman's men declared the appearance of their mahdi near the holy Ka'bah and demanded that the pilgrims, trapped inside the Grand Mosque, pay an oath of allegiance to the terrorist leader. Without caring to find out the facts, the Arabs reacted by blaming Iran.[67]

Like a toothless tiger, the Arab League was meeting in Tunis at the time. But its members refused to meet the Iranian emissary who had flown to Tunisia to reassure the delegates that Iran had nothing whatsoever to do with the assault on *Masjid al-Haram* (the Grand Mosque in Makkah). But they were not interested in hearing anything in defence of Iran.

It eventually transpired that under the very nose of Prince Nayif ibn Abd al-Aziz, the home minister at the time, and the chief mufti of Saudi Arabia Bin Baz, the plot was organised with the participation of the

---

67 Trofimov, pp. 63–69.

Wahhabi elements from several countries. All the captured members of the Juhayman gang were later beheaded. But until this day, the gang leader, Juhayman, has left his heritage in much of the thinking and plots within the Wahhabi establishment. This story has been analysed in greater detail in a work of Yaraoslav Trofimov, *The Siege of Mecca* (New York: Doubleday, 2007).

In conclusion, it is noteworthy that amid a network of plots and conspiracies against countries, like, Iran, Iraq, Syria and Yemen that refuse to bow down to the absolute authority of the Wahhabi establishment of Saudi Arabia, it has been discussed in international media that there are rivalries and divisions even between members of the royal family. In the latest failed coup against the President of Turkey which has left, according to Turkish sources and media reports, around fifteen thousand military, political and academic personnel being put behind the bars, with more arrests yet to come, it transpired that two Saudi princes were involved in supporting the coup in Turkey. The President of Turkey was supposed to be a close ally, whom the Saudi establishment included in every military alliance of Sunni countries against the Shia Iran. But the Saudi establishment is now getting entangled in its own web of plots, from which, it may not get a safe return to its senses.

Chapter 9

THE MISREPRESENTED PHENOMENA

MISCONCEPTION OF JIHAD

The misuse and misconception of jihad have been going on for centuries, since the time of the dynastic hegemony over the Muslim world. Undoubtedly, jihad is one of the principles of religion but with strict conditions and prerequisites. No other principle of Islam has been as misunderstood and misinterpreted as the concept of jihad. Due to this misrepresentation, tyrants like Saddam and Gaddafi had the audacity of declaring jihad as it suited their political interests and for protecting their autocratic reigns. Today, the loudest noises in the name of jihad are made by the violent extremists, who do not have any credentials for declaring jihad.

The word 'jihad' is derived from the Arabic root word 'jahada', which means 'to exert utmost effort' or 'to strive'. Jihad is classified into two categories. The first type is the struggle of the inner self against the self's base desires in order to overcome the temptation to commit evil acts. The Prophet called this type of jihad a 'greater jihad' in one of his widely reported authentic traditions. The second type of jihad is armed struggle for self-defence to repel aggression. This type is called 'qital' in the Quran. The Prophet called it a 'lesser jihad'.

Many radical enthusiasts believe that the term 'jihad' means nothing but armed struggle. This contention can be refuted by quoting an incident in the lifetime of the Prophet. A companion sought permission to go to a battle. The Prophet asked him whether his mother was alive, and he replied in the affirmative. The Prophet ordered him, 'Then stay with her, for paradise is at her feet'. The moral derived from this story is that abandoning one's dependants to live a life of poverty and destitution is not permitted in Islam even if it was for fighting jihad in the company of the Prophet.

As the concept of jihad has caused hysteria at an international level, two extreme views are analysed in this discussion. One is the attitude of the current jihadi movements that have declared war against 'infidels' and, by implication, against Muslims who do not subscribe to their views, who they count as enemies of Islam. Second is the mayhem caused by the ancient Khariji movement, which shares most characteristic traits with the present-day militant takfiris, who form dozens of terrorist groups.

Islamic ethics of warfare require that even if the adversaries kill and maim civilians, Islam does not permit the Muslims to retaliate. The Prophet did not react 'like with like' against his foes. For example, when Hind, mother of Mu'awiyah and wife of Abu Sufyan, the then-chief of the polytheists, disfigured the corpse of Hamza, the Prophet's uncle, by cutting out his liver, nose, ears, and other parts of his body and wearing them as a necklace after the Battle of Uhud (3 AH/625 CE), the Prophet did not retaliate.

The radical groups are in the habit of neglecting the legal and moral aspects of armed struggle, as proclaimed in the Quran and Sunnah. Any warfare in Islam which does not vigilantly guard the life of civilians and the places of worship of other religions and their sources of livelihood and does not treat human life with compassion cannot be called jihad. There are many examples in the Islamic sources which illustrate these points. Yet humanitarian values attached to the armed struggle in Islam are conveniently shelved by the extremists.

Compassionate and merciful are the two attributes of God with which each chapter of the Quran (with the exception of the chapter named 'The Repentance') commences its message. If a Muslim does not exhibit these attributes in his character, then his faith is considered deficient. In a state of war, compassionate treatment to the enemy has been stressed by the Prophet. The enemy has to be forewarned that the purpose is not to grab his wealth or to deprive him of life or freedom. War has to be a matter of last resort after all other peaceful means have been exhausted. If it is unavoidable, Muslims must not be the aggressors. Peace has to be the main objective of war.

The Battle of Badr (2 AH/624 CE) was fought by the nascent Muslim community against the Makkan aggressors after the migration of the Muslims to Madinah. The captives of this battle were fed by their captors with the best food available to them. This was in compliance with the Prophet's instructions. Those who were able to pay ransom were set free. Those who were not able to pay ransom were set free by pledging not to fight the Muslims again. Those who could teach ten Muslim children reading and writing were set free. When the Prophet heard the wailing of the captives, he became restless and could not sleep until the ropes with which they were tied up were removed. The Prophet took the initiative of freeing the captives, and others followed him.

The Prophet abolished the barbaric practices of the pre-Islamic era: torture, corporeal mutilation, driving out eyeballs from their sockets, and splitting the bellies of pregnant women. Disfiguring the dead bodies, stealing their possessions, killing the non-combatants and priests (of any religion) in their monasteries, and destroying trees were all prohibited acts. Destruction of the sources or means of livelihood was prohibited. Burning crops and destroying cattle were forbidden. Therefore, if Muslim powers and the extremist groups today revive all these practices, they are betraying their religion and committing treachery against Islam in the name of Islam. Among the people classified by the Prophet and entitled to the most severe punishment on the Day of Judgement are unjust rulers and mutilators of the dead.

Human life is inviolable according to the Quran, which asserts, 'Take not life, which God has made sacred, except by way of justice' (6:151). The Quran grants a single human life the same honour as the life of the whole of mankind, irrespective of religion, colour, or race. The Quran asserts, 'If anyone kills another person, except as a punishment for murder or for spreading mischief in the land, it is as if he killed the whole mankind. And if anyone saves a life, it is as if he saved the whole mankind' (5:32). The law has to take its normal course, and the legal procedure has to be enforced equally on the rulers and the ruled. But the modern-day concept of justice in the Muslim world has become deviated. The influential and powerful are exempted from persecution for crimes and murders they commit. This is tantamount to making a mockery of law and justice.

The Quran lays down the rule of restraint in hostility: 'And fight in the way of Allah with those who fight against you, but do not commit aggression. Allah does not like the aggressors' (2:190). The Quran proclaims self-restraint in the most trying circumstances to uphold respect for human life. Self-control is most difficult in the theatre of war. But this is a prerequisite of the concept of armed struggle in Islam. A misconception prevails concerning what is known as a holy war. Nowhere in the Quran has jihad been named a holy war (Arabic: al-harb al-muqaddasah). The concept of holy wars as such does not exist in Islam.

When the Prophet entered into a truce after a series of battles with the Makkan aggressors, the Quran called it a manifest victory. On the occasion of the peace treaty of Hudaybiyyah, jihad was fought through a truce, amidst objections by the close companions, against the Prophet's judgement. Yet preference was given to peace. Consequently, reversion to Islam multiplied manifolds.

In contrast with the slogans of the present-day jihadi-cum-takfiri movements, the Prophet used to issue instructions to the warriors: 'Do not kill any old person, any child or any woman'; 'Do not kill the monks in monasteries...Do not kill the people who are sitting in places of worship'. After a combatant surrenders or is overcome, he must not be attacked or tortured. The Prophet prohibited assaulting the wounded. In one of the battles, he was informed that some children of the enemies were caught up in crossfire and were killed. He expressed sadness and displeasure as some companions pleaded that after all they were children of the polytheists. He laid strict humanitarian rules for handling the prisoners. He said, 'No prisoner should be put to the sword'. The killing of captives and the looting of property, farms, and cattle were strictly forbidden under the Islamic concept of jihad. The corpses of the enemies were not to be disfigured or mutilated in revenge for what they did. The Prophet set the example of clemency even towards his deadliest enemies. On the final conquest of Makkah, he forgave his avowed foes.

The sanctity of human life is protected through the concept of justice, which is a central theme in the Quran. Judging with equity and bearing witness only for the sake of God is construed a vital duty (4:135). Under the Islamic concept of justice, and not the modern-day miscarriage of justice prevailing in the Muslim world, a person cannot be arrested arbitrarily. He is considered innocent until proved guilty. Grudges or hostility towards other people cannot be allowed to overcome the irrefutable principle of justice.

Several verses of the Quran and traditions of the Prophet also speak of life as being a form of trust from the Creator. Therefore, committing suicide is ranked as a major sin and considered injustice against one's soul. The Quran declares unequivocally, 'And whoever kills a believer intentionally, his punishment is hell; he shall abide in it forever, and Allah will send His wrath on him and curse him and prepare for him a painful chastisement' (4:93). There is not an iota of vagueness in the verdict of the Quran, and it leaves no loopholes for manoeuvring. Under this principle, the suicide bombers of the present-day takfiri militant movements cannot justify their acts of indiscriminately killing combatants and non-combatants alike.

When armed struggle was sanctioned for the first time, the conditions and objectives were clearly laid down: 'Permission to fight is given to those who are being fought against, as they are oppressed; and most surely Allah is able to assist them' (22:39). Hence, those fighting jihad were not on the offensive side but the defensive side. They were not aggressors. They did not start hostilities, but they were fighting in self-defence to repulse aggression. The next verse continues to describe their predicament: 'Those who have been expelled from their homes without a just cause, only because they said: "Our Lord is Allah"' (22:40). This indicates that the Muslims endured persecution for the sake of their faith.

The Muslim community at the dawn of the Prophet's mission was uprooted from its land and possessions. The believers were separated from their nearest kith and kin and suffered physical and mental torture. In sanctioning armed conflict, humanitarian objectives were spelled out. The same verse of the Quran continues, 'And had there not been God's repelling some people by others, certainly there would have been pulled down cloisters and churches and synagogues and mosques in which God's name is much remembered' (22:40). Therefore, the aim of armed jihad was to protect the rights of the people of other faiths to also practise their faith in peace, without compulsion.

The believers were fighting the polytheist aggressors and the non-believers who were adamant about usurping the rights of the religious communities. This explains why Islam gives protection to all places of worship and exhorts the Muslims to honour this pledge. Abd al-Rahman Azzam writes, 'Another principle stressed in the Message of Muhammad and extremely important in our times is that a pledge may never be betrayed. Islam forbids the betrayal of a pledge, secretly or openly'.[68]

Ibn Kathir, the student of Ibn Taymiyyah and the exegete of the Quran, whose exegesis is widely read in the Sunni world, gives the ruling of Abu Hanifah that a Muslim could be killed for killing a non-Muslim. He substantiates this punishment with the declaration of Umar during his caliphate that, 'If all the residents of Sanaa in Yemen collaborated in killing him (an innocent boy), I would kill them all [the population of Sanaa]'. Remarkably, if the rationale of the caliph is upheld today by the court jurists and the radical ideologues, then all members of the terrorist groups, the agent provocateurs, and the supporters and financiers of international terrorism have to be prosecuted.

The most important aspect of jihad, which is struggle of the self against base animal desires and lust, is shelved by the masses due to their unawareness and by the extremists due to their misinterpretation of the concept to justify their violent stratagem. The Prophet describes the highest form of jihad succinctly—that it is 'to confront a despotic ruler with the word of truth'.

Therefore, it is clear that jihad is not an outright war against non-Muslims or against Muslims of other sects, as the fanatical radical ideologues habitually portray through their rhetoric and polemics and implement into action through their killing sprees, which has surpassed the notorious agnostic Tamil Tigers in ruthlessness.

---

68 Azzam, p. 128.

CRITICAL REVIEW OF AN ACADEMIC STUDY

The voluminous book of Professor Natana Delong-Bas called *Wahhabi Islam* is perhaps the most sympathetic study conducted in the West on the movement of Ibn Abd al-Wahhab, with the bulk of information and financial support (as acknowledged by the author) coming from the King Abd al-Aziz Foundation for Research and Archives in Riyadh.

DeLong-Bas rebuts the belief that Wahhabism is a threat to the West. She disassociates any Wahhabi connection with the 9/11 terrorist attacks or even with Bin Laden. She emphasises that the movement has been very charitable in building mosques. But she does not mention that one of the main conditions of their donations has been the right of appointing imams in the mosques, which are built with their charitable contributions. This attracted much criticism[69] because the indoctrination process into Wahhabism continues targeting the worshippers and congregations in these mosques.

DeLong-Bas claims in her book that nowhere in his corpus of literature did Ibn Abd al-Wahhab encourage the Muslims to seek martyrdom.

It is to be noted that for anybody professing Islamic faith, martyrdom is only a corollary to jihad and results in fighting jihad with its strict preconditions, regulations, and restraints. In all their armed conflicts, the militants of the Wahhabi sect failed to meet the minimal preconditions of jihad. Any warfare where civilians are intentionally targeted and the sources of livelihood of other people are destroyed cannot be called jihad, and those killed cannot be called martyrs.

Ironically, Ibn Abd al-Wahhab may not have encouraged his followers to seek martyrdom because he might have sensed that the peculiar type of jihad his followers would fight around the world would not be

---

69 See Schwartz, pp. 124 and 239.

worth the name of jihad as defined in the authentic Islamic sources of the Quran and Sunnah.

DeLong-Bas continues that Ibn Abd al-Wahhab believed that the only way to face those who violated monotheism was 'to fight such people until they adhere to monotheism'. How could that be possible without resorting to violence in the name of jihad and seeking martyrdom?

The professor writes that Ibn Abd al-Wahhab considered adherence to the 'past juridical rulings' equivalent to associating and being partners with God. He had used the term *qital* (fighting) for jihad, according to her. No matter which terms he juggled, his followers fought the adversaries of their ideology brutally and without a shred of mercy in their hearts. She, however, alleges that the process of fighting was not to kill or annihilate people.[70] This is absolutely amazing as the bloodshed resulted in mass killings and maiming the victims. More often than not, innocent people were massacred.

Ibn Abd al-Wahhab's concept was 'to carry out the duty of jihad at least once a year', the professor alleges. She also claims that the contemporary extremists consider jihad an individual duty when he considered it a joint duty. Ibn Abd al-Wahhab believed that the opponents must be given a fair chance to convert to Islam.

Even if he considered it a joint duty, what was the alternative if the opponents did not convert after the lapse of a 'fair chance'? The dilemma created by Ibn Abd al-Wahhab contradicts his own views on jihad. The professor summarises her findings that he did not call for the destruction of Jews and Christians. Neither did he call for an offensive warfare against foreign occupation nor for the restoration of Muslim power.[71]

---

70 DeLong-Bas (2004), pp. 59–64.
71 Ibid., pp. 201–205, 238, 242.

It can be deduced that Ibn Abd al-Wahhab did not see the Jews or Christians as his opponents. His opponents were Muslims of other schools, especially the Shias. He wanted to convert them to his weird brand of Islam by force. His ideology was vehemently opposed by none other than his own father, Shaykh Abd al-Wahhab, and his own brother, Shaykh Ismail ibn Abd al-Wahhab, both of whom were noble and respectable jurists in their time. This also indicates that he knew that the main threat against the power acquired by him and his followers through bloodshed and treacheries would come from the Muslims themselves and precisely from the people of Arabia.

The alliance that Ibn Abd al-Wahhab formed with the House of Saud exclusively depended on the protection offered by foreign powers. In return for the deals on oil exploration and purchase of heavy arms and weapons, foreign powers became the main underwriters of the Saudi/Wahhabi alliance. The voices being raised in the Wahhabi circles at present, appealing to all Arabs to unite to face their common enemy, is specifically directed at Iran only. This proves that they do not see any other foreign powers as their adversaries.

Professor DeLong-Bas writes that Ibn Abd al-Wahhab argued that memorising the Quran is an innovation. If so, then undoubtedly he opposed what was already a well-established practice from the time of the Prophet until his day and from his days until now. Memorisation of the Quran forms an integral and most vital part of the Islamic studies curriculum in all the Saudi Wahhabi seminaries and even non-Wahhabi seminaries around the world. Almost all the exegeses of the Quran emphasise that the earliest Muslims used to memorise the Quran. The professor covers in detail Ibn Abd al-Wahhab's qualms with the scholars of other legal schools. He accused them of committing *shirk* (associating other deities with God), which DeLong-Bas quite rightly calls 'the worst of all sins in Islam'.[72]

---

72 DeLong-Bas (2004), pp. 43 and 48.

In the aftermath of the covenant entered between Ibn Saud and Ibn Abd al-Wahhab, the exclusive right of political leadership was to be the prerogative of Ibn Saud and his progeny (the amirs), and the exclusive right of religious leadership was to be the prerogative of Ibn Abd al-Wahhab and his progeny (the imams). Ostensibly, this is not how the present Wahhabi establishment works. During the Friday sermons and in the *tarawih*, extra-supererogatory prayers offered every night in the holy month of Ramadan, congregational supplications are offered in favour of the king, who is popularly referred as the 'imam of the Muslims', which indicates that the religious wing is subservient to the political wing. This practice is followed in all religious ceremonies in Saudi Arabia.

In 1940, the chief mufti, Bin Baz, had issued a fatwa against the presence of non-Muslims in the Arabian Peninsula, in line with the thinking of Ibn Saud's Ikhwan (and, much later, Bin Laden). The fatwa fell foul with King Abd al-Aziz. The king (political wing) jailed Bin Baz (religious wing). In this regard, Yaroslav Trofimov writes, 'Bin Baz learned the lesson: a lengthy career that took him to the pinnacle of the Saudi religious establishment'.[73] Hence, in this case, too, the religious wing had to give way to the political wing of the Wahhabi establishment.

The Wahhabis portray themselves as the original Sunnis and the followers of the virtuous predecessors and act as their spokesmen. Their propaganda apparatus works round the clock on the Wahhabi-sponsored media to drive a wedge between Muslims by alleging that the Shias abuse the companions of the Prophet and the first three caliphs in particular. On this basis, they declare the Shias heretics. YouTube is flooded with polemical outbursts against the Shias by foul-mouthed clerics. The contradiction between what Ibn Abd al-Wahhab personally believed and the ways in which his followers have manipulated this issue can be comprehended through a few instances.

---

73 Trofimov, p. 20.

DeLong-Bas writes that Ibn Abd al-Wahhab was in stark disagreement with the other four Sunni legal schools because he believed that at times the rightly guided caliphs themselves 'introduced innovations [*bidah*] that deviated from the Quran and the Sunnah', as she puts it. She continues that he rejected diversity of opinion as a 'source of chaos (*fitnah*)'. He described Abu Bakr's decision that the caliph is a paid official of the State as 'the most astonishing part of his ignorance'. He rejected Umar's ruling on three divorces in one sitting. He accused Abu Bakr of using zakat (alms) 'for his own private and personal use'. He stressed that Abu Bakr's precedent on this matter should not have been followed by the latter caliphs.[74] This means that even the caliphs who are considered by all Sunnis as righty guided have not escaped the wrath of the founder of the Wahhabi sect.

DeLong-Bas writes that Ibn Abd al-Wahhab distinguished between *mushrikun* (associationists who associate partners with God or polytheists) and *kuffar* (unbelievers), with the latter being more serious, as she claims. This contention complies neither with the Quran nor with the Sunnah and does not comply with what the professor has stated earlier on that associationism is the 'worst of all sins'. Her claim that Ibn Abd al-Wahhab rarely charged other Muslims of apostasy does not comply with the fundaments of this movement, which were built on declaring that all Muslims have fallen into *shirk*, or polytheism, which, according to the Quran, is the worst of all sins. It is precisely on this point that Ibn Abd al-Wahhab's own father and brother opposed him vehemently.

Having labelled Muslims who fight Muslims as 'apostates', he simply ignored the fact that all his victims were Muslims. He hated those people who called themselves Muslims but did not succumb to 'his interpretation of Islam', according to DeLong-Bas. This in itself illustrates his intolerance and bigotry. It speaks about his superiority complex, as if he had appointed himself as 'all-knowing, all-wise' sole representative of

---

74 DeLong-Bas (2004), pp. 54–56 and 303.

God on earth. It means that he considered only those who subscribed to his interpretation of Islam as Muslims, dismissing all others as apostates and heretics.

In her work, DeLong-Bas keeps on referring to 'the extremist Rafidah sect of the Shias'. She writes that the godfather of the Wahhabis believed that 'they had rejected Islam altogether' and that they are at par with the Christians, Jews, and Magis.[75] Nowhere does she mention that this is the mainstream branch of the Shias, and they share most religious tenets and principles with the Sunnis. They believe in the same God, they believe in the same Quran, they believe in the finality of the same Prophet, they pray in the same direction, they pray five times a day, they fast for the month of Ramadan, they perform pilgrimage to Makkah, and they share the same modes of worship and values with the Sunnis.

Perhaps that is why Shaykh al-Azhar, Ahmad al-Tayyib, the highest religious authority of the Sunnis, bluntly refused to give way to the pressure of the Wahhabis to withdraw Al-Azhar's recognition of the Shias and their jurisprudence. He said that they pray behind us, and we pray behind them.[76] The problem with the founder of the Wahhabi sect was that he saw himself as the supreme authority over the faith and fate of all Muslims. Only his followers, who were, and still are, a minority among the world Muslim population, were considered true Muslims.

With sincere spirit, the Shaykh al-Azhar thwarted the project of the Wahhabis to further divide the Muslims. The Wahhabis have mustered two main weapons since the commencement of their movement for preaching their creed: coercion and petro dollars. Under the charge of associationism, Ibn Abd al-Wahhab did not spare even the Sunnis,

---

75 Ibid., pp. 48 and 82–85.
76 'Sheikh Al-Azhar Rejects Wahhabi Extremist Call for Withdrawal of recognition of Shia doctrine', http://abna.ir/data.asp?lang=3&id=192741, 20 June 2010.

labelling anybody who dared to differ from his rigid theological interpretation as infidels. He did not go as far as labelling the Sunnis as the
'products of Jews', 'worse than Jews', and 'more deceptive than Jews', as
he and his followers had and have been labelling the Shias up to this
day. One can have a complete picture of their mind-set by logging on to
the websites run by the extremists and listening to their preachers when
they emit poison into the minds of their followers to instigate violence
and hatred against the Shias.

Professor DeLong-Bas speaks of a prominent hadith that 'Muhammad
debated with God the wisdom of appointing a caliph after his death'.
She attributes this so-called hadith to the Shias.

No such hadith exists in the Shia sources. It is a complete concoction
which has flowed from the mind of the founder of the Wahhabi movement and Ibn Taymiyyah before him. The proof of this is that Dr Nasir
bin Sa'd al-Rashid, a staunch Wahhabi himself, in the course of his research came across a handwritten manuscript of Ibn Abd al-Wahhab,
on the basis of which he published his paper narrating this incident of
the so-called debate with God. The research paper of Dr Al-Rashid is
discussed later on. This illusionary debate can be refuted from various
angles.

One of the classical books on the life of the twelve imams from the
house of the Prophet is the ancient source *Kitab al-Irshad* (*The Book of
Guidance*) by Shaykh al-Mufid, the pioneering classical scholar of Shia
Islam. He covers the complete historic event of Ghadir, where the
Prophet received the Divine Order to appoint Imam Ali as successor
after him, which he did in compliance with God's command.[77] There
is not a word about the so-called debating with God in the Shia version
taken from authentic sources. This famous historic incident of Ghadir is
also narrated in many classical Sunni sources.

---

77 Shaykh al-Mufid, pp. 123–125.

Ayatollah Jafar Subhani, in his acclaimed book *Doctrines of Shi'i Islam*, has discussed the Hadith of the appointment of Imam Ali as the successor of the Prophet and the incident of Ghadir. Again, there is not a word about the so-called debate with God. He writes, 'The hadith of Ghadir is accounted *mutawatir* (most authenticated) [with continuous and multitude chains of narrations] being related by the companions, the followers of the companions...110 companions, 89 of those in the succeeding generation, and 3500 scholars of Hadith have transmitted this hadith'.[78]

This is one of the most prominent hadith, thoroughly researched by the Shias. The late Abd al-Husayn Amini (d. 1970) compiled eleven volumes of *Al-Ghadir* in his lifetime, followed by three more volumes published after his death on this historic episode, taken from ancient and modern Sunni and Shia sources.

The Shias do not believe in any narration which says that the Prophet 'debated with God'. They unequivocally believe that the Prophet never had even an infinitesimal doubt about the commands he got from God. He implemented all the commands revealed to him unerringly in his capacity as the most obedient servant and messenger of God. Therefore, this so-called hadith is totally fabricated and has been manufactured by the adversaries of the Shias.

Wilfred Madelung, Laudian professor of Arabic at the University of Oxford, in his celebrated book *The Succession to Muhammad*, gives references from ancient sources, which will remain an important source of reference to the English readers and students of history. In his elaborate and well-researched book, he, too, has not mentioned anything about 'debating with God'. Dozens of references from primary sources can be quoted to refute this allegation of Ibn Abd al-Wahhab and his followers.

---

78 Subhani, pp. 104–107.

Continuing with the critique of the work of DeLong-Bas, she alleges, without giving any reference, that Ali accused the Prophet's wife of 'adultery and whoredom', thus accepting Ibn Abd al-Wahhab's version at face value. Based on his allegations that the Shias accuse the wife of the Prophet of 'prostitution', he justified 'fighting and even killing' them because of their 'defamation of God and Muhammad', according to his witchhunting. This completely nullifies the contention that his movement was 'nonviolent' and 'peaceful'. In light of the fact that, in a clear verse, the Quran absolves the wife of the Prophet from marital infidelity, even the verbal use of such descriptions is improper and insulting.

The Prophet's companions themselves were directly involved in rumour-mongering against the wife of the Prophet, and the rumour spread like wild fire in Madinah. The Prophet stayed away from his house until the revelation absolved his wife from unfounded rumours. But as is quite normal with the followers of Ibn Taymiyyah and Ibn Abd al-Wahhab, at every opportunity they could grasp, they make sure that they hurl some accusations against Imam Ali and the Shias of Ali to incite the masses against them—and, to a large extent, they have been successful. Nevertheless, to accuse the Shia community *en masse* of abusing the wife of the Prophet is, to say the least, mischievous and libellous. It is tantamount to saying that as Salman Rushdie abused the wife of the Prophet in his novel, and as he was born into a Sunni family, so all Sunnis are guilty of insulting the Prophet's wife.

Not only in the case of the Prophet Muhammad, but in regard to all the Prophets without any exception, the Shias believe that the wives of the Prophets were protected by God from marital infidelity. In the case of the wives of Prophets Noah and Lot, the Shias believe that they were not involved in sexual infidelity but infidelity against the religious teachings of these two Prophets.

Ironically, DeLong-Bas writes, 'At no point did he ever suggest that violence of any sort should be used against the Rafidah or Shias'.[79] By studying the history of the Wahhabi movement and the writings of the founder of this movement, from its inception until now, one cannot escape observing that this was the most violent movement which has claimed the lives of thousands of innocent people, especially the Shias. Through his allegations against the Shias, Ibn Abd al-Wahhab dropped the bombshell which proved to be lethal for igniting violence against them from his times up to this day, with the ensuing damage to inter-Muslim relations. Professor Esposito writes, 'Like the Kharijites, the Wahhabis viewed all Muslims who resisted as unbelievers (who could be fought and killed)'.[80]

While discussing legal and jurisprudential matters, DeLong-Bas writes that Ibn Abd al-Wahhab sharply differed with the Sunni Maliki school by giving precedence to the companions' consensus in Madinah, on the basis of which Abu Bakr had authorised, according to him, 'unlawful spending of Zakat for the purpose of bribery' in the public interest. He charged Abu Bakr's stance as an 'awesome lie'.[81] This charge did not deter Ibn Abd al-Wahhab himself from ruling that a simple choice should be given in the public interest to the male captives of, whom he considered as nonbelievers: either an imminent death or payment of poll tax.

DeLong-Bas writes that Ibn Abd al-Wahhab was so concerned about the rights of women that he even preferred the hadiths transmitted through the wife of the Prophet, Ayishah, to those transmitted by Abu Hurayrah, whom he did not count 'at all authoritative', in the words of DeLong-Bas, in the matter of women's rights. She considers Abu Hurayrah to be the 'most misogynistic'. Hence, she supports Ibn Abd

---

79 DeLong-Bas (2004), pp. 86 and 90.

80 Esposito (2002), p. 48.

81 DeLong-Bas (2004), p. 102, quoting Ibn Abdul Wahhab's work *Fatawa wa Masa'il*, p. 40.

al-Wahhab's contention that he showed preference for hadith transmitted by a woman over the hadiths narrated by man.[82]

DeLong-Bas concludes that Bin Laden owes his violent ways to the teachings of Ibn Taymiyyah and his student Ibn Qayyim and Qutb but not to Ibn Abd al-Wahhab. However, Qutb did not advocate use of violence[83] by killing civilians of the adversaries, to which Bin Laden and his fellow terrorists were zealously committed. She is right that the missionary goal is totally absent in Al-Qaeda's approach.

One would be flabbergasted to note that Professor DeLong-Bas claims that the classification of the Saudi monarchs as 'not truly Muslims' was a 'prominent theme in Ibn Taymiyyah's works', as she puts it, and not in Ibn Abd al-Wahhab's.[84] Ibn Abd al-Wahhab and the Saudi monarchy did not even exist in the times of Ibn Taymiyyah. They came into existence centuries later.

DeLong-Bas quite rightly confesses in her notes that many scholars believe that allegations made of un-Islamic superstitious practices prevalent in the times of Ibn Abd al-Wahhab are blown out of proportion, notably to distinguish his teachings from his predecessors'.

In fact, the great fallacy of the so-called superstitious practices became the rallying point to canvass support of the Bedouins in his days and up to our times. This evolved into theological contesting feuds between the Wahhabi movement and all other Muslim schools to show that Wahhabism was different from the rest. Concealed in the marriage of convenience between the Wahhabi movement and the Saudi dynasty, there was a deep-rooted ambition of enforcing their hegemony over all the Muslims in religious and political fields.

---

82 Ibid., pp. 100–102, 126, 207.
83 Ruthven, p. 37.
84 DeLong-Bas (2004), pp. 268, 273–277, 306.

While defending the Wahhabi movement, DeLong-Bas does not re-but the claims made time and again that under the present Wahhabi system in Saudi Arabia, women are not even allowed to vote or hold public position. In fact, Bin Baz, their late chief mufti, had issued a fatwa prohibiting women from driving cars.[85] This is still a contentious issue in the country.

Delong-Bas narrates Ibn Abd al-Wahhab's biased view that infringement of women's rights was committed by the *rafidah* (derogatory nickname for the Shias), which, he believes, served as further evidence of 'their failure to adhere to Islam'.[86] This contention, based on caprices, is typical of the Wahhabi sect, meant to mislead public opinion by acting as prosecutor, judge, and jury against their opponents. To conceal their intolerance and bigotry, they kick the ball into somebody else's court without a prick of conscience that this type of cunningness is employed by those who do not have any confidence in their own convictions.

The Wahhabi clerics formed a squadron against women's rights by promoting their own peculiar interpretation of certain narrations to disenfranchise women from civil rights. At present, there is a movement spearheaded by Saudi female activists in the West, demanding basic civil rights for women in their country. The reports of human-rights agencies bear testimony to the fact that the Saudi regime has faced criticism at an international level for depriving women of their rights.

It was improper and malicious for Ibn Abd al-Wahhab to blame the Shias for infringement on women's rights. This view was as bigoted in the days of Ibn Abd al-Wahhab three centuries ago as it is in this twenty-first century, where, shoulder to shoulder with men, women stand for parliamentary elections and manage one-third of the civil service in Shia Iran, where more than 60 per cent of university students in the

---

85 Schwartz, p. 118.
86 DeLong-Bas (2004), p. 90.

country are women. In contrast, in the Wahhabi state of Ibn Abd al-Wahhab, women are still treated as mere chattel and enjoy no rights to vote or be elected in any type of elections.

DeLong-Bas claims that the writings of Ibn Abd al-Wahhab do not support the view that he admired Ibn Taymiyyah.[87] This claim can be challenged on many grounds. The latter's teachings were adopted *ipso facto* by Ibn Abd al-Wahhab on all matters of theology, including his very hostile attitude against building graves and tombstones. Anybody monitoring Friday sermons delivered from the mosques in Saudi Arabia could tell that Ibn Taymiyyah is often quoted as a religious authority, which means that they follow his interpretations in all theological matters. He reinstated the teachings of Ibn Taymiyyah when all the four Sunni schools of law had rejected them. In his own writings, Ibn Abd al-Wahhab quotes Ibn Taymiyyah frequently.

Professor Khaled Abou El Fadl gives glimpses of the ideology of Ibn Abd al-Wahhab. Any jurists who did not follow the methodology of Ibn Taymiyyah for interpreting Islamic law literally without the aid of reason, logic, or rational argument were considered misguided. All the Shias and the jurists with Shia inclinations were considered apostates; hence, killing them was lawful.[88]

In regard to the practice of destroying tombs, DeLong-Bas alleges, 'The hadith record Muhammad's command to destroy tombs and shrines'.[89] Had such a command ever existed, then leaving the Prophet's tomb intact would have been a flagrant violation of the alleged hadith of the Prophet. She overemphasises that Ibn Abd al-Wahhab was merely following the footsteps of the Prophet. Independent researchers have totally refuted that such a command ever existed. It is based on a

---

87 DeLong-Bas (2004), p. 21.
88 Abou El Fadl (2005), p. 48, citing the work of Ibn Abdul Wahhab's son in *Majmuat al-Tawhid*, pp. 466–493.
89 DeLong-Bas (2004), p. 25.

fabricated hadith, whereby the narrator was assigned the duty, by whoever had employed him as a mercenary, of narrating only this hadith, and then he disappeared into oblivion. Scholars have produced elaborate academic studies on this subject to prove that this hadith was concocted in the name of the Prophet.

There is a world of difference between wiping out idols, which were objects of worship in pre-Islamic Arabia, and wiping out graves, which have never been objects of worship in Islam from the time of the Prophet until now. The Wahhabi scholars implemented the 'death penalty' and carried out 'shedding the blood and confiscating the property' of anybody paying respect to the tombs, according to DeLong-Bas. She writes apologetically that Ibn Abd al-Wahhab condemned these actions because, as she consistently maintains, his teachings were 'peaceful' and 'nonviolent'. However, she accepts that he destroyed some tombs with his own hands. This was perhaps a gesture of peace and nonviolence! He himself laid down the precedent of destroying tombs, and his followers imitated his tradition and caused divisions among Muslims up until now.

STARK CONTRADICTIONS BETWEEN WORDS AND DEEDS

The Salafi and Wahhabi schools have focused all their attention on accusing the Shias of abusing the companions of the Prophet. The Shias do not believe and have never pretended to believe that all companions of the Prophet, who are more than 100,000 in number, are equal in status. How could those who had accompanied the Prophet from the earliest time and dedicated themselves completely to the mission of the Prophet be equal in status with those who had opposed him and fought him until they could not continue with their hostilities? They define a companion of the Prophet as one who met him in his lifetime, even if very briefly. Such companions of the Prophet generally enjoy equal status with those who rendered all the sacrifices for the protection of his mission. The political undertone is quite transparent in this regard. The idea was to raise the status of the deadliest enemies of the Prophet, who had embraced Islam much later as a matter of last resort, with the most devoted and sincere companions.

The scholars of hadith literature have categorised the hadiths narrated in the name of the Prophet into four categories: *sahih* (right or reliable), *hasan* (good), *mawthuq* (authentic), or *daif* (weak). All four categories were narrated by the Prophet's companions. Therefore, there were those companions who spoke the truth and narrated authentic hadiths, and there were those whose narrations were considered unreliable and unauthentic. Yet, at the end of the day, those who were trustworthy were given equal status with those who were considered untrustworthy. It was the Shias who were to bear the brunt of offences committed by their opponents through stark contradictions. The position adopted by Ibn Abd al-Wahhab on the policies of the earliest caliphs or the close companions, discussed earlier, speaks for itself.

The Shias do not believe in the doctrine formulated around some weak and unreliable narrations that all the companions of the Prophet are like stars; whomsoever one follows, one will be guided to the right path. There is overwhelming evidence in the Quran, in the Sunnah, and in history that all the companions of the Prophet were not and cannot be at an equal level. No two human beings are equal in their conducts, perceptions, knowledge, attitudes, and characters. It is a fictionalised dogma to give equal status to two human beings, never mind more than 100,000 companions of the Prophet.

The warnings in the Quran in the chapters called Al-Munafiqun (The Hypocrites) and Al-Tawbah (The Repentance) reflect on the characteristic traits of the hypocrites, which cannot be overlooked in the light of some generalised weak narrations. The hypocrites lived in the surroundings of the Prophet, witnessed every aspect of his life, and interacted with the Prophet for a good part of their lives. But they conspired against him in the theatres of war and in peacetime, forged lies against him, fabricated narrations in his name, defamed his righteous character, and opposed his commands. Among the converts, there were those who had fought pitched battles against the Prophet and against each other.

The Umayyad caliph Mu'awiyah ibn Abi Sufyan, who, with his father, had converted to Islam after the final conquest of Makkah, initiated a vile practice of cursing the chief of the companions of the Prophet and his caliph, Imam Ali ibn Abi Talib, in public, on pulpits, and in Friday sermons. This practice continued throughout the reign of the Umayyads to satisfy their dynastic malice against the closest family and the household of the Prophet.

The Shias can never succumb to any pressure for giving equal status and honour to the hypocrites just because they carry the brand of being the companions. If the followers of the Umayyads had and have the audacity of claiming that there were no hypocrites among the companions and in the surroundings of the Prophet, then the stern warnings in the Quran against the hypocrites expose their lies. Moreover, the warnings in *Sahih Bukhari*, the most authentic book of hadith collections of the Sunnis, draw a scenario on the Day of Judgement, when, in front of the Prophet, some companions will be dragged into the fire of hell. As the Prophet recognises them, he will shout, 'My companions, my companions'. He will be told that he is not aware what they did after him. Of course, these companions could not be the loyal, sincere, and devoted ones but only the hypocrites, whose words contradicted their deeds.

Hence, the evidence overwhelmingly suggests that all the companions cannot be equal in status and equal in knowledge. But the political interest of the rulers, in particular the Umayyads and Abbasids, caused them to misuse the machinery of the state for manufacturing hadiths under which the insincere and disloyal companions were given a safe passage to paradise. This became the blueprint for the schools of Ibn Taymiyyah and Ibn Abd al-Wahhab to follow.

THE CULTURE EMBEDDED IN VIOLENCE

A trend has developed in the past few decades that some converts from the West proceed to the Wahhabi seminaries in Saudi Arabia on scholarship. When they return after graduating, they become preachers. Many of them specialise in promoting Shiaphobia in compliance with their training. One can monitor their tirades on some Wahhabi TV and YouTube channels. The Wahhabi establishment counts upon them to spread the Wahhabi creed among the new converts.

The graduates of the Wahhabi seminaries in Pakistan have converted a whole generation into extremists. As their proselytising mission was encouraged and supported under the dictatorship of Zia-ul-Haq and remained unchecked thereafter, the second generation of extremists has become violent and embedded in crime against the Shias. This found its outlet in suicide bombings, targeted killings, and genocide, with the connivance of some influential people in the government and the country's security apparatus.

The godfather of the Wahhabi movement left no stone unturned in promoting the culture of violence. Dr Nasir ibn Sa'd al-Rashid, a devotee of the Wahhabi movement, embarked upon what he thought was a noble task of introducing one of the handwritten manuscripts of Ibn Abd al-Wahhab after researching its authenticity. The paper was published in Saudi Arabia and freely distributed. It is worth examining its contents to quell any apologetic approach towards his teachings.

Apart from misrepresentations and distortions of the Shia faith, Ibn Abd al-Wahhab compares the Shias with Jews. He writes that the 'ugliness' of the Shias has many resemblances with that of Jews, including their 'shortening or completely shaving the beard and leaving the moustaches; this is the religion of Jews and their brothers in kufr. And conversion of Jews into apes and pigs has [also] been related for some Rafidah [Shias] in al-Madina al-Munawwara and other places that their faces were converted at the time of death and God knows best'.[90]

This type of garbage has emanated from the founder of the Wahhabi sect. He sought to propagate his mission with such indecent and vitriolic manners. If the leader of the sect were alive today, perhaps he would have dropped dead from a heart attack after observing his own closest devotees and followers, especially the entire House of Saud, from the king to the pauper, either shortening or completely shaving their beards. But in all probability, he would have wavered from his position and taken about-turns, blaming the Shias for forcing them to do so. The ideologues of this movement can easily change position on any issue. Never mind about the leader of the movement; even an illiterate man would have thought carefully before passing such remarks, which his own devotees and followers are violating day in and day out.

Then the godfather of the Wahhabi movement compares the Shias with Christians writing that 'they worshipped the Messiah; and similarly the exaggerators among the Shias worshipped Ali and his family...and they go with their wives from the rear side as the Christians do with their women when they are in their menstrual period; and [they resemble with Christians] dressing up like them'.

How can anybody posing as an intellectual engage in demonising others solely on the basis of his lunatic whims? But this is precisely what

---

90 Al-Rashid, pp. 43–44.

he did, passing sweeping accusations as if he had witnessed what people do in the privacy of their homes and in their beds.

This explains the verdict of the Quran: 'The Arabs of the desert are the worst in unbelief and hypocrisy, and most fitted to be in ignorance of the command which Allah has sent down to His Messenger. But Allah is All-knowing, All-Wise' (9:97). It should not surprise anybody that the Saudi youths are reportedly turning towards agnosticism and leaving the faith of their forefathers.

The making of irresponsible allegations carries a strict penalty according to the Quran. If the godfather of the Wahhabis could not prove what he alleges, then his evidence cannot be accepted. The Quran asserts, 'And those who launch a charge against chaste women, and produce not four witnesses (to support their allegations), flog them with eighty stripes; and reject their evidence ever after, for such men are wicked transgressors' (24:4).

His outright condemnation of dressing up like Christians means that the founder of this movement thought that his followers among the House of Saud would never dress up in three-piece suits and neckties. Again, this emanates from a lack of imagination.

Then he compares the Shias with *majus* (Magians) in that 'they believed in two gods, god of light and god of darkness; and the Shias too believe that God created good and the Devil created evil. The Magians married prohibited women [mothers, daughters, sisters] and the Shias do the same'.[91] With blatant lies and a venomous tirade against the Shias and people of other faiths, the founder of the Wahhabi movement heavily relied on the writings of Ibn Taymiyyah, except that in the process of converting people with a sword on their necks, Ibn Abd al-Wahhab broke all the records of brutality, taking refuge behind the power of Ibn

---

91 Ibid., p. 46.

Saud. Even today, the progeny of Ibn Abd al-Wahhab and the progeny of Ibn Saud are so intertwined that they cannot survive without each other's support.

He then calls the Shias 'children of adultery'. He continues, 'May God save us and you O community of Ikhwan from the followers of the steps of Satan'.[92] After having taken a few quotes from his malicious writings, further quotes from this obnoxious work are withheld to refrain from causing offence to the Shias and people of other faiths. Any leader operating in the name of religion has to have foresight and a positive attitude.

Anybody offended by his short-sightedness would have wondered how he would have reacted if he had noticed his own followers and devotees adopting a vulgar lifestyle. *The Guardian* reports, 'US diplomats describe a world of sex, drugs and rock'n'roll behind the official pieties of Saudi Arabian royalty'.[93]

The reference to Ikhwan in the writings of Ibn Abd al-Wahhab shows that he wrote these lines when his murdering clique called the Ikhwan (Brothers) were in power and were converting people to Wahhabism by force and by committing the most outrageous massacres in the history of Arabia. The quotes from his writings expose the mind-set of the founder of this movement, which has deceived Muslims by frivolously using religious slogans and rhetoric. Under the Islamic penal code, punishment has been prescribed in the Quran against any Muslim who dares to accuse others of adultery without producing four eyewitnesses for each case.

---

92 Ibid., p. 42.
93 Heather Brooke, 'WikiLeaks cables: Saudi princes throw parties boasting drink, drugs and sex', http://www.guardian.co.uk/world/2010/dec/07/wikileaks-cables-saudi-princes-parties, 7 December, 2010.

Three centuries after intense misrepresentations, it is quite natural for militants and fanatical ideologues to be conceived in the womb of this movement. The Wahhabis have always accused the Shias of committing *shirk* by seeking assistance and help from other than God. The Shias have religiously abided by the concepts of intercession and seeking help from God through intercessors. But the Wahhabis charge the Shias of committing polytheism, although these concepts are ordained in the Quran and Sunnah.

The essential feature of the Wahhabi movement is that they contradict themselves whenever they deem it expedient. For instance, when the Ikhwan gangsters became a pain in the neck of Ibn Saud, he sought help from the British imperial power to liquidate the Ikhwan, which he did effectively, but only after the British came to his aid. Therefore, when it was politically convenient, they forgot all about God or invoking God directly without an intercessor. Instead, they sought help from Britain. They would never have succeeded in defeating the Ikhwan without the help of the British. Yet the rant about polytheism never applies to them. It always applies to their opponents.

Aburish relates in his book *The House of Saud* that David Howarth, Ibn Saud's critical biographer, had passed his verdict: 'Not even Ibn Saud could say where he would have been without British help, protection and advice'.[94]

If seeking help from other than God is polytheism, as the Wahhabis religiously believe, then what could be said about seeking help and military assistance from the Western powers by entering into contracts worth billions of dollars with them? Shouldn't they have been entering into such deals directly with God without any medium?

---

94 Aburish, p. 23.

We have very briefly explored contradictions in the offensive writings of the pioneers of the Wahhabi movement. We will continue exploring other aspects of these contradictions.

Chapter 10

TOLERANCE AND FREEDOM HELD HOSTAGE

On February 20, 2009, the Shias of the eastern region of Saudi Arabia had gathered in large number in Madinah, outside the cemetery of Al-Baqi, to commemorate a very tragic day in the Shia calendar, that of the death anniversary of the Prophet Muhammad. The peaceful gathering of the mourners was attacked by the Saudi secret police, and several people were injured. No voice of protest was heard in most of the Muslim countries. Nevertheless, this incident is covered in the Human Rights Watch (2009) report.

The clashes continued for five days consecutively. In sympathy with this incident in Madinah, there were sporadic clashes in the eastern region of the country, where arrests were made, which included children, according to the said report. In 2008, King Abdullah led the call for tolerance among the world's religions at the UN General Assembly, but he acted in exactly the opposite way against the Shia population when he returned home. Despite the pledge of the king at the United Nations, the state mufti in March 2012 called for the destruction of Christian churches. The call was condemned by none other than the religious scholars in Iran.

WITH SWORD ON THE NECK

According to the Human Rights Watch (2009) report, despite solemn agreement with the Shia representatives, the Saudi government did not fulfil the promise to curb intolerant statements and discrimination against the Shias. The report highlights an offensive episode that took place on 5 August, 2007, when Sayyid Al-Qazwini was told by the religious police in the Grand Mosque of Makkah that 'the Shias worship the dead (and) stones and rocks'. He was told that all Shias are cowards and that they (the police) will purify the Holy Mosque from the Shias. Indeed, this is their unfulfilled dream since the Wahhabis invaded and took over Hijaz. They notoriously accuse their Shia citizens of fabricated charges, claiming that they insult God or the Prophet or the companions and that they practise witchcraft or sorcery.

On the basis of these false charges, they succeed in getting judgements against the arrested Shias in religious courts for the punishment of lashing or imprisonment, if the accused are lucky. Otherwise, thousands of Shias are being held without any charge or trial for decades in Saudi dungeons. If the United States and other allies of the Saudi regime show determination to remedy or counter the flagrant abuses of human rights, the situation could change forthwith.

With the connivance of the Saudi ruling elites, their counterparts among the Wahhabi clergy signed a statement on 30 May, 2008, stating that the 'Shia sect (is) an evil among the sects of the Islamic nation, and the greatest enemy and deceivers of the Sunni people'. This Shiaphobic statement was signed by twenty-two signatories, but when a Shia religious scholar, Shaykh Tawfiq al-Amir, replied to them in his Friday sermon on 11 June, 2008, he was immediately arrested.

The Wahhabis have irreconcilable differences in faith and beliefs with Hindus, Christians, and Jews, but they would never dare venture to express their spite against them in public because they know that they would not be able to sustain the reaction emanating from their allies in the West.

They have badly failed to bring the Shia communities under their orbit of influence. They have also failed to win over several noble and respectable Sunni communities on their side. They have not succeeded in influencing the most famous Sunni religious seminary in the world, Al-Azhar in Cairo, to withdraw its recognition of the Shia Jafari School and its jurisprudence. Therefore, the only tactic at their disposal is to instigate the Sunnis into believing that the Shias are their greatest enemy. Thousands of Sunnis themselves had been killed by their militias in cold blood in Ta'if and all over the Arabian Peninsula as they were struggling to spread their creed by coercion among Muslims in the early days of the Wahhabi movement.

According to the Human Rights Watch (2009) report, on 24 February, 2009, a Shia religious scholar, Shaykh Jawad al-Hadhari from Ahsa, was stabbed at the entrance of the Prophet's Mosque in Madinah. The stabber shouted, 'Kill the rejectionists'. This was one of thousands of incidents whereby the radicals who have cultivated bitterness against the Shias among their followers through centuries of indoctrination bear the responsibility for crimes committed by their devotees. The Shias consider harming any soul in the precincts of the Prophet's Mosque as blasphemy and an insult to the Prophet. Just because the victim was a Shia scholar, nobody was charged or arrested, which means that the establishment itself was not bothered to punish the murderer. This incident was repeated as recently as July 2016, when a terrorist plot was uncovered to commit suicide bombings in one of the most sacred mosques, the Grand Mosque of Madinah, and to commit mass murder of worshippers on the eve of the feast of Eid at the end of the holy month of Ramadan. Not even the deadliest enemies of Islam would have planned this atrocious act as these psychotic extremists did.

The aforementioned report lists the names of minors who were arrested in the eastern region and held without trial. But, then, it is not uncommon to get sentences passed without trial in Saudi Arabia when the defendants are Shia citizens. Lately, in the holy city of the Prophet, Shia pilgrims have been assaulted by ruffians with the religious police of the state failing to make any arrests.

The Shias are quite aware that transgression is going to continue against them as long as the extremists have at their disposal colossal wealth to implant resentment and carry out false propaganda, which is spreading around the Muslim world like a contagious disease.

In Pakistan, the radical clerics are heavily influenced by the Wahhabi sect with the complicity and cooperation from the state's popular political parties and security agencies. Many of the conspirators in the clerical circles in Pakistan are graduates of the Wahhabi seminary in Madinah. Some political leaders are allegedly on the payroll of the Saudi establishment. Indeed, there are some sites on the Internet which have taken bold steps to name and shame them. Hence, in Pakistan, as in Iraq, even during the holy month of fasting for Ramadan, Shias were killed mercilessly by suicide bombers with hardly any arrests made. Even if they were arrested and charged, members of Al-Qaeda and the Taliban were granted access and safe passage after their supporters broke into high-security prisons and released their fellow militants.

The militants in Pakistan have carried out target killings and ethnic cleansing of the Shias in the country. On one university campus in the United States, two members of the Sipah-e Sahaba (Soldiers of the

Companions) terrorist organisation told their fellow Shia students that they have been informed that it is *haram* (prohibited) even to talk to the Shias because they use black magic on the Sunnis. These students realised that they were duped by their own leaders. But the members of the terrorist organisations in Pakistan, who are drowned in the blood of innocent people, might never realise how their destinies have been ruined by their leaders.

In Saudi Arabia, authorities readily grant permission, with generous government grants and public donations to the Sunnis, to build mosques in the country. The Shias are barred from building any mosque. Even their existing mosques are closed down or demolished, and congregational prayers held privately at homes are banned. In areas where the Shias are in substantial numbers, they are not permitted to hold public prayers or religious gatherings. One could never understand this type of mind-set which believes that, through suppression, it will succeed in changing the faith and beliefs of other people.

These odious measures violate the UN Charter of Human Rights, international law, and the Geneva Convention, but the United States and European nations, who are in the position of being able to exert real pressure, have not shown genuine interest.

Lately, one of the Saudi princesses has taken bold steps to speak out in the media, drawing the attention of the international community towards the repressed status of women in Saudi Arabia, which, according to her, is worse than the condition of women during the pre-Islamic period of Ignorance. Princess Basmah bint Saud, the niece of the king of Saudi Arabia, accused the authorities of corruption and of pocketing $21 billion in US dollars earmarked for the expansion programme of the Grand Mosque. She protested that the wealth of the nation is concentrated only in the hands of a few members of the royal family, while

95 per cent of people in the country live under the poverty line.[95] The princess voiced her concern in interviews on several Arabic channels.

Soon thereafter, another Saudi prince, Khalid ibn Farhan al-Saud, defected from the royal family. Speaking on the Russian TV (RT network) on 12 August, 2013, he said that the authorities suppress freedom of speech and expression and exercise brutality and oppression. Political prisoners have surpassed forty thousand in the kingdom, according to the commentator on the programme. All the power, wealth, and resources of the country are concentrated in the hands of a few members of the royal family, and they are not prepared to listen, silencing all voices of dissent through arbitrary arrests, torture, and long-term prison sentences, according to the prince. He said that the authorities are scared of the Arab revolutions. They enforce arbitrary law, depriving state employees of their salaries. He continued that the ruling regime is not guided by justice. The police and the judiciary are under the interior ministry, which even overturns court orders for releasing political prisoners against whom no evidence is found.

Saudi intelligence forces chase the opposition members inside and outside the country, said the prince. The authorities react with violence and persecution, instead of dialogue, against the opposition who demands freedom. The interviewer asked the prince why, despite human-rights violations in his country, the West and the United States in particular turn a blind eye to all abuses of human rights. The prince replied that their political and economic interests dictate that they maintain the status quo and not offend the royal family. So much for the 'nonviolent' and 'peaceful' nature of the Wahhabi movement.

The UN Declaration on the Elimination of All Forms of Intolerance and Discrimination Based on Religion or Belief specifies that 'discrimi-

---

95 'Princess accuses Riyadh of corruption', http://www.defence.pk/forums/world-affairs/127625-princess-accuses-riyadh-corruption.html, 2 September, 2011.

nation between human beings on the ground of religion or belief constitutes an affront to human dignity'.

In this age of freedom and liberty, the Shias in Saudi Arabia are being oppressed just because they refuse to surrender to the paranoia of the repressors. They have passed through tumultuous upheavals in their history in order to preserve and protect their faith and identities. It is their patience and steadfastness in the face of unjust policies of the rulers and court clerics that has safeguarded their faith.

Professor Mahmood Mamdani vividly draws a picture of the spread of Wahhabism in Arabia. He writes that tens of thousands of unyielding people who were not prepared to convert were massacred, especially the Sufis and the Shias. There followed raids of lootings on the Shia sacred places in Karbala and Najaf, where civilians were slaughtered.[96]

Discussing the same issue in historical context, Stephen Schwartz asserts that in 1802, the Wahhabis took over Ta'if, where they killed men, women, and children.[97] Professor Abou El Fadl writes that under the Saudi-Wahhabi alliance, '40,000 public executions and 350,000 amputations' were carried out.[98] One can visualise a full picture of Ibn Abd al-Wahhab's so-called 'peaceful' and 'nonviolent' movement after studying the history of Wahhabism from its authentic sources, where pages after pages are filled with their massacres and genocides of people of other sects.

A research paper presented by the Islamic Study Circle of Education Department of the Central Mosque in Leicester in the United Kingdom states the contention of Ibn Abd al-Wahhab that 'for the previous 600 years all Muslim had become Kafir/Mushrik [unbelievers/polytheists].

---

96 Mamdani, p. 220.
97 Schwartz, p. 77.
98 Abou El Fadl (2005), p. 64.

Whosoever killed such Muslims would go to paradise'. It further states that at the time of taking an oath of allegiance, he required that Muslims declare that previously they were polytheists and that if they had already performed pilgrimage, then they would reperform it, that their parents died polytheists, and that the well-known religious scholars of the past died polytheists.[99] In this way, he sought to legitimise his political movement, which lacked the basic etiquette of religious principles and ethics.

A study conducted by NGO Freedom House found Wahhabi literature in mosques in the United States preaching to their followers that they should always oppose the infidels 'in every way' and 'hate them for their religion...for Allah's sake', that democracy 'is responsible for all the horrible wars of the 20th century', and that Shia and certain Sunni Muslims are infidels.[100]

Karen Armstrong writes that as the Ottomans did not concur with Ibn Abd al-Wahhab's vision of his so-called 'true Islam', he declared that they were 'apostates' and 'worthy of death'.[101]

Professor Vali Nasr writes that Saudi Arabia's leading cleric, Bin Baz, sanctioned fatwas declaring the Shias apostates. This gave a green light to the Wahhabi clerics to support the killing of Shias. The late Ibn Jibrin, member of the Higher Council of Ulama, clearly advocated the killing of Shias.[102]

There is overwhelming evidence in history that initially Ibn Abd al-Wahhab personally, and then top members of the Wahhabi hierarchy, incited the fanatics to use violence in the name of religion under the pretext that their opponents were infidels, apostates, or polytheists. This

---

99 M. S. Raza, 'The Wahhabi Movement', http://www.islamiccentre.org/presentations/wahhabi.pdf, 12 October 1997, accessed 17 May 2012.

100 http://en.wikipedia.org/wiki/Wahhabi, accessed 17 May 2012.

101 Armstrong, p. 114.

102 Nasr, p. 236.

became one of the rallying points for the spread of the culture of terrorism in the world and provided food for thought to the militants, who are spreading havoc and anarchy as the basis of their political philosophy. The direct result of this philosophy was the birth of the Taliban, al-Qaeda, al-Nusra, and ISIL, the most ruthless and inhuman among all.

The fatwas of the radicals among the Wahhabi clerics were taken by the so-called jihadists as if they were the revealed words of God. From the inception of the movement, Ibn Saud nurtured his gang of Ikhwan and armed them to commit heinous crimes. They became involved in spilling the blood of their opponents under various religious pretensions. The strategy of this movement was based on marketing itself as the only 'true Islam'. Therefore, in the initial period, either the Muslims had to confess that all the previous generations of Muslims were misguided and infidels or let the swords decide their fate. The intellectual works of Shaykh Sulayman ibn Abd al-Wahhab, the brother of the godfather of the movement, are banned in Saudi Arabia because he reacted with revulsion against his brother's movement, which he considered to be blasphemous and misguiding.

Contrary to what the authors sympathetic to the Wahhabi movement suggest, history of this movement is soaked with blood. Thousands had to die just because the godfather of the Wahhabi movement and his followers wanted to coerce others into their brand of Islam. Thousands are dying in this enlightened century of respect for human rights and international law just because the followers of his school are bent on acting on the precedents laid down by Ibn Taymiyyah and Ibn Abd al-Wahhab irrespective of the fact that in the history of religions, no religious leader had adopted the method of preaching hate and violence as Ibn Taymiyyah and Ibn Abd al-Wahhab have done.

If they had followed the teachings of any of the Prophets, then no person would have been killed mercilessly and mutilated in front of his family members and children as they have been doing in Pakistan, Syria, Iraq, and Yemen. The Shias are paying the heaviest price because the Taliban, Al-Qaeda, and other terrorist gangs associated with them have decided that the Shias are not true Muslims, and, therefore, their lives are not worth living. They act as if they have a mandate from God to supervise and assess whose faith is based on pure monotheism and whose faith is not. In his book *Wahhabism and Monotheism*, Shaykh Ali al-Kurani, a renowned scholar in Qum, has discussed the Wahhabis' concept of monotheism from its sources, in which he shows categorically how it violates and contradicts the laws of the Quran and Sunnah.

In his well-researched book *The House of Saud*, Aburish draws a dreadful scenario of massacres carried out by Ibn Saud and his gang of Ikhwan in various cities, including massacres of innocent women and children, in order to conquer and subdue Arabia to comply with the Wahhabi rule.[103] Under the forced conversion strategy of this movement, both Sunnis and Shias living in Arabia had to pay a heavy price with their blood and the blood of their children, who were considered legitimate targets. Three centuries later, civilians killed in 9/11, 7/7, and hundreds of other terrorist attacks were considered legitimate targets.

THE POLITICS OF *BIDAH* (INNOVATION)

The blatant double standard of the Wahhabi establishment is observed in their austere attitude in prohibiting the celebration of the birthdays of the Prophet and other religious personages under the pretext that the Prophet's companions did not celebrate it and, therefore, it is an innovation in religion. Their opponents have a right to ask if the companions celebrated the national festival of Al-Janadriyyah, which the House of Saud have innovated and are adamant in celebrating despite objections from some of their own clergy.

---

103 Aburish, pp. 23–24 and 27.

The year 2012 was the twenty-seventh year of these festivities, with music, dancing, and mixing of males and females, all of which are supposedly strictly prohibited under the Wahhabi religious order. In reply to the objections of their clergy, the son of the king, the Protector of the Two Sanctuaries, publicly defended the festival that it is a cultural event. When they introduce innovations, they totally exempt themselves from the criteria by which they accuse others of being innovators and violators of Islamic piety and injunctions. Did the companions celebrate the National Day of the State, which they do, by declaring it a public holiday? Yet no public holiday has been declared on the anniversary of the Prophet's birthday.

By labelling any act as an innovation in religion, their extremist ideologues find themselves in a dilemma. Most of the modern amenities, discoveries, and instances of scientific and technological progress did not exist in the time of the Prophet. Should these be discarded? There were no automobiles or air travel in the time of the Prophet. People used to travel mostly on camels. Should the mode of travelling on camels and mules be revived? The companions led congregational prayers wearing robes, while, in a number of countries today, the imams leading congregational prayers wear three-piece suits and smart neckties. This was not the attire of the Prophet and his companions. Paradoxically, once they are outside the boundaries of their mosques, the same clerics start lamenting about the spread of *bidah* or innovation. No Wahhabi mufti has publicly denounced the clerics for adopting Westernised dress codes in congregational prayers because they know that they cannot afford to enter into a feud with their fellow clerics in the Sunni communities of Egypt, Lebanon, and Jordan.

The pretensions or duplicity behind the slogan of *bidah* can be unveiled by considering a few practical examples. The Grand Mosque in Makkah did not have a tiled floor in the time of the Prophet, it did not have tall minarets, the Ka'bah was not of the same size it is now, and the slaughter of sacrificial cattle as part of the hajj rites used to take place within the boundaries of Mina, not outside its boundaries as is done at present.

Superficially, the Wahhabis believe that the belief system should be practised as it was practised by the virtuous predecessors. Hence, they have developed resentment against the study of philosophy and logic simply because these disciplines, according to them, are not in the Quran and the Sunnah.[104] Their discourses carry minimal references to philosophy and logic because they believe that these disciplines are the products of infidels. But the establishment of a stock market and of speculative investment, directly borrowed from the Western capitalist system, is quite permissible in their society.

When telephone lines were first introduced in Saudi Arabia, the Wahhabi muftis issued a fatwa that this was the act of Satan. Ibn Saud sought to solve this predicament. So a representative of his muftis was asked to listen to the telephone call, wherefrom a voice on the other side recited the testimony of faith: 'There is no God but Allah and Muhammad is the Messenger of Allah'. He asked them, 'What type of Satan might this be to have recited the testimony of Islamic faith?' So the problem was solved.

One of their clerics issued a fatwa that in order to stop the mixing of men and women during pilgrimage, the Grand Mosque in Makkah should be demolished and a new one built with separate facilities for men and women. But in this case, the cleric did not need any precedent from the lives of the Prophet or his companions simply because there was none. Never has pilgrimage been performed with separation of men and women around the Ka'bah. So whenever it suits their wishes and psyches, they have no hesitation in superimposing their conjectures on the Sunnah of the Prophet and his companions.

---

104 Faqihi, p. 227.

One can virtually count hundreds of new phenomena in mundane and traditional life which were simply nonexistent during the time of the Prophet. Yet the concept of *bidah* is being overstretched to express resentment against anything that the ideologues do not like. On multitudinous points of duplicity, one can cite some more interesting instances which make this movement, and its clerics and media, the last on earth to judge other people and hurl abuses and accusations at them.

In his book, Schwartz talks about 'airport Wahhabis', who, as soon as their private jets left the airport runway, would unveil their real faces. In the circles of the rich elites, bottles of whisky would appear, and women's veils would disappear. He draws a scenario of Saudi luxuries and 'sexual enslavement and the exploitation of children'.[105]

BETWEEN DEMOCRACY AND TYRANNY

Whatever diplomatic immunity the oppressive caliphs of the Umayyads and Abbasids and other tyrants could have aspired to, it was granted to them by their prominent court jurists. This was a mockery of the Quran and Sunnah because the caliphs and dynastic rulers were not considered accountable for their misdeeds and crimes against the state and its people.

In the wake of the Arab awakening in 2011, the public unreservedly rejected the juristic rulings which kept on urging the masses to obey the depots and not to rise against them or else risk breaching the shariah. The masses in Tunisia, Egypt, Libya, and Yemen decided that it was high time to lay down counterprecedents by overthrowing the dictators and opening up avenues for changes in the countries afflicted with similar predicaments.

---

105 Schwartz, pp. 116–117.

The juristic rulings urging passivity in favour of oppressive rulers took no heed of the Prophetic admonition which says that there is no obedience to the creatures in disobedience to God. To oppress the creatures of God is the worst disobedience to God and His Prophet, as could be proved from many verses of the Quran and Sunnah. If the community reaches an agreement to install someone in power who does not follow the guidance of the Quran and the Prophet, can that community be called a community of believers? Professor Abou El Fadl rightly comments in his well-researched scholarly books that 'the obedience traditions were part of the Umayyad campaign against their opponents'. The same weapon was later on used by the Abbasids against the Umayyads. Both of them saw the direct descendants of the Prophet and their followers as their rivals and the biggest challenge to their autocratic authority and oligarchic reign.

The history of nations indicates that power obtained through usurpation and repression lacks stability, even if it is supported by military force. One of the core principles of Islam is to abide by justice and to adopt moderation. This cannot be done by violating the dignity of fellow humans. This is why the Islamic community is called the 'middle nation', according to the Quran (2:143), free from any extremes. But, sadly, the court jurists played a major role in demoralising the Muslim community and in imposing upon them unrepresentative rulers.

In his elaborate study, Kamali discusses the essence of democracy that it is based on freedom of self-expression but not freedom to offend. The individual's right to voice his opinion on matters pertinent to him is guaranteed in Islam. He further states that *hisbah* (calling towards right and preventing evil) is a collective obligation of the community. He discusses the central role this concept plays in keeping the authorities in check. This is allied with the right of consultation in the affairs of the community.[106]

---

106 Kamali 1997, pp. 11, 28, 31 and 41.

In practice, it is not as straightforward as that. All the dictators that fell from grace in the Arab awakening claimed that they ruled by consultation and that Islam was the law of the state, when they were miles away from Islamic polity and piety. Even heads of the states under absolute monarchs are claiming that they rule on the principle of consultation. Yet it is public knowledge that the vast majority of their citizens are disenfranchised. If there was anything called principles of consultation and democracy in their political order, they would not have jeopardised the interests of their own states by creating menace in neighbouring countries.

Noorani quotes V. A. Syed Muhammad, a distinguished lawyer, who summarises the principles of democracy in Islam as the right of 'life, liberty and security...freedom of religion, thought and expression; freedom of movement; right of education'. He further quotes, in the same source, the Prophet's tradition: 'He who knowingly lends support to tyranny is outside the pale of Islam'.[107]

Today, debate is raging in the Muslim world over the need to reform antiquated political systems. This debate has led to questioning whether Islam and democracy are compatible at all and whether universal suffrage of men and women can be implemented in Muslim countries in the twenty-first century. There are constraints which cannot be overlooked. Secularists believe that religion must be separated from politics. The advocates of Islamic political order insist that religion is part of politics. The radical ideologues hasten to pronounce the verdict of *kufr* and polytheism on whosoever dares to advocate democracy or the democratic system.

Shaykh Faysal, a graduate from Madinah University in Saudi Arabia, writes in his book *Islamic Psychology* that the cause of nationalism is the collapse of the caliphate. He turns a blind eye to the fact that the

---

107 Noorani, p. 100.

institution of caliphate itself was totally undemocratic and had reached the apex of corruption and abuse of power before its dissolution. The caliphate had become rotten at the core. But the proponents of caliphate are not interested in exploring the underlying factors that caused its doom. Rather, they believe that its reestablishment will solve all the problems Muslims are facing. Had they cared to study historical facts rather than espouse dogma, they would have discovered the extent of corruption and injustices that had plagued the Muslim community during the era of the tyrannical dynastic caliphs. In their zeal to establish caliphate, as soon as ISIL declared that new caliphate has been established in the Syrian town of Raqqa, with Abu Bakr al-Baghdadi as the new caliph of Muslims, the fanatical ideologues rushed from many Muslim countries to avow him the oath of fealty. The world has seen nothing but destruction and suicide bombings since this so-called caliphate came into existence. The latest condemnation has emanated by none other than the chief of al-Qaeda, who called it 'an evil caliphate' and accused the caliph of ISIL of perpetrating crimes against and murder of innocent Muslims.

Shaykh Faysal claims, in his study referenced above, that Ahmad ibn Hanbal, with whose school the Wahhabis claim affinity, had memorised one million hadiths.[108] He does not explain why, if he had taken the pain of memorising such an incredibly vast number of hadiths, he chose to collect only a few thousand in his encyclopaedic *musnad* (confirmed collection of hadiths), available in libraries and on line. What was the point in memorising all these hadiths, the vast majority of which he had to discard and write off anyway? To allege that he memorised one million hadiths, there must have been at least two just witnesses, according to the requirement of the shariah law, who could vouch for this fact impartially. These witnesses must themselves have been knowledgeable about the contents of the alleged one million hadiths, testifying

---

108 Faisal, p. 45.

to their authenticity and genuineness. But history has not recorded the narrators and transmitters who had heard one million hadiths from the Prophet.

Continuing to review the exaggerated and incredible claims of Shaykh Faysal in his work referred above, he denounces the Muslims who believe that elections or democracy are the only avenues of gaining power. He stresses that the only language the *kafirs* understand, is jihad. Many references have been made in his work to jihad while denouncing democracy. When the public is hammered with this type of preaching, the net result is fanaticism as it promotes the idea that the only means available to the Islamic parties is to acquire power through violence.

CONTRIBUTION OF THE WEST IN BREEDING MUSLIM EXTREMISM

Karen Armstrong, a modern British writer and ex-nun, has written extensively about Islam and discussed the issue of what she calls 'fundamentalism'. She defines this term as 'a form of nationalism in religious disguise'. She writes that rarely has IRA militancy been branded as 'Catholic terrorism', nor has such a description been given to the fundamentalism in Israel or to the Christian right in the United States. As a result, she dismisses the term Islamic or jihadist 'terrorism'. Armstrong rightly asserts that Muslims take offence at the distorted representation of their faith. She is pragmatic in her observation that Qutb entered Nasser's prison as a moderate, but the physical and mental torture converted him into a hardliner.[109]

The distortions of Islam to which Armstrong briefly refers have played a vital part in instigating extremism in Muslim societies. The

---

109 Karen Armstrong, 'Blame Politics, Not Islam', *The Hindu*, http://www.thehindu.com/2005/07/12/stories/2005071206991100.htm, 12 July 2005; posted in *The Guardian*.

Prophet, the Quran, and Islam have all come under persistent attacks in the writings of many Orientalists. In his elaborate book, Jabal Buaben of Birmingham University critically analyses medieval and twentieth-century Orientalist writings. He quotes Norman Daniel that these distortions were viewed by succeeding generations 'through the eyes of their predecessors'.[110] In this way, a negative legacy has been perpetuated.

The worst assault in living memory on Muslim–Western relations was the saga of *Satanic Verses*, the most offensive novel by Salman Rushdie, the aftereffects of which have been researched by Professors Kidwai and Manazar Ahsan, the director general of the Islamic Foundation. Muslim leaders and intellectuals campaigned for freedom of speech to be distinguished from vitriolic language. In the said novel, pornographic and abusive expressions were used against the Islamic faith, Islamic sanctities, and revered personages.

In a democratic society, religious communities are free to practise their tenets and to preach their faith and beliefs publicly. At the same time, nonreligious communities are also free to remain agnostics or atheists if they choose to. They have the right to criticise religious dogmas in public. To bar freedom of expression in this area is tantamount to restricting civil liberties, according to the protagonists of the system. But Muslims argue that they are not against criticism. On the contrary, they have faced and replied to criticism against their religion and beliefs for centuries.[111] It is also one of the features of a democratic society to promote congenial and peaceful community relations and to stop flagrant abuse of the system under the pretext of freedom of expression.

Ahsan and Kidwai point out that contradictory overtures appeared in the name of free speech. They quote several instances when censorship

---

110 Buaben, p. 304.
111 M. H. Faruqi, 'A new "value" in new world order?', *Impact International*, vol. 28, no. 5, May 1998.

was voluntarily accepted by the press and media.[112] The overwhelming majority of Muslims saw Rushdie's novel as a premeditated attempt to blaspheme the most revered personages of Islam. The West stood united against withdrawing the book despite the testimony of the chief rabbi, bishops, Lord Shawcross QC,[113] and several other dignitaries that the book was very offensive and provocative. President Jimmy Carter wrote, '*The Satanic Verses* goes much further in vilifying the Prophet Muhammad and defaming the Holy Koran'.[114]

Ahsan and Kidwai, through several examples, illustrate the self-censorship prevailing in the West. At times, offensive books have been withdrawn and pulped. They write that in this case, the offences on the Quran and the Prophet were defended in the West in the name of freedom of speech amidst many objections. Muslims argued that if the author had used scurrilous language against a living person in his novel, there would have been recourse to the law of defamation. He portrayed the Prophet Muhammad and his wives in the most obscene manner imaginable, which he had planned consciously and not in a dream. And yet they could not bring any legal action simply because the law of blasphemy in England only applies to the Christian faith.

The Danish newspaper *Jyllands-Posten* published cartoons depicting the Prophet as a 'terrorist'. Despite worldwide protests, the Muslim community was snubbed in the most insulting manner as these cartoons were subsequently published in many newspapers in Europe under the pretext of freedom of expression. These double standards encouraged the Dutch filmmaker Geert Wilders to conceive of making an offensive film against the Quran and calling it *Fitna* (*Mischief*).

---

112 Ahsan and Kidwai (eds.), pp. 163–164.
113 Ibid., pp. 86–89 and 123–125.
114 Ibid., p. 90.

On 12 February, 2006, a cartoon showing a bomb with a burning fuse attached to the Star of David was cancelled in European newspapers as it would have offended the Jews. But the sentiments of Muslims carried no comparative value. It did not matter to the European countries concerned that they were discriminating against their own citizens on the basis of religion or race.

Many examples of self-censorship can be cited where Western newspapers and media have voluntarily imposed upon themselves restrictions or have succumbed to the pressures of some pressure groups. The *Muslim News* editorial writes that in 1989, a film called *Vision of Ecstasy*, depicting St. Teresa of Avila caressing the crucified body of Jesus, was banned in the United Kingdom. In 2003, an application to register Jesus as a trademark to sell jeans in Britain was refused and considered 'morally offensive to the public'. In January 2006, W. H. Smith removed two titles, *The Protocols of the Elders of Zion* and *The International Jew*, as they were meant to be offensive to Jews. A French court found Al-Oalam Publishing House guilty of anti-Semitism for publishing *The Other Face of Israel*. But if similar anti-Islam and anti-Muslim offences were committed, then no such action would have been taken.

A new offensive term, 'Islamofascism', was coined and used by neo-conservatives in the United States in the era of George W. Bush. In the wake of the foiled aviation terrorist plot, ex-President Bush himself said that the nation is at war with 'Islamic fascists'. Despite protests from the Muslim community worldwide, US Defence Secretary Donald Rumsfeld reiterated the same expressions two weeks later. The counterreaction came from the United States's closest ally in the Middle East in the Friday sermon from Makkah on 1 September, 2006, where the congregation was told that these types of descriptions and defamation of Islam encourage extremism and terrorism.

Another case in point is the scandal of the Dutch lawmaker Ayaan Hirsi Ali, of Somali origin. She had lied and committed forgeries on her asylum application to the Netherlands. Still, within a short period, she was awarded nationality and elected to parliament.[115] She had been preaching what certain political parties were vying to hear—hostility towards Islam. But the lies she spoke to obtain asylum were already public knowledge before she was elected, and her forgeries had been exposed even before the immigration minister faced resistance from political parties to revoke her nationality.[116] Yet she won an offer of employment from the neoconservative think-tank the American Enterprise Institute as she contemplated leaving the Netherlands.[117] On June 30, 2006, the Netherlands government collapsed on resignation of the Prime Minister, because of this scandal. One may wonder that if Hirsi were not anti-Islam or pro-Israel whether she would have been given the same VIP treatment. Was the Hirsi affair worth the scandal and political crisis in the country? This is the effect of bigotry prevailing against Muslims in the West.

The communiqués of human-rights groups are replete with records of torture of political prisoners in most Muslim countries. But if the dictatorial and repressive regimes are close friends of the West, they face very little or no condemnation at all. The societies that systematically practise torture are the ones that produce the largest number of fanatics and violent extremists.[118] The undesirable backlash combined with sensational media coverage is responsible for what is called 'Islamic terrorism'. Professor Mamdani observes that both genocide and terrorism have a common denominator—both deliberately target civilians.[119] Parvez Ahmed writes, 'A word search on news stories published in major

---

115 http://news.independent.co.uk/europe/article485483.ece, 17 May 2006.
116 'Dutch minister under fire over MP asylum row', www.reuters.co.uk, 17 May 2006.
117 'Somali-born Dutch lawmaker welcome in US: Zoellick', www.reuters.co.uk, 19 May 2006.
118 Abou El Fadl (2005), p. 166.
119 Mamdani, p. 11.

newspapers over the past decade shows that reporters are one hundred times more likely to associate Islam with terrorism or militancy than all other faiths combined'.[120]

It may be concluded that Muslim masses are losing confidence in the policies of the West and believe that it applies different standards to the oil-producing countries because of its unquenchable thirst for their oil. If Western nations had abhorred and condemned unequivocally the repressive policies of their allies and if they had supported demands of the masses for representative governments, then no ally of the West would have carried out brutal repression, torture, and intimidation against political opponents as they do. But the application of two different standards, depending on whether the abusers are their political allies or adversaries, has emboldened the dictatorial regimes to continue suppressing their public and turning people towards extremism.

In a TV interview given by President Asad of Syria on the American network NBC on 14 July, 2016, he said that the terrorism of ISIL could stop forthwith if only Turkey, Saudi Arabia, and Qatar would stop supporting and financing them. Unfortunately, all three of them are the sweethearts of the West, especially the United States. If the United States could not put pressure on its allies, then the least it could do is get their funds in all the Western banks frozen in favour of the victims of terrorism. As these lines are being written, news is coming in of the dreadful massacre committed in the French tourist town of Nice, where eighty-five civilians, most of them tourists, were killed in cold blood, and hundreds were injured. The savage ISIL proudly claimed responsibility. If the accounts of the sponsors of international terrorism are frozen, and when they realise that they might have to live on charity for the rest of their lives, this lunacy might stop; otherwise, it will continue, taking the Western countries and the world at large for a rough ride.

---

120 Parvez Ahmed, 'A Sensible Way to Describe Terrorists', CAIR-DFW Newsletter, 23 May 2006.

Chapter 11

RADICALISED DOCTRINES

There are many cultural and customary impediments in Muslim societies which degrade the honour bestowed upon women in Islam. Because of these impediments, people in the West think that Islam is exploitative towards women and repressive of their rights. But as they have different roles to play, they are treated differently in view of their emotional and mental conditions. For instance, Islam takes into consideration that there are some physical duties that women are not suited to perform.

The daily scene which has now become too familiar is that woman stands side by side with man in the revolutions of the masses in several countries. She suffers the same repressive measures and takes all the beatings on the streets while demanding democratic rights and freedom.

Islam does not adopt the view that a woman is the 'root of human misery'. Man and woman are seen as a source of love and affection, sharing duties and responsibilities in society.

RADICAL PORTRAYAL OF WOMEN

Human society is a male-dominated, chauvinistic institution in Muslim as well as non-Muslim cultures, in the West and the East, and in the North and the South. In pre-Islamic Arabia, females were considered mere chattel with no basic rights and treated as sexual objects[121] to be used and then disposed of. But under Islamic laws, they emerged as partners with males and were accorded unprecedented rights and status.[122] Women were given the right of inheritance from their parents' and husbands' sides[123] Functional roles or duties in socity and family structure were distinguished on the basis of physical and emotional formation and strengths and weaknesses.[124] The Prophet said that paradise lies at the feet of the mothers,[125] stressing the special respect that Islam attaches to the unique status of the mother.

Humans came into existence without their own will and power. According to the Islamic faith, the omnipotent power determined for them their attributes, potential, and abilities and supported and guided them with values. In Islam, the ties of universal kinship and family are derived from the ties with God. The Prophet said, 'The tyrannical aggression and the severance of the ties of kinship are punishable in this life and the Hereafter'. Neither the role of man nor the role of woman is dispensable in human society. Their nature makes them mutually complementary.

Professor Abou El Fadl criticises the views of radicals which says that 'women will constitute the vast majority of the residents of hell' and that 'most men in hell will be there because of women'. These types of narrations vitiate the respect accorded to women in Islam. The motive

---

121 Haykal, pp. 318–319.
122 Osman, pp. 853 and 858.
123 Mutahhari, p. 157; Osman, pp. 850– 852.
124 Mutahhari, pp. 64–67.
125 Afzalur Rahman, p. 394.

of every single injunction on women in the Quran is 'to protect women from exploitative situations'.[126]

But if this matter is examined in the context of the attitudes of extremists and their ideology, then the wide disparity between them and the true Islamic perspective becomes clear. Putting a ban on women's education and work simply does not comply with human dignity and values. The traditions of the Prophet emphasise the need for women to acquire knowledge. Yet these specific instructions did not deter the destruction of girls' schools by the Taliban[127] during and after their downfall. During their reign, they had closed sixty-three girls' schools.[128] Their brutality defied human dignity. This is one of many situations where the extremists behave as if the Quran and Sunnah have to be subservient to them and surrender to their whims and caprices.

The Quran draws equality but not similarity in physical structure between men and women (33:35). The nature of men and women is nurtured around these characteristics. In disparity with the values reflected in the Quran and in the Prophet's Sunnah, emphasising respect towards women, there is a male-chauvinistic bias in the radical juristic attitude. For instance, some weak traditions are narrated, which have been given legitimacy by juristic rulings, that say that a man must refrain from sitting where a woman once sat lest he is sexually aroused and that he must wait until the woman's bodily heat fans away in the air.[129]

---

126 Abou El Fadl (2005), p. 262.

127 'Girls School Attacked in Afghanistan', *Feminist Daily News Wire*, 24 June 2005, http://www.feminist.org/news/newsbyte/uswirestory.asp?id=9118, and Greg Bearup, 'Girls poisoned by militants for going to school', 3 May 2004, http://www.guardian.co.uk/afghanistan/story/0,1284,1208299,00.html.

128 Ruthven, p. 111.

129 Abou El Fadl, *And God Knows…*, pp. 18–19, quoting Ibn Ahmad al-Makki, *Manaqib Abu Hanifah*, p. 132.

The Prophet is widely reported to have stood up for the funeral of a Jewish woman. When his companions objected, he reminded them that she was, after all, a human soul. Among the hadith compilers, Al-Tirmidhi and Al-Nasa'i concurred on the Prophet's practice of standing up on such occasions as a sign of respect. Malik, Abu Hanifah, and Shafi'i believed that the practice was abrogated. Ibn Hanbal and Ibn Ishaq (d. 282/896) believed that this was a matter of individual choice.

Professor Abou El Fadl gives several examples which, as he states, are based on fabricated traditions meant to degrade the status of women in Islam. Al-Nawawi believed that standing for a funeral is not preferred, whereas others said that it is recommended. 'Al-Sanadi said that sitting down is permissible but standing is preferred'. This means that on one single tradition of the Prophet, prominent jurists differed among themselves between standing and sitting and between permissibility and prohibition for standing in honour of anybody at all. This shows that a very simple ethical issue was transformed into a juristic contest and disagreement.

Ibn al-Jawzi (d. 597/1201) rules that a woman is a slave of her husband; she cannot refuse sex even if her husband demands it on the saddle of a moving camel in the course of travelling and that she should 'lick his puss-filled ulcers if need be'. The jurists tend to abide by the text and literal meaning of the tradition if it is quoted in what they consider to be authentic sources. For example, *Sahih Muslim* reports that the majority of the dwellers of hell will be women and that harm done to men is because of women.[130]

Sahih al-Bukhari narrates that the wife of Umar, the second caliph, reported to him that the Prophet's wives were argumentative with the

---

130 *Muslim* book 36, *hadith* nos. 6596, 6597, and 6603, http://hadithcollection.com/sahihmuslim/164-Sahih%20Muslim%20Book%2036.%20Heart%20Melting%20Traditions.html, accessed 8 April 2012.

Prophet, and one of them abandoned him from morning till night. Ibn Hajar narrates that one of the Prophet's wives angered him through her arguments.[131] But the Prophet never abandoned his lenient and compassionate disposition towards them. Despite the widely reported compassion and mercy in the life of the Prophet, Ibn Hanbal reports that the Prophet said, 'Beware of this world and beware of women, for the first affliction that the children of Israel suffered from was that of women'.

Ibn Kathir, the student of Ibn Taymiyyah, quotes his sources that if the wife declines to come to bed when her husband requires her, 'the angels will keep cursing her until morning'.

Abou El Fadl produces a list of references which claim that the husband must be obeyed even if he is 'unjust and oppressive'. He expresses his concern that Islamic discourse is falling prey to certain ideologies that tend to interpret the text as if they enjoy exclusive authority over it. He believes that the specific points of law should be evaluated in the light of the universals in scripture. Human lethargy and scepticism towards intellectual challenges should not be construed as 'God's Will'. Commitment of ugly acts should not be blamed on God's intent. Instead of indulging in fantasies, one should have the guts to face the ugliness within oneself. Human interpretation is fallible. When it acquires 'ugly authoritarianism', it tends to act as an antithesis to everything that is represented by God's beauty and morality in the scripture.[132]

The negative attitudes of the radical ideologues in relation to the status of women emanate from a superiority complex under which a woman is not allowed to drive a car, lest she drives a stranger when she is alone in her car. But this mental complex does not apply if the woman travels in a taxi as a passenger with a stranger.

---

131 Abou El Fadl, *And God Knows...*, pp. 57–67.
132 Ibid., pp. 74, 152–155.

As a reaction to the attitude of the radicals, feminists believe that although the Quran improved the status of women, many of the reforms introduced by Islam in regard to the rights of women were simply ignored by the later generations. Consequently, the position of women in Muslim societies far worsened since the time of the Prophet.

Fatima Mernissi is among the outspoken Muslim feminists who developed a critical approach against the traditionalists' interpretation of the Quranic text in the light of certain hadiths, especially those narrated by Abu Hurayrah, one of the main narrators of *hadiths* in Sunni Islam. She sees him as a misogynist. She believes that the companions who narrated hadiths on women attributed their personal views, superseding those of the Prophet. Such hadiths, she believes, achieved dominance in the traditionalist interpretation of the Quran and provided justification to the theologians to discriminate against women. Mernissi humanises the companions of the Prophet to prove that they were fallible.

This viewpoint clashes with the idealist image portrayed in Sunni Islam, until the present time, indicating that the companions are of equal status; that they are like stars in that whomsoever one follows, one is bound to be guided on the right path; and that theirs was the best generation ever to have come into existence, no matter that they fought fierce battles against each other and abused and cursed each other, as is widely narrated in history. But if the historic facts contravene the idealistic image portrayed by the radicals, then history has to be falsified so that the thinking and conjectures of the ideologues remain uppermost and unchallenged. Sadly, this matter has acquired a despotism of ideology commensurate with despotism of a political order. When stretched to the extremes, it becomes tantamount to fraudulent misrepresentation of history and puts shackles around scholarly endeavours to present objective research.

Conclusion

THE CHALLENGES
CONTINUE UNABATED

The prevalent oligarchic political order in the Muslim world is responsible for the sufferings of the masses. But it is much more convenient to throw one's garbage at the doorsteps of others and blame others for the misfortune that has befallen Muslims worldwide. Corruption is the main factor behind the failure of civil society. Hence, human dignity guaranteed by Islam is treated as a relic of the past. There has been hue and cry for the need to reform Muslim nations. But nepotism and favouritism are driving away any attempt at reforming society.

Class structure is causing incongruity not only in the field of education but also in matters of justice. In the Muslim world today, even the judiciary is not free from corruption. If the aggrieved are from a poor class, they are left with no other option but to accept corruption imposed upon them as the norm or to go on suffering for the rest of their lives, trying to obtain justice. This causes resentment among the masses. Societies formed on these bases cannot be healthy, positive, and constructive. They cannot enjoy peace, tranquillity, and serenity.

The absence of a sense of justice in the present Muslim political order, whether monarchical or republican, has made the Muslims a laughingstock among other nations of the world. If Hitler had sought refuge and immunity for war crimes he had committed, hardly any power in the West would have volunteered to grant him asylum. But in the Muslim world, the more crimes the political leaders commit, the more respectable they become. When examining the plight of the deposed dictators, no country of Europe or the United States was prepared to offer refuge or asylum to the shah of Iran, although he had been the policeman of the region and their closest ally.

If a ruler is accused of involvement in mass killings, no Western power would be willing to offend international law or obstruct the course of justice by assisting him to escape justice. But this abnormality is reserved for some Muslim countries which show willingness to challenge Islamic and international law by offering asylum and support to the political leaders involved in committing crimes against humanity. Some of these nations had spent billions of dollars to obstruct the trials of fellow despots in neighbouring countries, as happened in the case of Saddam. If they could not respect international protocols and treaties to uphold the cause of justice, how could they be trusted to administer justice domestically?

This is the tragedy of Muslim countries, where, more often than not, top officials of the state are involved in making a mockery of justice. Because of that, grassroots movements have lost confidence in the prevailing systems. Even in this twenty-first century, treacheries, betrayals, breach of covenants, lust for power, deception, forgeries, and fraud are considered indispensable parts of polity, thanks to the political orders which have neglected the principles of truth and justice for many centuries. In return, Muslims get theatrical talks about the restoration of past glory in the media and in Friday sermons.

The world has been reacting with abhorrence against the terrorists who rejoice in killing innocent people. But rarely has the world's attention focused on those who harbour them, finance their activities, and provide them with facilities to move across borders freely. Every single calamity facing the Muslim world has a direct link with past history. Every single catastrophe facing the Muslim world will impact on future generations. What is needed is a fundamental change in thinking and a complete reformation.

Violence and terrorism, insurgency and insurrection, corruption and usurpation of civil rights, dictatorship and autocracy, despotism of ideology, misrepresentation and misinterpretation of the views of others, gang wars and state terrorism, invasion and occupation, hostage taking and hijacking of nations, and massacre and genocide have become institutionalised and implanted in the heart of the Muslim world. There seems to be unlimited funding to nurture, encourage, and support ideological imperialism and violent extremism, thus causing havoc in the lives of innocent people. When is the Muslim world going to wake up to these realities which defame the name of Islam and of the community at large?

ABOUT THE AUTHOR

D r. Mahmood Yoosuf Abdulla received his PhD from Loughborough University, his MA from Portsmouth University, and a diploma with distinction in freelance writing from the London School of Journalism.

He has been a fellow of the Association of Chartered Certified Accountants for thirty-five years and has lectured in eighty community centers across four continents. Having given back to the community through service and executive posts in community organizations since he was sixteen, he now dedicates his time to writing.

BIBLIOGRAPHY

BOOKS

Abdullah, Mahmood Y. (1996), *Islamic Heritage*, Leicester: Tawheed Publications.

—— (2005), *Tampering with the Text and Meaning of the Qur'an*, Leicester: Academia Press.

Abou El Fadl, Khaled, M. (2001), *And God Knows the Soldiers—The Authoritative and Authoritarian in Islamic Discourses*, rev. ed. Maryland and Oxford: University Press of America.

—— (2001), *Conference of the Books: The Search for Beauty in Islam*, Maryland: University Press of America.

—— (2001), *Rebellion and Violence in Islamic Law*, Cambridge: Cambridge University Press.

—— (2001), *Speaking in God's Name: Islamic Law, Authority and Women*, Oxford: Oneworld Publications.

—— (2004), *Islam and the Challenge of Democracy—A Boston Review Book*, Princeton and Oxford: Princeton University Press.

—— (2005), *The Great Theft: Wrestling Islam from the Extremists*, New York: Harper San Francisco.

Aburish, Saïd K. (2005), *The House of Saud*, London: Bloomsbury.

Afzalur Rahman (1980), *Islam: Ideology and the Way of Life*, London: The Muslim Schools Trust.

Ahsan, M. M., and Kidwai, A. R. (eds.), (1993), *Sacrilege versus Civility*, rev. ed., Leicester: The Islamic Foundation.

Al-Alayli, Abdullah (1986), *Al-Imam al-Husayn* (Arabic), Beirut: Dar Maktabat al-Tarbiyyah.

Algar, Hamid (2002), *Wahhabism: A Critical Essay*, New York, Islamic Publications International.

Ali ibn Abi Talib (tr. Syed Ali Reza) (1996), *Peak of Eloquence* (translation of *Nahj al-Balaghah*), 6th ed., New York: Tehrike Tarsile Quran.

Al-Mufid, Shaykh (tr. Howard, I.K.A.) (1981), *Kitab al-Irshad* (*The Book of Guidance*), New York: Tehrike Tarsile Quran.

Ameer Ali, Syed (1974), *The Spirit of Islam—A History of the Evolution and Ideals of Islam*, 10th ed., London: Chatto & Windus.

Al-Amin, al-Sayyid Muhsin (n.d.), *Kashf al-Irtiyab* (Arabic) (*Uncovering of Doubts*), Sanaa: Maktabat al-Yemen al-Kubra (Bookshop of Greater Yemen).

Al-Aqqad, Abbas Mahmud (1974), *Al-Husayn Abu al-Shuhadah* (Arabic), (*Husayn the Father of the Martyrs*) in *The Complete Works of Abbas Mahmud al-Aqqad*, vol. II, Beirut: Dar al-Kitab al-Libnani.

Armstrong, Karen. (2002), *Islam: A Short History*, London: Phoenix Press.

Azzam, Abd al-Rahman (1965), *The Eternal Message of Muhammad*, New York: Mentor Books.

Buaben, Jabal M. (1996), *Image of the Prophet Muhammad in the West—A Study of Muir, Margoliouth and Watt*, Leicester: The Islamic Foundation.

DeLong-Bas, Natana J. (2004), *Wahhabi Islam—From Revival and Reform to Global Jihad*, New York: Oxford University Press and London: I. B. Tauris.

Esposito, John, L. (1988), *Islam the Straight Path*, New York: Oxford University Press.

———— (1999), *The Islamic Threat—Myth or Reality*, United States: Oxford University Press.

———— (2002), *Unholy War: Terror in the Name of Islam*, Oxford: Oxford University Press.

Faysal, Abdullah Shaykh (1997), *Natural Instincts: Islamic Psychology*, London: Darul Islam Publishers.

Faqihi, Ali Asghar (tr. Iqbal Haydar Haydari) (2006), *Tarikh-e Wahhabiyyat* (Urdu), (*History of Wahhabism*), Qum: World Ahlul Bayt Assembly.

Haykal, Muhammad Husayn (tr. al-Faruqi, Ismail Ragi A.) (1976), (translation from 8th ed.), *The Life of Muhammad*, United States: American Trust Publications.

Hazleton, Lesley (2010), *After the Prophet: The Epic Story of the Shia–Sunni Split*, New York: Anchor Books.

Hitti, Philip K. (2002), *History of the Arabs*, 10th ed., New Hampshire and New York: Palgrave Macmillan.

Husain, Ed. (2007), *The Islamist*, London: Penguin Books.

Ibn Kathir, Abu al-Fida Isma'il al-Qurashi al-Dimashqi (1984), *Tafsir Ibn Kathir* (Arabic), 4 vols., vols. I and III, Beirut: Dar al-Fikr.

Jordac, George (1982), *The Voice of Human Justice*, Karachi: Islamic Seminary.

Kamali, Mohammad Hashim (1997), *Freedom of Expression in Islam*, Cambridge: Islamic Text Society.

——— (2002), *Freedom, Equality and Justice in Islam*, Cambridge: Islamic Text Society.

——— (2002), *The Dignity of Man: An Islamic Perspective*, Cambridge: Islamic Text Society.

Al-Kurani, Ali (tr. Badr Shahin) (2009), *Wahhabism & Monotheism*, Qum: Ansariyan Publications.

Ma'ash, Jalal (2005), *Al-Husayn wa al-Wahhabiyyah* (Arabic) (*Husayn and Wahhabism*), Beirut: Dar al-Kari.

Madelung, Wilferd (1997), *The Succession to Muhammad*, Cambridge: Cambridge University Press.

Malik, Aftab, A. (ed.) (2005), *With God on Our Side: Politics & Theology of the War on Terrorism*, Bristol: Amal Press.

Makarim Shirazi, Nasir (tr. Muhammadi, Mustafa) (2011), *Wahhabism at the Crossroad*, Qum: The Ahl al-Bayt World Assembly.

Mamdani, Mahmood (2004), *Good Muslim, Bad Muslim—America, the Cold War, and the Roots of Terror*, New York: Pantheon Books.

Mawdudi, Abu Ala (1976), *Human Rights in Islam*, Leicester, United Kingdom: The Islamic Foundation.

Al-Misri, Abu Hamza (n.d.), *Khawaarij and Jihad,* Birmingham: Maktabah al-Ansar.

Mohy-ud-Din, Ata. (1983), *The Arabian Prophet His Message and Achievements,* Lahore: Islamic Book Foundation.

Mutahhari, Murtada (tr. Abidi, Sulayman H. et. al.) (2004), *Divine Justice* (Persian title, *Adl-e Ilahi*), Qum: International Centre for Islamic Studies.

Moussalli, Ahmad S. (2001), *The Islamic Quest for Democracy, Pluralism, and Human Rights,* Florida: University Press of Florida.

Mughniyyah, Muhammad Jawad (1985), *The Despotic Rulers,* Karachi: Islamic Seminary Publications.

Nasr, Vali (2007), *The Shia Revival,* New York and London: W. W. Norton & Co.

Noorani, A. G. (2002), *Islam & Jihad: Prejudice versus Reality,* London and New York: Zed Books.

O'Neil, S. and McGrory, D. (2006), *The Suicide Factory,* London: HarperCollins Publishers.

Osman, Fathi (1997), *Concepts of the Quran—A Topical Reading,* Los Angeles: MVI Publications.

Pickthall, Mohammed Marmaduke (n.d.), *The Meaning of the Glorious Koran,* New York: The New American Library.

Qarai, Ali Quli (2004), *The Quran With a Phrase-by-Phrase English Translation,* London: Islamic College for Advanced Studies Press.

Qutb, Sayyid. (1977), *The Religion of Islam* (English translation of *Hadha al-Din*), Damascus: International Islamic Federation of Student Organizations.

Al-Rashid, Nasir ibn Sa'd (n.d.), *Ibn Abd al-Wahhab Fi al-Rad ala al-Rafidah* (Arabic) (*Answering back al-Rafidah*), Riyadh: Dar Tiba for Publication and Distribution.

Ruthven, Malise (2004), *Fundamentalism: The Search for Meaning*, Oxford: Oxford University Press.

Said, Edward (1981), *Covering Islam*, New York: Pantheon Books.

Schwartz, Stephen (2002), *The Two Faces of Islam—The House of Saud from Tradition to Terror*, New York: Doubleday.

ash-Shaykh as-Saduq (tr. Asaf A. A. Fayzee) (1982), *A Shi'ite Creed* (*I'tiqadatu 'l-Imamiyyah*), Tehran: WOFIS.

Subhani, Jafar (tr. Jalil Durrani) (1996), *Wahhabism*, Tehran: Naba Organization.

———— (2005), *Al-Wahhabiyyah bayn al-Mabani al-Fikriyyah wa al-Nata'ij al-Amaliyyah* (Arabic) (*The Wahhabism between the Structure of Thought and the Practical Results*, Qum: Organisation of Imam al-Sadiq.

———— (tr. and ed. Reza Shah-Kazemi) (2001), *Doctrines of Shii Islam*, London and New York: I. B. Tauris.

Al-Suyuti, Jalal al-Din (1986), *Tarikh al-Khulafa* (Arabic) (*History of the Caliphs*), Beirut: Dar al-Qalam.

Tabataba'i, Muhammad Husayn (n.d.), *Shiite Islam*, Karachi: Shia Institute of Pakistan.

Trofimov, Yaroslav (2007), *The Siege of Mecca*, New York: Doubleday.

Viorst, Milton (1998), *In the Shadow of the Prophet: The Struggle for the Soul of Islam*, New York: Doubleday.

Yusuf Ali, Abdullah (n.d.), *The Meaning of the Glorious Quran*, 2 vols., Cairo: Dar al-Kitab al-Masri and Beirut: Dar al-Kitab al-Lubnani.

WEBSITES

ASHARQ AL-AWSAT newspaper
http://aawsat.com/english/news (11 June 2006).

ABC local services, Australia.
http://abclocal.go.com/wpvi/story (2 July, 2006).

ABC-klubben – för användare av alla slags datorer
www.abc.se (7 September 1996 and 11 September 2009).

Ahlul Bayt News agebcy
http://abna.ir/data (20 June 2010 and 29 June 2013).

News website
www.adnki.com (28 April 2006).

Ahlul Bayt Islamic Mission
www.aimislam.com (1 September 2009, 9 February 2010, and 12 April 2012).

Al-Islam
www.al-islam.org (8 April 2012).

Al-Mayadeen Lebanese Independent TV channel
Al-mayadeen, https://www.youtube.com/watch?v=jDMUqYjpfls, 10 August,
 2016.

Al-Riyadh news channel
www.alriyadh.com/ (8 April 2011).

Al-Watan Arabic news
www.alwatanye.net (4 April 2012).

Imnesty International webite
Amnesty International, www.amnesty.org.uk/content.asp?CategoryID=
 10224 (19 May 2012).

Second look at the Saudis (**warning: the website infested with virus**)
www.asecondlookatthesaudis.com/ (4 June 2008)

The ongoing ethnis cleansing in Pakistan (**warning: the website is
infested with virus**)
http://aut.abis.org.nz/the-ongoing-ethnic-cleansing-of-pakistan/ (17 May
 2012).

Council on American-Islamic relations
www.cair-net.org (21 July 2003).

Cair – Calls for bias crime probe
www.ccc.nps.navy.mil (6 April 2006).

Channel 4 news
www.channel4.com/news (15 November 2005).

Child Help
www.childhelp.org (8 April 2012 and 28 May 2013).

Daily Mail newspaper
http://www.dailymail.co.uk/ (30 May 2012).

Pakistan Defence website
www.defence.pk/forums/world-affairs (2 September 2011).

People's Daily newspaper
http://english.people.com.cn (10 November 2005).

Wikipedia Encyclopedia
en.wikipedia.org (31 May 2007 and 17 May 2012).

Fairness and Accuracy in Reporting
www.fair.org/ (November/December 2001).

Feminist Majority foundation
www.feminist.org (24 June 2005).

Foreign Policy online magazine
Foreign Policy online magazine, http://foreignpolicy.com/, July/August 2016.

Gatestone Institute
www.gatestoneinstitute.org (9 February 2012).

Global Research, Canada. www.globalresearch.ca/ (16 August 2011).

The Guardian newspaper
www.guardian.co.uk (3 May 2004, 11 November 2004, and 7 December 2010).

Haaretz newspaper
www.haaretz.com (1 April 2009).

Hadith collection:Sahih Muslim
http://hadithcollection.com/sahihmuslim (8 April 2012).

Hazara.net
http://www.hazara.net/persecution/pak-persecution.html (17 May 2012).

Human Rights Watch website
http://www.hrw.org/node/107909 (12 June 2012).

Human Rights in Islam website
www.human-rights-in-islam.co.uk (30 December 2011).

Human Rights Watch
Human Rights Watch, https://www.hrw.org/ (11 July 2016).

International Business Times
www.ibtimes.co.uk. (27 April 2013).

The Independent newspaper
http://www.independent.co.uk. (13 June 2012).

Shafaqna newspaper
http://india.shafaqna.com/shafaq (20 July 2013).

Institute for Strategic Dialogue
Institute for strategic dialogue in London, http://www.strategicdia-logue.org/, accessed on 11 August, 2016.

International Centre for the Study of Radicalisation: TERRORISM RESEARCH & ANALYSIS CONSORTIUM
http://www.trackingterrorism.org/resource/international-center-study-radicalisation-icsr, accessed on 11 August, 2016.

Islamic Centre.org
www.islamiccentre.org/presentations/wahhabi.pdf (12 October 1997).

Islam Daily
www.islamdaily.org/ (19 November 2004).

Media Monitors.net
www.mediamonitors.net/ (8 October 2002).

Rubin Center Research in International Affairs
meria.idc.ac.il/journal (issue 4, 2002).

Milli Gazatte
www.milligazette.com (31 August 2005).

National Council of Churches
www.ncccusa.org/news (7 October 2002).

BBC News
news.bbc.co.uk/1/hi/england/manchester (25 November 2009).

The Independent newspaper:news.independent.co.uk/world/ (19 April
    2006 and 17 May 2006).

Media Monitors
www.mediamonitors.net/ (8 October 2002).

Rubin Center Research in International Affairs
http://meria.idc.ac.il/journal/2002/issue4.

Nahrain news
www.nahrainnet.net (19 July 2007).

New statesman
www.newstatesman.com (18 July 2005).

Reuters
www.reuters.co.uk (17 and 19 May 2006).

Salon news
Salon news, http://www.salon.com/2016/08/15/atrocious-attack-u-s-backed-
  saudi-coalition-bombs-4th-msf-hospital-in-yemen/, 15 August, 2016.

Sunnah.org
www.sunnah.org (11 March 2012).

Swiss info.org
www.swissinfo.org (2 July 2006).

The Hindu.com
www.thehindu.com (12 July 2005).

The USA today
http://usatoday30.usatoday.com/news/world/2002/02/06/saudi.htm.

US Information State government
usinfo.state.gov/ei/Archive/2004/Dec (22 December 2004).

Voe Smart
http://votesmart.org/public-statement/17524.

Why Islam?
whyislam.org/forum/ (5 August 2008).

Women in Judaism
wjudaism.library.utoronto.ca (vol. I, no. 2, 1998).

http://www.youtube.com/watch?v=zAG72Dq9rW4.

http://www.youtube.com/watch?v=-e-J2977xB4.

https://www.youtube.com/watch?v=Wp3B4p-iorw.

http://www.youtube.com/watch?v=gD9IYQXRE_0&feature=youtube_
  gdata_player (17 July 2013).

JOURNALS, MAGAZINES, AND ACADEMIC PAPERS

Brandeis University *Crown Paper No. 2*, July 2009.

CAIR-DFW Newsletter, 23 May 2006.

Daily Telegraph, 27 October 2009.

FT Magazine, 17 May 2013.

Globalpost, 28 December 2011.

Impact International, vol. 28, no. 5, May 1998.

Islam Daily Observing Media, 7 December 2004.

Islamica Magazine, no. 15, 2006.

Jewish Week, 10 February 2009.

MERIA Middle East Review of International Affairs, vol. 6, no. 4, December 2002.

The New York Times, 27 January 2011 and 27 July 2013.

The Washington Post, 16 May 2012.

INDEX

Tunisian, 24, 34, 173

Turkey, 28, 38, 46, 48, 64, 114, 143, 144, 157, 199, 201, 252

Turki al-Faisal, 5, 172

Turkish, 37, 38, 58, 157, 186, 201

Turkish president, 157

Turmoil, 27, 110, 145

TV channel, 76, 80, 97, 99, 100, 128, 169, 272

TV channels, 17, 21, 46, 48, 55, 75, 76, 90, 93, 98, 101, 102, 112, 126, 128, 157, 169, 178, 183, 192

TV serial, 123, 124, 125

Twelver Shias, 191

Twelvers, xxvi, 31

Twentieth, 123

Twenty-first century, 7, 141, 189, 220, 245, 260

Twin babies, 83

Twin towers, 19

Tyranny, 27, 66, 243, 245

Tyrant, 25, 63, 98, 121, 132, 155, 159, 163, 164, 165, 166, 167, 168, 170

Tyrants, 16, 28, 40, 68, 165, 168, 170, 202, 243

U

U.S.-backed, 197

Ulama, 28, 54, 155, 182, 192, 238

Ulama of Sham, 54

Ultimatum, 72, 179

Ultra vires, 166

Ultranationalists, 31, 132, 158, 171

Umar, 60, 65, 84, 87, 124, 140, 208, 213, 256

Umar ibn Abd al-Aziz, 140

Umar ibn Sa'd, 87

Umayyad, 23, 40, 41, 55, 63, 84, 121, 138, 139, 148, 150, 224, 244

Umayyad dynasty, 23, 40, 41, 84, 121

Umayyads, 57, 60, 62, 64, 123, 140, 142, 153, 182, 224, 225, 243, 244

Ummah, 2, 59, 170

UN Charter of Human Rights, xvi, 235

UN General Assembly, 231

UN Human Rights, 38

Unaccountability, 40, 134

Unbelievers, 74, 213, 218, 237

Undertone, 77, 223

Undiplomatic, 36, 50

Unemployment, 24, 100, 112

Unique status, 254

United Arab Emirates, 35

United Kingdom, 80, 109, 237, 250, 268

United Nations, xv, xvi, 9, 38, 48, 53, 114, 133, 155, 166, 186, 197, 199, 231, 235, 236

United States, 5, 6, 8, 9, 10, 12, 21, 25, 30, 35, 44, 45, 47, 48, 49, 50, 51, 63, 67, 70, 84, 86, 104, 105, 113, 115, 129, 133, 146, 153, 155, 160, 164, 169, 184, 196, 197, 228, 232, 234, 235, 236, 238, 247, 250, 251, 252, 260, 267, 276

Made in the USA
Charleston, SC
28 February 2017